CRITICS PRAISE *DARING THE SEA*

"Readers who enjoy tales of humans pitted against the elements will find this work by freelancer Shaw thrilling."

—*Publishers Weekly*

"Shaw, equally experienced as writer and yachtsman, is singularly well qualified to produce this excellent account of George Harbo and Frank Samuelsen . . . who became the first men to row across the Atlantic. . . . May this book help two fine sailors become as well known as they deserve to be."

—*Booklist*

"The year was 1896. The daring oarsmen were George Harbo and Frank Samuelsen. Their story—told in novelish narrative similar to that of Sebastian Junger's THE PERFECT STORM—is mind-bending."

—*Chesapeake Bay Magazine*

"In DARING THE SEA, Shaw's colorful language vividly re-creates the characters, allowing them and their victory over the Atlantic to inspire present-day adventurers."

—*Offshore* magazine

"A well-told and warmly written tale."

—*The Independent*

"DARING THE SEA is a great sea yarn, fast-moving and gripping."

—*Our Time*

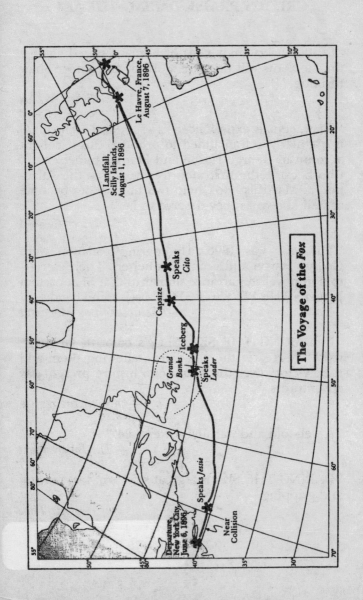

The Voyage of the *Fox*

Departure, New York City, June 6, 1896
Near Collision
Speaks *Jessie*
Speaks *Leader*
Iceberg
Grand Banks
Capsize
Speaks *Cito*
Landfall, Scilly Islands, August 1, 1896
Le Havre, France, August 7, 1896

Daring the Sea

The True Story of the First Men to
Row Across the Atlantic Ocean

DAVID W. SHAW

PINNACLE BOOKS
KENSINGTON PUBLISHING CORP.

www.pinnaclebooks.com

For my wife, Elizabeth,
and all the men and women who brave the sea.

Acknowledgments

I am deeply grateful to the many people who played a part in making this book a reality. I want to thank my good friend and editor, Gary Fitzgerald, for showing an interest in the story from the very beginning and my agent, Jill Grinberg, for her faith in the project and her belief in my ability to bring the story to life. The families of both Harbo and Samuelsen also deserve my gratitude for spending hours with me on the telephone and in person and for sharing personal documents and photographs. Joan Minnis, George Harbo's granddaughter, and Spencer Samuelesen, Frank Samuelsen's grandson, were particularly helpful in my effort to learn all I could about the lives of the voyagers.

Tom Laverty, curator of the Twin Lights Historic Site, Highlands, New Jersey, provided access to the many documents related to the voyage as well as the original logbook, which was donated to the museum by the Harbo family. Tom Hoffman, historian for the Sandy Hook Unit, Gateway National Recreation Area; members of the Long Branch Ice Boat and Yacht Club; the Sandy Hook Pilots Association; patient librarians at Princeton and Drew Universities; and my wife, Elizabeth, who helped with the research, all have my heartfelt thanks.

Preface

To bring the tale of the *Fox* alive required a profound knowledge of the sea, which can only come through experience, though, to a certain extent, one can learn about it from books written by seasoned offshore sailors. In my travels aboard my little sloop, often single-handed, I became a student of the sea. I found it both a cruel and a kind teacher, one I respect and love deeply.

The sea taught me to reckon with its many moods and all that goes into creating them. The tidal currents and their effect on waves and a compass course challenge the most experienced navigator, particularly in the Gulf of Maine, where the water rises and falls in the foggy reaches of the far eastern borders of the state more than twenty feet every six hours. I learned how current and wind and shoals influence the size and shape of waves and how changes in cloud formations, wind shifts, and fluctuations of barometric pressure can help predict the weather just over the horizon. I experienced firsthand what it is like to ride out a gale, how tired one can get of the incessant noise and the violent motion of a small boat, and how absolutely terrifying the ocean can be. To take to the sea in small craft demands skill, courage, and not a little luck.

But to write this book also required great attention to detail and nearly a year of research on a wide variety of subjects. By far the most important documents were the original logbook George Harbo wrote while at sea and the expanded account of the journey he dictated to an anonymous writer before his death in 1908. Using both documents, which I obtained from the Twin Lights Historic Site, I was able to piece together the voyage and transform the dry words into what I hope were vivid scenes.

I stuck purely to the facts, and took no literary license. I wrote of George Harbo and Frank Samuelsen's fears and pain but did not elaborate further on what they had reported. For example, I know from reading many accounts of men who crossed the Atlantic in small open boats that the combination of moisture and friction caused most to suffer greatly from boils and horrible pain in the buttocks. Harbo never mentions any such thing. I suspect he may have thought it unnecessary to record, but he does note the condition of their hands, the painful, raw skin of their noses, how their skin was burned almost black from exposure to the elements. In short, I did not feel inclined to add boils to their suffering, even though I would bet that they did grow crops of them during their time at sea. If such information wasn't in the log, I didn't introduce it into the narrative.

In most cases the dialogue in the book was taken right from the expanded log, or fashioned from direct expressions of emotion and thought by George Harbo. In a few cases, I reconstructed dialogue, based on deduction and logic, from details provided by the members of George and Frank's families and occasionally from press reports which quote the men directly.

One of the most taxing of all aspects of this project derived from the stuff of legend which has grown up around the tale. The most enduring myth holds that Richard Fox offered $10,000 to any team successful in rowing the Atlantic. Every press account of the voyage written in the twentieth century includes this bit of information, apparently as a means by which to justify why the men set off on their journey. I looked through rolls of microfilm of the news accounts published just before, during, and after the men arrived in Le Havre as well as those published in March 1897, when the men arrived back in New York harbor. None mention the $10,000 prize.

More important, neither does George Harbo, though he does refer to contact with Richard Fox. He states quite specifically that he and Frank named the boat after the publisher because he had promised them *Police Gazette* medals if they successfully completed the voyage. Fox did this often, and it is a fact that his paper did give them their medals in 1897. The medals Frank received are locked up in a vault in Norway. As to the $10,000, none of the members of either family could state with certainty whether the money was either offered or received, though most say the men got nothing from Fox and very little from the exhibitions of the boat. They, too, had little to go on besides the primary documents and reams of often spurious press accounts written long after the men died. In short, I kept to my promise: if it wasn't in the log, it didn't go into the book.

Another myth also cropped up in the press accounts written in the twentieth century. The story goes that when the steamer the men shipped out on was returning to the United States, it ran short of coal about two hundred miles off Sandy Hook. The captain supposedly wanted to burn the *Fox* for fuel at the height of a gale, but the men, quite naturally, refused to do so. Instead, they put off from the storm-tossed ship and rowed home. This is pretty amazing stuff, making for excellent copy in the pulps. But it never happened.

The file I obtained from Twin Lights included dozens of such stories reported as fact, some of which appeared in very prestigious national periodicals. The story had truly taken on a life of its own as one reporter after another read the old clips and rewrote them for use in his or her newspaper or magazine. I decided to completely dismiss every story written in the twentieth century.

Although journalists in the nineteenth century did a better job, there still appeared in their stories some strange discrepancies. For example, the reports all say that Frank's sister was very upset when the two men left the Battery on June 6, 1896. They all list her name as Lena. Spencer Samuelsen has never heard of Lena; she didn't exist! The woman the reporters saw on the dock was Caroline. I saw her name myself in a giant volume listing the inhabitants of the Farsund area, which included the Samuelsen family, and which Spencer was kind enough to show me. Where did this Lena come from? Possibly it was a nickname.

Again, the reports even at the time the men undertook their voyage could not be trusted completely. They were, however, invaluable when one or more newspaper provided the exact same information; two sources are far more trustworthy than one.

The families provided me with details about both men no one but descendants could possibly know. They described to the best of their ability the character of each man, the lives of the families, the chronology of events. They shared personal documents, including family Bibles, letters, diary entries, and anecdotal data passed down from George and Frank's children and their relatives. For this I am indebted, for even with the logbooks it would have been impossible to bring the men to life without help from the families.

Numerous books were helpful in my research (see bibliography). Some of them make for exciting reading. I particularly recommend the firsthand accounts of others who rowed or sailed small craft across the seas. For storm buffs, *Heavy Weather Sailing*, by K. Adlard Coles, a true classic, presents hair-raising and useful information about handling small vessels in horrid weather. The book was invaluable in my efforts to re-create the sea conditions the men encountered and, I hope, in my effort to impart a glimmer of understanding of how the ocean and wind work for those of us who have never, and will never, take to the sea in a mere cockleshell of a vessel.

Introduction

Back in the mid-1980s, I heard about a rather strange man whose dream was to row across the North Atlantic in a tiny boat not much larger than a beer can. He left from Cape Cod, his boat loaded with a cargo of peanut butter, bread, and cases of Coca-Cola. The newspapers treated the event as great sport, poking fun at the man in every article. The U.S. Coast Guard, which has the right to turn any vessel back from the sea if the craft is deemed ill-suited to the rigors of ocean travel, cruised out and retrieved him. He tried again, and this time he went terminally missing, as the British are fond of saying. He was by no means the first to try such a seemingly impossible crossing. The list is long and includes Robert Manry, who sailed a thirteen-and-a-half-foot sloop nonstop across the Atlantic in 1965, and Hugo Vilhen, who, in 1968, transited the Atlantic in a six-foot sailboat called, quite appropriately, *April Fool*.

Why would men do such a silly thing? The sea is no place for fools. It is vast, uncaring, and often fierce. I have heard ship pilots who drive big freighters in

and out of harbors say they would never put to sea
in anything smaller than a battleship. But I have also
known sailors who think nothing at all of thrashing
off to Bermuda on a twenty-foot sloop.

For many of us today the earth appears a mostly
tame place. We look to outer space as the setting for
the next real challenge, the arena in which human
ingenuity and determination will ratchet us up
another step on the ladder of evolution. Some among
us still look closer to home for the challenge; and
others die trying to reach deep within the soul, body,
and mind, to the limit of human endurance, then
push on even farther. To do so is not unusual. To
reach for the stars, literally and figuratively, is what
it means to be human.

For some adventurers the high peaks of the Himalayas beckon. For others it is the sky or a wild river.
Many also still look to the sea, perhaps the most
awesome of any place on the planet, for its ability to
test one's character.

Just last October a group of avid rowboat lovers
took up a challenge to win the longest rowing race in
history—across the Atlantic Ocean. The two-person
teams (women also participated in the event) set off
from Los Gigantes in Tenerife, one of the Canary
Islands, and rowed some 2,700 miles to Bridgetown,
Barbados, in roughly fifty days. Each team rowed an
identical twenty-four-foot boat designed to right itself
if capsized. Satellite navigation systems, water-making
machines, emergency-positioning devices to facilitate
rescue, and all kinds of other state-of-the-art techno-
logies played a vital role in making the race as safe
as possible, though no such venture is ever safe, which
is part of its attraction.

This event is the most recent in a long line of epic
adventures aboard small craft that all share a common
thread: The participants underwent the peril and
physical hardship voluntarily. They weren't castaways

like the men who sailed with Captain Bligh in one of the *Bounty*'s lifeboats on a forty-eight-day passage of 3,600 miles across the Pacific. They were willing actors on a dangerous stage of their own making.

As far back as the mid-1800s individuals have set out to challenge the sea in all manner of small boats, unlike past voyages made in earlier centuries for the noble pursuit of exploration or the necessity to get from point A to point B to find freedom in new lands. These journeys were made for other reasons—chiefly to set records and test human endurance. Sails powered most of the boats, and the transatlantic voyages of the last century, those that succeeded, that is, created a stir on both sides of the Atlantic. The daring feats touched the hearts of people who cared nothing for boats, or the sea, except for what it provided in the way of a tasty dinner. They wouldn't know a bow from a stern, a gaff from a bowsprit. But no matter. They read about the foolhardy souls who attempted to set world records at risk of life and limb, and for a time they were transported out of their day-to-day grind. They saw in these attempts the universal aspiration to achieve what seems impossible.

In the late 1800s airplanes, the atomic bomb, and space stations would have seemed impossibilities. But to strive individually to achieve the improbable struck a chord in most everyone, and still does, because it is the one characteristic we all share. It is still something we hold close to our hearts, and that is why we thirst for tales that illuminate the greater meaning behind a seemingly insignificant event.

On June 6, 1896, two Norwegian fishermen briefly captured the attention of common folk and nobility alike in Europe and the United States by what appeared to all an impossible endeavor: to be the first to row across the North Atlantic with no sail, steam, or even a rudder to aid them. One of the men was an American citizen who had emigrated to the

United States more than a decade earlier, the other was a more recent arrival. They, like so many others at the time, suffered from the class distinction of being on the poor end of the stick, with no middle ground to work toward.

The theaters were filled with adventurers giving lectures on their travels for good pay. In fact, the word *travelogue*, meaning a dialogue based on one's travels, derives from this time in American history. The men dreamed of a better life for themselves and their families, and so they set out to row from the Battery, at the tip of Manhattan, more than 3,000 miles to Le Havre, France. They hoped to give lectures and display the boat in Europe and the United States and, with the money earned, to buy their way into an American dream that had hitherto eluded them.

Experience had already proved to me that in challenging the sea I had picked an implacable adversary. But it is in the nature of man to better his own achievement; it is normal and healthy to strive continually for new records. Each newly established record, after all, makes a positive contribution by setting the limits of human achievement. . . .

What drove me to test my strength of mind and body to the utmost? I realized that no one answer would satisfy me; the urge for adventure, the quest for scientific knowledge—both played a part. I told myself that man has always searched for the new frontier, pushed for further boundaries and that I, as a man, would have to accept that for my answer.

—From *Alone at Sea,* by Hannes Lindemann, who paddled and sailed a dugout canoe and a rubberized foldboat, a kayaklike craft, across the Atlantic on two voyages, between 1955 and 1957. He was the first to cross the ocean in a dugout canoe.

The field of freak enterprise in crossing the Atlantic under unusual conditions is being gradually narrowed. Several have made their way across in small sailboats, and now two foolhardy adventurers have arranged to row an eighteen-foot boat from this port to Havre. If they succeed, the next aspirant for distinction in that special line may have to announce his intentions of swimming across in order to attract interest.

—From the *New York Times,* June 3, 1896, p. 1.

Daring the Sea

Cattle die.
Kindred die.
Every man is mortal.
But the good name never dies of one who has
done well.
—From the Norse poem "The Speech
of the High One"

1

A steamer appeared over the horizon off the coast of New York, visible only as a dark smudge in the clear, hard light of the early-afternoon sun of March 9, 1884. Gradually, its superstructure and finally its hull hove into view against the seemingly infinite backdrop of the Atlantic Ocean it had just crossed. A trail of black smoke blew aft from its funnels, snatched up and carried off in the wind that swept the ship as it moved forward through the sea at twelve knots and vanishing soon after on the wings of the northwesterly gusts that had come almost as far as the ship, originating deep in Canada's interior plains, thousands of miles away. One of the smaller iron types, under 5,000 tons, the ship wasn't old, but it was already outdated. The introduction four years earlier of larger steel ships taking the transatlantic shipping business yet another leap forward had seen to that.

Speed topped the list of requisites for ocean crossings, and the fastest steel express steamers grew larger by the year, able to make the run from Liverpool to

New York in a mere week. Lucrative mail contracts and rates of $150 for first-class suites and $15 per head for steerage spurred the technological progress. The thirst for profit acted every bit as effectively on the development of better ships as the desire to win wars. Stiff westerly winds had made for a slow passage of the iron steamer from Southampton—nothing unusual so early in the season—but almost three weeks to cross meant additional tons of expensive coal consumed to fire the inefficient boilers that drove the screws.

The pilots on station aboard their swift schooners in the steep seas beyond the Sandy Hook Lightship awaited the arrival of this ship with as much excitement as a grocery clerk for a delivery of fresh produce from the fields or a shipment of beef from the slaughterhouses. With their pay based on the length and draft of each vessel they guided safely into port, the little steamer plowing through the seas toward the coast meant no pot of gold. Had it been one of the sleek new liners, one of the true greyhounds of the sea, it would have already taken on a pilot. The competing boats from New York and Sandy Hook ranged far offshore in search of the best and the largest ships, with their heftier fees.

A crewman aboard the steamer had hoisted the international signal flag for the letter G upon closing the coast. Seeing its yellow and blue stripes alerted the men aboard the schooners that the ship was ready to take on a pilot for the last leg of the voyage to the piers along the Hudson River. It touched off a miniature race among the boats, all of which made directly for the steamer, their skippers anxious to arrive first and collect the mandatory fee, however humble it might be, for services rendered. Another flag on a different halyard also flew from the mast. Solid yellow and faded from much use, the quarantine signal snapped in the cold breeze, indicating that the ship had come from a foreign port and would require a close inspection of passengers and crew before it docked in Manhattan.

The steamer turned its starboard side to the force of the wind and rolled piteously in the trough of the waves, creating a shadow of light air and smoother water to leeward. The schooner nearest the ship stopped, quickly launched its rowboat, and stout oarsmen rowed the pilot over to the rope ladder the crew aboard the steamer slung down the hull of the ship. He climbed it with the nimble, sure movement that came only after years of practice and made his way up to the bridge.

"You've arrived at a good hour. We'll have a fair tide over Sandy Hook bar," the pilot said, clasping the master's hand. From that point until the ship arrived safely in port, the pilot would be in command, repeating a transfer of power that had taken place off the shores of New York since 1694, when regulations requiring the presence of pilots aboard inbound ships first took effect.

The master nodded but did not smile. "Let's have her out of the trough, mister," the master said. "Fair tide or no, we're not deep enough for worry in Gedney Channel."

"Maybe, but a fair current up the bay is better than foul."

The steamer made its way slowly up the channel, across the sandbar, and turned north to the Narrows. Six miles below Manhattan, quarantine authorities boarded for the routine inspection before clearing the vessel for its final passage, with the aid of a tug, to a berth at the docks near the Barge Office at the Battery, a place which symbolized the rigid class distinction among transatlantic travelers. Officials would clear first-class passengers at once without their ever having to leave Manhattan; for immigrants, the story was different. Those passengers from steerage that could find a place on deck lined the rails and gazed in wonder at the busy port spread out before them.

Among the throng on deck was a nineteen-year-old Norwegian of medium height and build, with deep-red hair cut close, in the utilitarian style of the men who worked the fishing boats plying the Strait of Skagerrack, between southern Norway and Denmark, the North Sea, and far up the coast to Finnmark, deep beyond the Norwegian Sea, where the summer sun never fully set. His sharp, angular nose, blue eyes, and rounded chin gave him looks not unappealing to the ladies. A thick red mustache made him appear less of a youth. Dressed in a woolen overcoat pulled tight against the damp sea air, he was the antithesis of the city dudes, decked out in their silk toppers and black capes.

His given name was Gottlieb Roed. However, just as he had chosen to leave his home in Brevik, a little village in the rich, agriculturally hospitable lowlands of southeastern Norway, he had adopted a new name, George Harbo, for his time in a new land. The first was easier on the tongue and smacked of America, the last was his mother's maiden name, one he held dear to his heart.

George stared at the paddlewheel ferries, square-rigged ships, the fishing sloops and schooners, the seagoing sailers with more mast than fingers on one hand, and the steamships. The harbor was thick with vessels, as were the docks. A thicket of masts fenced the uneven skyline on the Hudson River side. To the east, the Brooklyn Bridge towered above all else. Already, a thin, sooty patina, from the coal burned to heat the city over the previous harsh winter, covered the bridge, in use for less than a year after it married Brooklyn to Manhattan so that workers on the Long Island side could cross the East River even when it froze solid and the ferries couldn't run. Off to the port side of the steamer, hundreds of men worked on Bedloe's Island to pour the concrete foundation for the Statue of Liberty, which was still in France, fully assembled and a big attraction among the Parisians strolling along the rue de Chazelles.

The customs and emigration officials from the Landing Department boarded the steamer, now securely moored to the quay. George, along with the rest of the passengers in steerage, found himself herded aboard a small launch packed with luggage and people reeking from their own sweat and sodden clothes. The boats took them the short distance to the tip of the Battery, to an enormous circular building situated on a narrow spit of land made of fill harvested from the city proper as the tide of humanity swept over the tiny island, denuding it of trees, burying streams and creeks, reaching outward, and finally upward, to claim every available inch of space.

The line of passengers trudged down the docks to the building, Castle Garden, and passed under the arched entrance into organized bedlam. The voices of many nations echoed through the cavernous rotunda, dimly lit in the twilight that sifted through the skylights in the domed ceiling, seventy-five feet above the queues. Hissing gas jets, placed not for efficiency but for lighting the great hall for operatic performances that took place there decades earlier, produced long shadows and areas of near darkness punctuated with the white of tired faces and clasped hands.

Worn out, in desperate need of a bath, and hungry, George looked around him, excited, anxious, and homesick all at once. He thought of his bride-to-be, Anine, a beautiful woman with silky dark brown hair and bright blue eyes that lit up her rounded face when she smiled. In just about a month she would turn eighteen. The thought of missing her birthday both depressed him and fed his ambition to earn enough money to bring her over from Brevik as soon as possible. At that moment, as he waited for his interview with the officials, he dreamed of a happy, comfortable life, times of love with Anine, and the joy of raising a family.

George, like the nearly 3 million other immigrants since 1880 who had found themselves in Castle Garden after crossing the Atlantic, came with the hope of finding a better life in an America firmly in the grip of the Industrial Revolution. Abundant opportunities to earn wages far better than in Europe attracted the masses. Advertisements promoting the land of promise flooded the countrysides of Scandinavia, Germany, Ireland, France, and Great Britain. Sensing the profit potential, the shipping companies actively recruited immigrants, sending scouts far inland to praise the riches across the sea that were waiting for any who cared to work hard and take the risk of embarking into the unknown for a life abroad.

Back in Norway, more than 300,000 of George's countrymen, out of a total population of just over one and a half million, left the dairy farms, tucked away in valleys at the feet of steep fjords, or little fishing villages on the coast. They left not because of famine, which touched off the first wave of Irish emigration, political unrest, or war, but out of simple economic imperatives. Norway's tiny population occupied a land more than a thousand miles long from north to south, with only 3 percent of the soil suitable for cultivation of crops and vast reaches of rocky coast which offered fishing or whaling as occupations and nothing else. The pressure exerted on the people during the mid-1800s as a result of a population boom meant that children could expect a standard of living below that achieved by their parents.

The young men shipped out in the merchant marine or came to America, for the most part heading to the Midwest to farm the rich soil of the prairie. Others remained in the East, though only a small fraction of the total number that came from Scandinavian countries put roots down there. They came at first in a trickle starting in 1825, and following the overall pattern of immigration cycles, they flooded into America in good economic times and slacked off during times of depression and during the Civil War, when Quebec became a lot more appealing. By the end of the age of unbridled immigration, no other country besides Ireland would give more of its young in proportion to its total number, though the overall impact on American culture of the Irish, Germans, and Italians at George's elbows as he waited in the queues was far greater than that of the relatively small group from Norway that eventually landed on American soil.

At last, George came before the registration official.

"Name?" the official asked.

George knew little English, just enough phrases to get by.

"Name?" the official asked again.

Despite feeling confused and nervous, George looked the man straight in the eye and in a quiet voice said, "George Harbo."

"Nationality . . . country?"

"Norway."

"Town of birth?"

George didn't know what the man was asking.

"Where in Norway were you born? Where?" the man asked, impatient, though he had been through this routine thousands of times. All the officials were trained to ask the same questions time and again, and after the months, then years, of repetition, it was natural for them to lose patience with these hopeful souls. All the humanity of the moment had been sucked away, the souls turned to mere cattle, warm bodies to be dispensed with as quickly as possible.

"Norway," George said.

After a few more minutes, the interview was over,

with his place of birth established as Sandefjord, his
town of former residence, Brevik, and his destination
in the United States, Brooklyn, where a burgeoning
enclave of Norwegians and other Scandinavians had
begun to take root and flourish. George moved on
to the row of troughs set out in a section segregated
for the men to bathe. A similar sanitary section was
set up for the women. The luxury of a bath was not
a pleasure, however. Like cattle, the men crowded
together and attended to their basic needs, using
water black with the dirt of hundreds. It was dehuman-
izing for the young man, whose quiet sense of dignity
found itself increasingly assailed.

After eating a meager, tasteless meal provided gratis
by the authorities of the great, shining city, George
spent his first night in America on a crowded bench
in the cacophonous dark of Castle Garden, too wary
to sleep lest he find his few belongings gone in the
morning. When dawn arrived, he turned in his kro-
ners for dollars at the Money Exchange in the rotunda
and with some difficulty found seats on a series of
grimy horse-drawn omnibuses that lurched him into
Brooklyn.

2

As the population of New York soared to well over 1 million in the 1880s, the demand for all manner of goods increased. The city needed coal, lumber, and steel for its enterprises and to proceed on its envisioned path to greatness. It needed fresh water from the Catskill Mountains and food from as far away as the Midwest to nourish the population. Although New York harbor ranked as one of the best natural havens for ships on the entire East Coast, the island of Manhattan was in a sense a victim of geography. It sat at the edge of a natural demarcation zone between the land of the glaciers and the land of sandy coasts and barrier islands that extended all the way to Florida and the Gulf of Mexico.

New England's many natural harbors were created from ancient valleys enlarged through the passage of glaciers that scoured the land as far south as Staten Island. The valleys later became submerged when sea level rose after the climate warmed and much of the ice melted. Georges Bank off Cape Cod and the Grand Banks off Newfoundland, once dry land, owed their existence to the push and pull of natural forces at work during and after the Ice Age. The waters south of New York harbor, in New Jersey, however, never experienced such a direct influence. The long coastline remained almost unbroken, with few inlets to the large, shallow bays behind the barrier islands. It had no natural harbors to speak of, nor did the south shore of Long Island, and it had no rich fishing banks the likes of those up north.

The ocean up and down the eastern seaboard teemed with fish, though, and the fishing industry thrived, providing a food source much in demand at the time. Boston had its nearby port of Gloucester to sustain it. Seagoing fleets of schooners brought dorymen and their long lines to the fishing banks. New York, however, had no Gloucester of its own. As a consequence, vast quantities of fish from its New England neighbors ended up at the Fulton Fish Market.

Still, Manhattan's appetite for fish was sufficient to foster a profitable fishing trade closer to home as well, and despite the lack of natural harbors, a local industry took root. Tons of fish, caught on long lines and in enormous nets off the coasts of Long Island and New Jersey, flooded into the Fulton Fish Market by rail, steamer, and sloops engaged in coastwise transportation. Owing to geography, the local fishermen in New Jersey adopted a practice not duplicated anywhere else in the nation. They built their villages on the beach and launched their little boats through the surf day in and day out, making do with what nature provided and prospering where nothing but sand had once existed.

Just a few miles south of Sandy Hook, the shanties of Nauvoo, near present-day Sea Bright, dotted the beach. Galilee, a similar village near present-day Monmouth Beach, occupied the beach farther down the coast. With tarpaper or wood siding, a potbellied stove situated in the center of a single room and set up for cooking and eating on the first floor, and a loft upstairs for sleeping, the dwellings offered nothing for one desirous of luxury. In the summer, greenhead flies and mosquitoes robbed the inhabitants of sleep after a long day of fishing. In winter, the northeasterly winds took over, sending drafts through the heavy wool blankets that chilled their very bones, already stiff from cutting from the rivers and creeks blocks of ice for preserving their catches the following season.

Although the hundreds of fishermen living and working there led an austere existence, they did not go without the basics. The wives of the few married men attempted to make a home in the sand for their husbands and children. They kept the shanties tidy and carted soil from inland to the beach for the purpose of growing small plots of vegetables. On Sundays, a preacher held services on a crude wooden platform for any who cared to attend.

A typical fisherman earned roughly $1,000 a season; some with multiple boats did far better, even becoming rich, with annual profits as high as $15,000. Their lives weren't easy, but in contrast to the thousands of immigrants working in sweatshops doing piece work for pennies per item, in the factories and food processing plants, and on the multitude of construction sites throughout the region, life on the beach allowed families to earn a living with dignity while still keeping in touch with the natural world. George Harbo learned about the opportunities in Nauvoo from his fellow countrymen in Brooklyn and tried his luck there at the start of the fishing season in April.

Not long after his arrival in Nauvoo, he secured a position as a crewman aboard one of the boats. The proprietors of the vessels were, for the most part, Anglo-Saxon immigrants that came to the area during and shortly after colonial days. (Only one man, a fellow by the name of Hennessey, represented the more recent lot.) These were men, however, who had not forgotten the value of fresh views and the willing muscles of newcomers anxious to carve out their own slice of the American dream. Scandinavians, like George, off the ships that put into New York harbor, brought with them the skills of the sea, boat handling, and the craft of fishing. Though George found himself immersed in an unfamiliar culture, he soon felt at home despite the difference in mores and the flat, almost featureless land, with the exception of the highlands of Navesink, that in no way resembled Norway.

Every day, George rose before dawn in the company of six other unmarried men crowded together in a shanty and walked down to the beach to his surfboat, a seventeen-foot craft built for a crew of two. As the sky turned pale blue to the east, he stood at the bow of the surfboat, the spritsail and jib already set and flapping on the stocky mast, sheets eased to spill the air. Work pants rolled up to his knees, though this did little good, since the bowman always got wet, he firmly gripped the boat's rail and, together with his crewmate in the stern, ran her out into the surf. Both men leaped in as the boat rode into the backwash of an extinguished wave. Using the oars, they skillfully brought the bow into the breaking crests. The boat climbed the nearly vertical wall of the first, and then the second, and settled down after emerging from the surf.

They sailed the boat out to Shrewsbury Rocks, the light to the east now tinged gold with the rising sun, the air still cool from the night. These boulders, deposited on the ocean floor from melting drift ice as the glaciers to the north broke apart, created an ideal habitat for fish. The rapid tidal currents running along the coast stirred the nutrients in the sea and kept the food chain active. Once anchored over the rocks, the two men jigged or chummed. The smell of menhaden as George dumped it over the side amid a cloud of screeching gulls did not offend his sensibilities. Rather, it reminded him of days back home. Fishing and whaling came as naturally to Norwegians as it did to the men up north in Gloucester and those working the foreign fleets off the banks from other far-off places, such as Portugal.

By day's end, as much as 150 pounds of fish filled the boat. George cleaned the fish and pitched the entrails overboard, much to the delight of the crabs waiting below and the gulls hovering overhead. Once ashore, he and his crewmate placed the fish in baskets and carted it to an icehouse, shared with crews from other boats, where the cold work of layering the fish between slabs of ice kept them busy well past dusk. Coming from a land where ice was in no short supply, the odd-looking, conical roofs of the ice houses, protruding like half-opened umbrellas above the dunes, the depths inside reaching about fourteen feet below the surface, struck him as both ingenious and somewhat incongruous during the dog days of summer.

The work paid George well, though he had already made up his mind that life in Nauvoo wasn't the type of existence he wanted for Anine. Young and filled with ambition, he dreamed, not of fame and fortune but of a life that meant more than what he saw on the beaches. After less than a year in America, the first stirrings of wanting to make his mark, to strike off on his own on some as yet unseen path, began to move in a place deep in George's soul.

The following spring, George sailed for Norway with a pocketful of cash. Anine and he returned in the fall, were married in September, and settled down in a small apartment in Brooklyn. The following August, Anine gave birth to their first son, whom they named Andrew Jackson, after the American president George admired.

That October 28, 1886, with Anine cradling their two-month-old son in her arms, covered up warm and dry against the chill and rain, the young couple stood together among the crowds along the Brooklyn waterfront and peered through the mist enveloping the Statue of Liberty. In the harbor, a flotilla of all manner of boats surrounded the statue, and as the face of "Liberty Enlightening the World" was revealed to the dignitaries on Bedloe's Island, every vessel sounded its whistle. Sirens blared from nearby buildings, and cannons boomed. Anything seemed possible, for they were free, healthy, and most important of all, living together in America.

3

By the 1890s, the age of sail had largely given way to the power of the steam engine and its ability to provide reliable transatlantic service for the transportation of goods and passengers. The swift packet sailers, the clippers, and the multimasted windjammers, with clouds of canvas set to catch the wind that was free and able to take a ship the world over with no fear of running short of coal, had become anachronisms. Their stately beauty symbolized a simpler, purer time that was viewed with some considerable romance by those who had never experienced the hardships of the sailing ship.

Still, the coastal sloops and fishing schooners continued to frequent the port of New York. The square-riggers weren't altogether dead; they were actually sought after for the transportation of cargoes, such as guano, that required little profit from speed alone. They still found berths along the Hudson and East Rivers, though the largest of them no longer made the inside passage through Hell Gate to Long Island Sound; the Brooklyn Bridge didn't allow enough clearance for the topmasts. Like any doomed great enterprise, the road from good health to a lingering death took time, but any sailor with an ounce of brains knew the hourglass was nearly empty.

Life before the mast aboard these ships bred men of a particularly rugged nature. They were every bit as tough as the cowhands driving herds thousands of miles through the vast interior of the United States to rail depots that acted as gateways to civilization and the lucrative markets that were expanding urban centers throughout the nation. The sailors lived cramped together in the forecastle, with only a hammock and a duffel bag. They climbed the ratlines and inched their way out on footropes hung beneath the yardarms to shorten sail in ice storms that froze the canvas to sheets of rock hard enough to tear skin and break bones as it flogged in the grip of a gale. They lived hard and often died hard. But the open sea, the hum of wind in the taut rigging, and the trail of phosphorescence in the ship's wake during the blackest of calm nights resonated with the very essence of living and the value of toil, the prelude to a time of drunken boredom on the beach between voyages that most men alternately yearned for and longed to end.

Frank Samuelsen was one of these men. He had left his father's farm in the tiny village of Elunde, a cluster of one hundred or so cottages on the outskirts of Farsund in southern Norway, at the age of seventeen and, like many of the young men, shipped out in the merchant marine. His break with Norway occurred out of the natural course of events that compelled many others to leave. The little farm, bathed in the balmy southwesterly winds of summer and blessed with a climate moderated by the influence of the warm remains of the Gulf Stream, produced wheat, oats, and potatoes and sustained a number of dairy cows. However, for his parents,

Emanuel and Elizabeth, and their growing family, life remained difficult. It did not suit the temperament of a young man with adventure burning in his heart.

In 1887, Frank went to sea aboard sailing ships out of Farsund and other ports. The letters he sent home to his parents bore the postmarks of exotic places in the West Indies, South America, Africa, and the West Coast of the United States. The young man's physical presence and quiet but strong personality impressed his superiors. His imposing physique—he was six feet three and weighed more than two hundred pounds—made him a natural as a bosun's mate. He worked his way into that position at a very early age, driving the men who drove the ships to reach maximum hull speed whenever possible. Frank's natural inclination to look at any man directly with his piercing blue eyes, his squarish face speaking of quiet strength behind a gentle but stern spirit, led the crews to follow orders with little resistance and the captain and mates to treat him with the kind of respect accorded sailors with a talent for men, ships, and the sea.

After six years in the merchant marine, Frank began to wonder about what other opportunities the world had to offer. His was a life without connection to much else besides a family in a distant land, a place he missed and often thought about during his nights on watch. His reveries were set to the gentle wash and slap of the water against the hull of his ship as it moved through a sea of blackness under a sky spangled white with stars. The yearnings of a young man, at the age of twenty-three, led his thoughts to finding a wife and making a home where he could raise a family without spending months, even years, away at sea.

When his ship sailed up the lower harbor of New York in 1893, the crew busily tacking to avoid steamers that seemed intent on running the sailer down, his thoughts bordered on taking action and gradually grew stronger. Long lines of traffic, ranging in size from great liners to little scows dumping refuse from the city, clogged the tight channels. As Frank's ship slowly passed through the Verrazano Narrows and came around a protrusion of land on the Brooklyn side, the green smudge of the Statue of Liberty suddenly became visible. The skyscrapers of Manhattan, some of which reached more than twenty stories high, spoke of a world that held great promise. The windows caught the sun and reflected it seaward in flashes of white.

For years he had heard of a better life in America from sailors tired of the long hours and the dangers at sea. His younger brother, Jake, had set off from the farm several years earlier to find out if his dreams matched the reality of the new land. He settled in Leonardo, a small town near Sandy Hook. Frank had thought of him only a few hours ago. Based on what letters from home indicated, Jake seemed happy enough.

Frank's thoughts of joining his brother had remained merely a fancy, a longing for change. But he had chosen not to act. Rather, he regarded this land as a place where his ship put into port to offload cargo and either pick another up or sail off in search of one. As he looked at the skyline, the busy harbor, he fixed his eyes on Ellis Island's main building with mounting interest. The four-story towers, capped with slate-blue pyramids and the buff-painted walls, struck him as hospitable. The building resembled more a hotel for the rich than a processing station through which he would have to pass were he to stay.

In the end, the pull of the potential opportunities on land was too great for him to resist. He had come to think of America as a place to start on a new path, and now he would no longer ignore his desires. As he rode the ferry across to Ellis Island after collecting his wages and saying good-bye to his shipmates, the same excitement and anticipation that most immigrants experienced took hold of him. He smiled broadly, his eyes sparkling, the wind tousling his fine blond hair.

Frank headed straight for the fishing villages along the beaches of New Jersey and looked up his brother, where he stayed for a while until he got on his feet. Working as a fisherman in the area, sometimes with his brother, it wasn't long before he met George Harbo and the two became friends. They both found in each other something of the homes they had left behind, a feeling that came alive as they talked about Norway, their families, and their futures in America.

George had moved six years earlier from Brooklyn with his wife and son, Andrew, to the Atlantic Highlands, a town far more comfortable than Nauvoo. He had occasionally worked as a harbor pilot for one of the independent companies serving the harbor. Having studied advanced navigation in Brevik, he easily qualified for a pilot's position after he knew the harbor well enough to draw a chart of its every contour, shoal, and navigation aid onto a blank chart. This, in fact, was one of the tests every pilot underwent before he could guide a ship into port, that and a long apprenticeship. But piloting was dangerous work. In 1888 an early spring blizzard in March buried the city under snowdrifts. Out at sea, off the lower harbor, nine pilot boats sank, and seventeen pilots died. George knew some of them; all the pilots knew each other, or at least of each other. It was a close-knit fraternity that competed fiercely, pitting one boat against another.

George tried his hand at fishing, which he considered safer and possibly more lucrative. He owned a clam boat he had built with his own hands. It was like him to want something that was his, and his alone, to carve out a living on terms dictated by no other. Aboard the various pilot boats, there was always politics or lack of conformity to an ordered way of doing things. Being his own boss fit very much into George's view of himself and his place in the world. Frank joined him, and together they dug clams from the bays and rivers near Sandy Hook and shipped them to New York City.

The years 1886–1893 saw great change both in America and in George's personal life. As the two men set out in the early morning, rowing their beamy skiff to the clam flats, they shared stories, and a bond grew stronger between them as their friendship developed through the years, taking them through the hard times then at work shaping and irrevocably changing the nation and acting as an impetus on them both to make a seemingly desperate effort to achieve what they perceived as their only chance to truly make their mark in the world.

In the early 1890s the country sank into turbulent times. Strikes among workers protesting working conditions and stagnant wages became more frequent. The lists of suicides published on the front pages of the newspapers grew long, obvious signs of a country with problems that seemed beyond facing. Crop prices decreased, and transportation costs climbed ever higher, as did rates for goods and services. The flood of investment capital from wealthy European investors that had so helped buoy the economy during the relatively prosperous 1880s came to a halt with a panic in British security markets in 1890, setting the stage for far worse to come in the still very young nation across the Atlantic. That same year, the U.S. Census Bureau announced that America no longer had any frontier remaining. Sentiment toward immigrants soured and soon metamorphosed into outright hostility.

While many immigrants had grown to love their adopted country, a number decided to go home when the going got tough. The rate of immigration in the early 1890s began to slow as the economy hit hard times. In 1892 labor groups, and farmers primarily from the Midwest and the South, organized a third party, with idealistic hopes that great change could take place and transform an America with two distinct classes, the poor and the rich, into a more equitable society. They were known as the Populist Party, and their aim was to nationalize the railroads and the telegraph companies, institute an income tax, and allow for the unlimited coinage of silver. This latter reform would destroy gold as the measure against which currency was based, but since the silver dollar was the common man's currency and did not equal the value of a dollar in gold, the notion took on an appeal of its own. Had this reform occurred, however, it would have meant financial suicide for the United States.

Against this backdrop of uncertainty, George Harbo faced his own dark days. He had brought Anine and Andrew to the Atlantic Highlands in May 1887. The family lived a fairly comfortable life, one not nearly as austere as it would have been had he thrown his lot in with the people of Nauvoo. Anine gave birth to Annie Louisa the following August, on the twenty-second, the same date Andrew was born two years earlier. In June 1890, Anine had another daughter, Agnes Grace. It looked as though the future were bright, filled with the promise that had led George to America in the first place.

On August 13, 1891, Anine and the three children boarded a transatlantic steamer to return to Brevik. The reasons were both personal and in keeping with the compulsions exerted on many immigrants at that time to seek solace in the familiar, to get back in touch with the lands they had left behind in search of a perceived better life that somehow didn't jive with reality, particularly in view of the economic unrest then prevalent in America. Three days later,

Agnes Grace, only one year old, died at sea and was unceremoniously committed to the deep in a weighted sack. Upon receiving word from Anine of their daughter's death, George, alone and trying to find his place in the America he had grown to love, sank into temporary depression. He lost himself in his solitary work as a clammer, the monotonous labor a balm for his wounded soul.

Two years later, the entire country found itself in a deep depression. It became known as the Panic of '93 and was brought about in part by a decline in the treasury's gold reserve, due to decreasing federal revenue and heavy expenses, that threatened to topple the country off the gold standard. More than 4 million workers lost their jobs, companies went bankrupt, and banks closed. The stock market in New York City fell into a short-lived, though temporarily disastrous, decline.

George extended a helping hand to his fellow countryman Frank, who had had the misfortune of arriving in America at the height of the depression. Work was scarce everywhere; the prospects on the beach were likewise less than stellar. The two men labored with their heavy clamming tongs that summer, reaching deep into the sand to scoop up their daily bread in the form of hard gray shells, and managed to earn enough money to live on.

On Wednesday, August 23, they worked the clam flats as usual. However, the increasingly thick layer of clouds began to make them both feel uneasy. The sky took on an almost yellow appearance, and although very little wind ruffled the surface of the bay, white puffs of scud streaked away to the west, indicating extremely high winds aloft, blowing in from off the Atlantic. Huge numbers of seabirds flew overhead, headed inland.

"The air has a funny feel to it, George," Frank said, standing in the center of the boat, hands on his hips, eyes fixed on the birds retreating to the west. "I've seen it feel this way before only once, down in the West Indies before a great blow."

George had lived through plenty of storms at sea himself during his short stint in the merchant marine, prior to coming to America. However, he had never sailed into tropical waters, had no firsthand experience with the power behind the cyclonic storms that breed in the hot, humid temperatures of summer and early fall, born from deep low-pressure systems off the coast of Africa. Still, he, too, felt apprehensive. "I think we'd do well to head in, Frank."

His friend nodded but said nothing. When they got to shore, they pulled the boat far up the beach, much farther than necessary in ordinary times, and moored it to a stout old tree with thick manila lines. Down on the ocean side of the beach, some of the fishermen of Nauvoo came in early, hitched teams of horses to haul their boats on logs used as rollers, and pulled the little vessels well above the dunes.

As the afternoon progressed, the wind veered more to the northeast and increased to well above fifty knots. By eight o'clock, the full force of the hurricane lashed a swath of destruction more than one hundred miles wide all that evening and through the next morning. The incoming tide, all the higher from the storm waves, flooded up the bay and inundated lower Manhattan. Telegraph wires blew down, trees took brief, destructive flights, and the vessels in the upper harbor dragged anchor, ramming each other or running aground on the flats off Governors Island and Jersey City. People died, though the death toll wasn't very high because the storm's strong center passed over relatively unpopulated areas on the south shore of Long Island.

As the hurricane passed to the north, George and Frank went down to the beach, like most everyone else along the shore, to see what was left of their property. Although the boat had sunk at its mooring and partially filled with sand, it was easily put right. Others had not been so lucky. As they worked together, their friendship seemed all the stronger. Perhaps it was facing the hard times, the near disaster of the hurricane, and their shared heritage that bound the men together and provided the foundation on which they would build a dream three years later that to all observers seemed as impossible to attain as the stars.

4

A thick summer haze all but obscured the hills of the Atlantic Highlands, blending the green of the trees on the steep slopes into a blot dark against the blue-white sky. Hardly a breath of wind stirred the surface of the bay, shining like quicksilver in a sheen that heaved almost imperceptibly from the influence of long-spent swells. Every now and then the muffled report of the guns fired at the army's proving ground on Sandy Hook rumbled in the distance, a testament to the country's continuing push for better and better weapons and its deep-seated insecurity about foreign powers. The shrill blast of a steam whistle at regular intervals announced the coming and going of the ferries at the Atlantic Highlands terminal. The cry of a lone gull and the sound of the oars working in the tholepins that locked them into place against the rails of the clam boat punctuated the longer spans of near silence as George and Frank set about their daily business.

They followed a mind-dulling routine, first rowing the clam boat through the shallows that extended outward from the shore, particularly shallow at low tide, the most opportune time to tong for clams. At the prescribed spot, often marked with stakes driven into the sandy bottom of the clam flats, Frank stood up to work the clam tongs, scissorlike baskets used to unearth clams from the depths. His massive muscles strained as he gripped the rounded and smoothed mahogany handles, worn to fit the shape of his hands, and lifted a wedge of sand, heavy with slippery gray muck that smelled similar to rotted cheese, to the surface of the water. He tried his best to wash most of it away to reveal the catch and dumped the mass onto the culling board. George picked through the clams, broken shells, and other debris and threw the keepers into baskets.

After a time, the two men switched duties. Even though George owned the boat, his even-handed nature meant sharing in the work on equal terms with his friend. Their long hours in the boat together honed their ability to work as a team, to know the swings in mood of the other. Though both men were not given to sharp tempers or deep depression despite the hardships life dealt them, no man's spirit remained immune to the forces of emotion. They each knew when a joke or a word of encouragement was needed, and even more important, they each knew the other well enough to make words unnecessary.

This hot, humid day late in the summer of 1895 was just like any other, uneventful over the more than twenty miles they rowed in making the rounds of the clam flats. It merged with the hundreds of other days into a haze of memory every bit as obscure as the one that clung to the steamy hills of the Atlantic Highlands to the south of them and enveloped the telegraph tower rising one hundred feet to the east above Sandy Hook. Marine observers, stationed at the top of the tower, scanned the horizon for incoming ships and, upon sighting the flag of a specific line, telegraphed the shipping company in New York. As with the men in the clam boat, the humid air made their work more difficult.

On this day and others during the summer of 1895 the men worked with a bit more zeal than they had in past years, for they had found a purpose in the routine, a glimmer of hope that fueled their spirits. A shared dream had formed, one that had taken shape very slowly in George's mind and had gradually taken an inexorable hold on Frank after his friend told him his intentions. Any dream, whether it remains hidden in the recesses of one's mind or springs forth into the world and cries out to become a reality, exerts a strong pull on the soul. The dream shared between two people becomes all the stronger, almost impossible to forget and even more impossible to discard as something impractical.

On one of those countless days aboard the clam boat, while Frank worked the tongs, George straightened up from his hunched position over the culling board and simply said: "You know, I think two good men in a good sea boat could row across the ocean."

Frank, not a quick man to laugh but one whose laughter, once started, could shake the walls of a house, looked at his friend as though he were crazy.

"Stop laughing, Frank. I'm serious."

Frank set the tongs in the boat, sat down, and looked hard at George for a long time. He thought back to his days on the farm in Elunde, ten years ago, when a fellow from the nearby town of Farsund, William Jahnsen, had disappeared at sea after setting off from Ireland single-handed in a tiny sailboat to America, just for the adventure of it, and to establish a world record. The people of the village shook their heads at the loss of a man they thought both brave and stupid. The story made a deep impression on the fifteen-year-old as he worked with his father on the farm. For Frank, the death of Jahnsen was heroic, the very essence of adventure, one that had turned out badly but nevertheless stuck in his mind.

"Such a thing would be very dangerous," Frank said, suddenly as serious as George. "If it could be done at all."

"I know it would be. But think if we could do it. No one has crossed the ocean under oars alone. It's the only kind of small boat that hasn't done it, and I think there would be plenty of city people who would pay to hear the tale. With the summer westerlies and a push from the Gulf Stream, it could be done, Frank."

Frank remained silent, turning over in his mind the question of whether his friend had gone mad from the heat, but at the same time wondering if it could be accomplished and what it would mean to them both if they succeeded. At least two other men he knew of, on separate occasions, had made the voyage under sail. They received much attention and made lecture tours on both sides of the Atlantic. The lecture halls and little theaters in the larger towns often hosted other less adventurous travelers who gave talks on their experiences in far-off places. Famous authors, hunters, inventors, daredevils, and the like routinely presented their audiences with stories of the outlandish that, for at least a short while, swept the listeners away from their daily routines and ordinary lives to a world they could only dream existed outside the confines of their villages. With little else to do for entertainment, these lectures were very popular and lucrative for the presenters.

"It's something to think about," Frank said at last. "But I wouldn't mention this to anyone, George, or they'll think you've lost your mind."

George chuckled. "They'll know soon enough, Frank. They'll all know soon enough."

From that day on the two men kept the flame of the idea burning, and slowly, after living with it for a long time, it grew in them, somehow seeming a little less impossible with each passing month. What prospects did either of them really have in America? They had seen hundreds of people come to the land of promise with high hopes, only to find themselves blocked from the opportunity to earn fair wages and lead comfortable lives. They ended up working most of the time for the betterment of a boss, with little energy for the enjoyment of even simple things, like taking a walk with their children, or having a day of fun at Coney Island. The prospects didn't bode well for a pair of uneducated clam diggers. With the country still weak from the depression, it didn't look as if the future would hold the key to anything other than more of the same backbreaking toil.

George and Frank kept quiet about their plans, not breathing a word to their families back in Norway or the other fishermen on the beach. As George had said, if the plans were to become reality, everyone would know soon enough. Both men knew that when news got out family members would try to dissuade them from attempting what seemed a suicidal journey, and acquaintances would enjoy having a bit of fun at their expense as they joked that the clams the tongers caught were smarter than the both of them put together.

Late that October, George received word from Anine, who was living with Andrew and Annie Louisa with her family in Brevik, that she had given birth on the first of the month to a son conceived when George had returned to Norway for a brief visit in the dead of the previous winter. He read and reread the letter, overjoyed at being blessed with a son. He will be good company for Andrew, he thought. A boy should have a brother.

He and Anine had agreed that if the baby was a boy they would name him after Fridtjof Nansen, whom George admired for his courage. Nansen, also from

Norway, had braved the sea and ice of the high latitudes of the North Atlantic to reach Greenland in
1888. He then proceeded to explore the ice cap, a
truly great scientific achievement that advanced
man's understanding of the world. It showed that the
earth's most terrible places, locations so harsh one
would think mankind did not belong there, could in
fact beckon the brave soul who dared to partake of
adventure. Nansen had at the time embarked upon
another great adventure, which involved freezing his
trusty ship, *Fram*, into the pack ice and allowing it to
drift north to better position him for further explorations of the North Pole. So his son would bear this
great man's name, just as Andrew had been named
after a great American president. Fridtjof Nansen
Harbo—it had a nice ring to it.

The thoughts of his son clouded over somewhat as
he considered how his intended voyage would impact
on Anine now that Fritz had been born. Three children to take care of instead of two, all without a
husband. He knew Anine seemed content to remain
in Norway while the economy remained flat in the
United States despite the fact that she missed him
very much. She would not welcome the possibility of
losing her husband to the sea over what amounted
to a get-rich-quick stunt, at least in the minds of most
people. Although he had deep misgivings about what
might happen were he to die and leave Anine a widow
with three young children, he came to realize that
sometimes a man must take a risk to achieve his full
potential, as Nansen had. If he and his friend succeeded, it would mean the possibility of a better life
for his family. He put off writing Anine of his plans
for as long as he could.

Frank, with no responsibilities to a wife and children, nevertheless spent many sleepless nights gazing
out at the lighthouses, visible from the shore of the
Atlantic Highlands. His family loved him very much.

They had always cautioned him to take care while at sea, not to take foolish risks that might put an end to a long life ahead of him. They lived with the constant knowledge that he might never return from his voyages under sail while in the merchant marine. They had expressed as much in their letters to him and had been pleased when they learned he had taken up a safer, less risky trade in America. They, no doubt, would not think highly of this adventure. The safer way is always the easiest way, but that was not for Frank, and it never had been. As he looked out into the blackness at the tiny pinpricks of light from the lighthouses on Old Orchard Shoal, the West Bank, and Romer Shoal, just off Sandy Hook, he convinced himself that his family would understand. They would have to let him be free to try his best and to do as he saw fit, even if it meant something as strange as rowing a boat across an ocean that routinely sank large ships.

George and Frank worked with vigor and saved every penny for provisions and, most important, the boat, which they decided would have to be a custom-built, modified version of the surf-boats of Nauvoo. They talked at length about logistics, the most favorable month to depart, how long a passage to expect, and hundreds of other tiny details. The very dream of their voyage buoyed their spirits and infused their lives with a new meaning. At last they had found their chance to make a mark in their adopted land and, in doing so, escape conditions that restrained most common men.

5

In the heart of Manhattan's Franklin Square, a large-circulation national weekly newspaper called the *Police Gazette* had its headquarters. Its printing plant churned out millions of pink-sheeted pages filled with all manner of stories upstanding Victorians publicly labeled as trash but read on the sly, anyway, because its content revealed the base, the gritty, and the tawdry side of the human condition that most people, regardless of their station in life, find hard to resist. The *Police Gazette* let them step into a world in which the poor lived, and gave them a glimpse of the other half without getting their hands dirty in the process. Of course, the masses of workers throughout the country, whether on the farm or in the city, were the true target of the *Police Gazette*. They were the ones the proprietor and editor courted, with the help of wayward reporters recruited from the daily papers in New York who would write virtually anything for a ten-dollar bill, a meal, and a bottle on weekends.

Stories of murder, female pugilists, daredevil bridge jumpers, aeronauts killed trying to fly, fashion, gossip, and the sexy ladies of the theater—all illustrated with woodcuts plastered liberally throughout each issue— attracted a loyal following of readers who liked looking at the pictures and who could digest the short, telegraphic stories. The strange and bizarre sports that found their way onto the pages of the *Police Gazette* tantalized the country. Rat-eating dogs, fights between bulls, cockfights, even boxing matches pitting man against a rather dogged kangaroo—nothing was beneath the standards of the *Police Gazette* or its proprietor, Richard Kyle Fox. Shrewd, handsome, and ruthless, Fox had the genius to fashion a unique publication that had earned him millions of dollars since 1876, the year he had bought it from the previous publishers and immediately added his personal stamp of the tasteless to its pages.

Fox, a lean, dark-haired man with a silky handlebar mustache, sat behind a beautiful oak desk in the suite he had set aside for himself at the editorial offices of the paper and pored over press accounts published in other periodicals, looking for ideas to flesh out the issue ready to go to press. In this routine he had minions to act as helpers. But he always was a hands-on kind of editor, ensuring that each edition of the *Police Gazette* met his demanding standards, not for high-quality journalism but for the sensationalism he knew would sell papers. As he went about his business, he received visitors upon occasion. His door was always open to any who might provide an opportunity to further the paper or his own personal agenda.

Fox looked up from some papers on his desk, smoothed his hair, and raised an eyebrow at his secretary in a silent question.

"Some odd ducks to see you, sir," she said. "They're fishermen from down the bay. They say they're going to row across the ocean."

Fox smiled. He had heard it all by now—desperate fools who wrote him letters saying they would drink more water faster than anyone else, lift more weight with their teeth, wrestle gorillas, fly in weird inventions—and in most cases he encouraged the activity and sent reporters to write about what happened. If someone died, all the better. Blood made good copy for his pink pages. He also presented the successful players with *Police Gazette* gold medals, not worth much from a cash standpoint. But to those who received them, along with public adulation, the medals greased the wheels of the human tendency to outdo every other soul in accomplishing something that no one had ever done before, no matter how stupid it might appear to the practical observer.

"They say that, do they?" Fox said, mildly interested in meeting these two men. "Send them in."

Fox leaned back in his chair and looked long and hard at George and Frank as they entered his suite and stood before him. Their clothes were clean but made from coarse wool. The garments looked as if they had seen more than their fair share of Sunday church services, weddings, and funerals. Their derbies, clasped before them, appeared smudged in an effort to rid them of soil. Both men looked him directly in the eye, however, and that he respected. Although he enjoyed being held in high esteem, even awe, the truth of the matter was that he admired men, and women, with courage.

"Mr. Fox, my name is George Harbo, and this is Frank Samuelsen. We were hoping to speak with you about—"

"Yes, my secretary told me." Fox smiled, though only slightly, and kept both men fixed in a cool, calculating stare. Obviously, these rough-looking men hailed from Scandinavia, based on their accents, so thick that they sounded as if they had just stepped off the ferry from Ellis Island. Although Fox was an immigrant himself, he detested the newcomers from eastern Europe, especially Jews, whom he considered of equal status with Negroes. However, the Swedes, the Danes, and the Norwegians shared the same part of the world as his ancestors had. They seemed less strangers than distant neighbors. In fact, Fox's view of the Scandinavians was common among most Americans. The white Anglo-Saxons, with a work ethic bordering on the puritanical, allowed them to fit in almost as well as the Germans, who were considered excellent craftsmen and seldom represented a liability to society.

He thought back to more than two decades ago, when he had first gotten off the boat from Belfast. The Irish weren't part of the mainstream at that time, not really, not like now. Those who had come even earlier faced nothing but prolonged unemployment and a society that deemed them worth less than scum. His countrymen, driven to the land of promise out of starvation and the unjust rule of the British, slaved for pennies, when pennies could be had. They built the Erie Canal, made bricks in the factories at Haverstraw Bay, up the Hudson River, shoveled manure in stalls . . . anything to bring a little cash back to the tenements, the Irish ghettos that eventually thrived and became decent neighborhoods. Now the Irish were firmly entrenched in America. They owned businesses, served on the police force, and also had acquired considerable clout in the down-and-dirty political circles that ran cities and small-town local governments.

There had still been quite a lot of the same ill feeling toward the Irish when he had found himself on the docks of Manhattan in 1874, the grandson of a minister who knew the world had more to offer than the word of God and the meager existence one could expect in return for preaching it to the flock. He had clawed his way to the top selling advertising for the *Commercial Bulletin*, a financial publication read by the rich. In just two years, he finagled a buyout of the *Police Gazette*. He breathed new life into the newspaper and set the stage for success beyond his dreams. Yes, he thought, America still was the land of opportunity, and for some the streets really were paved in gold.

"You say you're going to cross the ocean in a rowboat," Fox said. "A daring feat—if you live."

"We believe we can do it," George said. "I've read the *Police Gazette*. I've seen you sometimes back people like us."

"Yes, that's true. But only when I think the event has something that will appeal to the readers. Two men who row off and are never seen again will not make for a very long story, I'm afraid. Hardly worth the ink to print it, wouldn't you say?"

Fox did not ask the two men to sit down just yet. He let them stand there, awkwardly shifting their weight from one foot to the other. "I'm aware that no boat has made it across under oar power alone, with no sail or rudder to help. As you know, I follow these endeavors carefully. I'm something of an expert, I should say. What makes you think you can succeed other than you've got a giant as part of the team?"

"George and I both know the sea. We have since we were boys. Where we come from, you take a boat to get to town, and you row. The ocean can always surprise you, though, even those who know it like us," Frank said. "But with the right boat—"

"It can be done!" George said, interrupting Frank. "And we're the ones to do it."

"Well, we shall see," Fox said, sensing the determination of these two Scandinavians. He found their idea interesting, at least to the extent that he would hear them out. If there was one thing about people he could believe in it was their propensity to reach for the impossible and their odd ability to achieve it given the right combination of luck and courage and intelligence, in that order. He motioned to two chairs. "Sit down, gentlemen, and tell me more about it."

Emerging from Fox's office that May of 1896, George and Frank were no richer for their efforts, though the publisher had assured them that were they to succeed in their crossing each would receive a special *Police Gazette* gold medal. Succeed, and one other thing, too. The boat would bear his name: Fox across the sea, worldwide attention. The idea came to his quick mind as effortlessly as had the chestful of others that made him a very rich man. His orchestration of the fight between John L. Sullivan and Jake Kilrain almost seven years earlier had created a national fervor; it helped legitimize the illegal sport of boxing, though the authorities in Mississippi, where the match took place, didn't quite see it that way. Where there was opportunity to grab the public's attention, Fox was sure to be nearby, ready to take advantage of a good thing when he saw it.

Fox shrewdly played the safe end of the game, motivating the men with the promise of medals but offering no help of substance until they actually completed the voyage. With their journey linked in part to his newspaper, headlines in all the dailies would, of course, include a mention of the *Gazette's* medals and its publisher and provide exposure valuable to Fox's interest in ever-increasing circulation. Free publicity never was something Fox turned away lightly, and if he could get it from the respected dailies, it would please him to have manipulated the press barons and pious editors. He knew that many of the latter would condemn the two men as nothing more than fools intent on suicide and, by the *Gazette's* indirect involvement, excoriate him as well for condoning the enterprise, if not encouraging it. But that troubled Fox not a bit.

For George and Frank's part, they left the decorous offices of the *Police Gazette* happy with the prospect that the publisher supported their idea, thought it possible to establish a world record, and might offer more than just medals if they succeeded.

There was the hint of a cash prize, a tribute to their bravery, but nothing more. They had made the rounds of the city's other major newspapers, told the editors of their intentions to row from the Battery to Le Havre, France, a major port every bit as important as Liverpool, Southampton, or Bristol, and were met with skepticism and in some cases outright indifference. This made Fox's words of encouragement all the more important to them, words they could hang on to. Nevertheless, despite the contrasting initial response both men received from the other newspapers, when they retrieved their little boat from the painter's shop in Brooklyn on May 25 and rowed it up the East River to Harlem for an exhibition at local rowing clubs, every major paper sent reporters to cover the story.

The reporters dubbed the two Norwegians foolish and suicidal, idiots who would risk their lives for a brief period of celebrity and the intangible reward of setting a world record—a negligible human achievement. While accomplishing such a feat would indeed speak of extraordinary courage and physical stamina, what did it really matter? Why undertake what amounted to a frivolous stunt, like a child trying to get attention by climbing the highest tree in the park just to alarm his parents? Others admired their courage, their determination. Still others, with the righteous indignation so common in the press during that time, the same type of sentiment that Fox hated and flouted in every way he could, called on the police to arrest them before they could leave the Battery on June 6, the day set for the start of the journey.

The gloom present in many of the press reports reflected the feelings of both men's relatives in Norway, who wrote letters at regular intervals during the early days of the year while they tested the boat and prepared for their long row, begging them not to try such a foolish thing. The assurance that the boat was the best one possible for a transatlantic crossing, that it had been fashioned by a renowned builder who supplied the fleets of Nauvoo with craft capable of weathering the worst of storms, provided no comfort to them whatsoever. Details about the boat's custom-built features, such as sturdy handrails fixed to the underside of the boat for use in righting the vessel in the event of a capsize, only served to aggravate and enhance their worry. Their families knew that the ocean was vast, and they had a great deal of trouble understanding what had taken hold of their loved ones. But by June, it became quite clear that George and Frank would indeed attempt the crossing, and almost everyone who heard about the voyage expected them to row off and never be seen again.

6

The month of June in the Northeast brings with it variable weather, a transition from the north winds and their accompanying cold and fog to the prevailing summer southwesterlies. These southern winds blow up the coast across thousands of miles of ocean, which grows constantly warmer with each sunny day, and carry the searing heat and energy-sapping subtropical humidity so common in July and August. The dog days of summer, when people in crowded city neighborhoods spent as much time as possible outdoors on their front stoops nursing cups of shaved ice topped with Vermont maple syrup, often sleeping on fire escapes to catch the evening breeze channeled between the tall buildings, were not unknown in June. George and Frank had decided that the best time for their departure would be between extremes of heat and cold, the beginning of a season maturing into consistency.

To leave earlier in the season meant the very real possibility of facing easterly winds impossible to row against, violent nor'easters, and bitter cold. Without the land to act as an enormous radiator, trapping the heat of a weak sun, those cool days of spring on the farms well beyond the coast were dangerously cold out at sea. To leave later, with the warmth of summer, its prevailing southwest and west winds behind them, meant the possibility of encountering an early hurricane. Both men, having experienced the fury of a strong, well-developed cyclonic storm three years earlier, had no desire to witness one thousands of miles offshore. Such a storm would quickly destroy their stout little boat. As it was, if easterly winds delayed their passage, a hurricane could easily overtake them well before they reached the frigid waters of the North Atlantic, where tropical storms can't live; the heat and humidity they thrive on removed, they soon dissipate.

Dawn on Saturday, June 6, came at five-thirty. As the rising sun bathed the upper harbor of New York in a reddish haze, George and Frank were awake to see it. One by one the windows of the buildings facing east toward the sea turned from gray to copper. The thunderous rumble of the trains on the elevated railway nearby increased in frequency as the city slowly came awake and set about its business.

"The day looks like it will be a fine one," Frank said. "And hot." He had long been aware of the old saying: Red sky at night, a sailor's delight; red sky in the morning, sailors take warning, which he knew was inaccurate as often as it was right. The weather seldom conformed to an old saw. He clapped George on the shoulder and looked down at the *Fox,* which was moored to a floating dock near the barge office, not far from Castle Garden, no longer in use for processing immigrants. Piles of provisions bought at Rafferty's Canned Goods and Fancy Groceries over on Front Street the day before would require long hours yet of careful stowing. "Not long till we're off," he whispered, more to himself than to his friend.

Frank thought of his sister Caroline, who had re-

cently come over from Norway and who would see
him off later that day with his brother Jake. At seventeen, slim, a beautiful young woman with fair hair
and a pleasing figure, she was filled with the hope
and optimism he had possessed at her age. She had
come to America with every intention of living a life
with far more to offer than was possible on the farm
in Elunde, and no words of discouragement damp-
ened her spirit. For her anything was possible, and
it was as simple as that. Not that Frank could blame
her; he understood what she felt more than even
she did, having lived through the same experience
himself. Brooklyn, with its burgeoning enclave of Norwegians and other Scandinavians, had beckoned, and
she had come. News of his adventure, however, had
caused her great anxiety. Even in her belief that
America offered a chance at the impossible, this
endeavor was too extreme. She, like Jake, was convinced that the voyage would end badly, that it was
nothing more than suicide.

His mother, Elizabeth, had responded to his letter
telling her of his intentions with similar sentiments.
She begged him not to pursue this folly. Emanuel
felt the same way and wished he would continue safely
shell fishing close to shore. Frank had a brother, born
in 1894, whom he had never seen. Her letter implored
him to think of little Sigurd, his three sisters, and his
brothers. Jake tried to talk him out of the trip as
well but soon gave up. He saw the determination in
Frank's eyes, his quiet way of showing annoyance at
being berated and called crazy, even by his own family.
He shrugged off these thoughts and set to completing
the tasks at hand.

As the day wore on, the stagnant heat of the wind-
less morning became oppressive. Sweat poured off
George and Frank's faces as they tried to make sense
of the pile of provisions, stowing each item into the
eighteen-foot open boat with an eye toward keeping

the balance of weight distributed as evenly as possible. The little boat was equipped with two watertight compartments lined with galvanized iron, one in the bow, the other in the stern. Into each of these went a barrel of sea biscuits, hard, brownish flat bread that tasted like wood. George's log, writing paper and pencils, charts, nautical almanac, and other important materials required for navigation, as well as boxes of matches to light their signal lamp, the tiny lamp for their compass, and the kerosene stove mounted in the bow were stowed in the stern's compartment. George took special care with the quadrant, a less sophisticated version of a sextant, an instrument used to find one's position using the sun or stars.

Cans of corned beef, roast beef, baked beans, ham and salmon, boxes of brown bread, jars of jam and mustard, bags of coffee, tomatoes, and green onions— all had to find a place in the *Fox*, which was only five feet wide and weighed just 250 pounds. A crate of 250 raw eggs, surrounded and covered with damp seaweed to keep them from breaking and to retard rotting, was wedged under one of the seats. Cakes of soap; tins of sugar, salt, and pepper; sixty gallons of water, stored in special galvanized iron tanks, fitted and secured to the bottom of the boat; sixteen bottles of wine—the sheer volume of provisions meant to last for two months or more posed a daunting task to stow properly during those last hours on land.

On the floating dock, ready for lashing lengthwise within the boat, were three pairs of oars built from ash, a strong, flexible wood, and two pairs of light spruce, a wood far less heavy than the latter. These were the workhorses. Designed for tandem rowing, the *Fox* would move through flat water at roughly five knots with both men rowing hard. Three pairs of sculls and two pairs of sweeps, long oars with considerably more leverage than the shorter, stouter workers, also had to fit somewhere. The varnished finish glistened in the hot sun. The metal wraps along each blade, to prevent splintering, conducted the heat, making the sharp edges hot to the touch. Bands of heavy leather sheathed all the oars where they would grind against the rail of the boat and the tholepins that held them in place.

With each passing hour the big clock at the Produce Exchange, a short distance away, struck the time. The sound carried over the voices of the crowd, drawn there after reading the stories in the local press. People had begun to gather early in the afternoon, which started as a trickle at first, then swelled to a veritable mob of more than one thousand not altogether well behaved souls. Lines of people watched the men work, shouting unwanted comments about where to stow the gear, the feasibility of the voyage, and the sanity of those preparing for it. For them, it was an outing on a Saturday off from work with nothing better to do than watch the *Fox*'s crew of two prepare for their date with Davy Jones's locker, where they would sleep an eternal slumber in the company of the many sailors who died at sea before them.

Caroline was there, too, silent, eyes locked on the boat, though she could not get near it. Her brother Jake stood silently at her side, just staring at Frank. They both looked at George, the man easy to blame for all of this. Caroline hadn't said as much to her brother, but she would have preferred that he had never met this short, stocky, red-haired man. His handsome looks, sharp nose, and sparkling eyes, seemingly benign features of manliness, represented the veneer over something wild and untamable, a bad influence on Frank, who was still very much a boy, even though he was twenty-six. Of course, she didn't understand yet why her brother needed to make this voyage or that George hadn't bewitched him at all.

As the clock ticked on, the crowd grew larger, as if swept in with the rising tide that churned and boiled

around the tip of the Battery on its way north up the
Hudson River 150 miles to Albany and eastward to
Long Island Sound via the East River. The bands of
white chop in the water and eddies behind the pilings
supporting the docks were the only visible signs of
the powerful current, but to any mariner its presence
was well known, an event that occurred every six hours
in a cycle begun long ago. George and Frank had
planned their departure to coincide with the start
of the outward-flowing tide, which would begin at
around 5:00 P.M. To start earlier would have sapped
their strength in a futile struggle against the elements.
Far better to have a helping hand from nature, to
seek a level of harmony with it from the outset rather
than charge off in a bold act of senseless defiance.

But with the gear stowed, the boat's red bottom
sunk under the weight so that only its white topsides
showed, the waiting on the tide went hard for both
men. Like actors in the wings of a darkened theater
before taking the stage, the anticipation and deep
anxiety had time to work on them, and the intense
heat didn't help matters. They stood, then sat, and
endured. Frank had spoken few words with Caroline;
they each knew, or thought they knew, what sentiments resided in the other's heart, and the enormity
of the event seemed to banish the need to talk more
about it.

George, alone in his thoughts, let his mind wander
to Anine, Andrew, Annie Louisa, Fridtjof Nansen, his
newborn son. George had met Nansen and admired
the man's determination to strike off into the
unknown, his zeal for adventure, and his ability to
find it. At such a great moment in his life, George
half wished his family were there to see him off; but
the sight of Frank's sister amid the crowd, obviously
distressed, tears welling up in her eyes, her face
creased with worry, made it clear that if his family
were among the onlookers on the dock, the moment

would have been unbearably painful for them all. As
it was, Harold, his brother, was standing as close to
the seawall as possible and not looking pleased. Like
his relatives in Norway, Harold didn't claim to understand the voyage.

George sighed and gazed out at the tide rips, less-
ening in fury with every passing moment. "It will be
good to be off," he said quietly to Frank. "I'm not
one for the waiting."

"We'll soon have our wish," Frank said, checking
his little pocket watch. He shoved it back into his
pocket.

"Gentlemen," said a man at the front of a small
group of well-dressed men with pallid faces emerging
from the crowd. They all wore the finest white shirts,
though slightly wet at the armpits and around the
collar from sweat. Despite the heat, their vests remained buttoned tight. Their topcoats, however, were
folded across their arms. Their top hats scarcely provided any relief from the sun, unlike the broad-
rimmed hats George and Frank wore. "We've come
for the certification. Is everything in order?"

The men, eight of them, represented the city's
largest newspapers and the local office of United Press
wire services. They had come to certify that the *Fox*
was not equipped with a mast or a sail. This was just
the first in a chain of certifications to follow, vital to
the formal establishing of a record, and both men
knew it. W. S. Merwitter of the *New York Times*, John
S. Still of the *New York Herald*, two reporters from the
Daily News, Benjamin F. Butler and J. M. Livingstone,
J. W. Longby of United Press local, and two others
examined the boat. Some of them frowned, not wanting to be part of this lunacy. Others, caught up in
the spirit of the moment, shook George and Frank's
hands and wished them well after signing the certification.

At last, when George and Frank could scarcely stand

the waiting any longer, the clock in the Produce
Exchange began to chime. Each of the five strikes of
the bell hung in the air, and for a moment, the crowd
went quiet, and time seemed to stop. As the last sound
of the bell faded away, the crowd cheered, clapped
their hands, and pressed around the two men on the
dock. The police moved in and formed a line, creating a narrow gully through which Caroline ran. She
reached Frank and held him close. He embraced her,
looked down into her face, and whispered, "I must
be off now. Please try not to worry about us."

Caroline refused to let her brother go. She clung
to him, felt his sweat, smelled the almost sweet odor
of honest work. "Don't go, Frank. Don't do this."

Frank took his massive hands, placed them gently
on her shoulders, and pushed her away. "It's done.
I can't turn back now. I love you, Caroline," he said,
and turned away to step down into the boat. George
was already seated in the stern seat, oars in hand.
When Frank looked back at the crowd to catch one
last glimpse of his sister, she had gone. Overcome
with emotion, she had fled the docks, unable to bear
watching the departure. Jake, and George's brother,
were invisible among the throng as well, their faces
having merged into a sea of humanity.

Some of the crowd, drunk on spirits and with emotions running high, jeered and shouted as if they were
witnessing a bad circus act. The prevailing view held
that the two men would be dead before the *Fox*
reached the deep offshore canyons about ninety miles
east of New York. One of the battery boatmen who
ferried passengers and goods back and forth across
the Hudson and East Rivers, a fellow named Pegleg
Connor, joked to his friends: "If they want to hand
in their chips, why don't they do it in the right way
and hire a room?"

"You've a date with Davy Jones," many on the seawall crowed.

A dark look passed over George's face. He pushed off from the dock, turned to the crowd, and yelled, "We'll get to the other side or meet you all in Hades!"

The men rowed slowly southward past Governors Island. Several tugs were waiting to carry some of the crowd down the upper harbor to the Narrows. But no one boarded the vessels. Instead, the crowd slowly departed, content that the show was over. Each man lingered, taking the time to drink in a last look of the busy upper harbor, the Statue of Liberty, Ellis Island, the piers along Manhattan and Jersey City. The scene depicted life as usual in a thriving metropolis and stirred memories of their first glimpse of New York. For George more than a decade had passed, but only three years had elapsed since Frank's arrival. Yet they had each arrived thinking that America held unlimited promise; that they had reached a point that bordered on desperation in the eyes of most people didn't really enter their minds. To them what they did made sense.

The contrast between the sights they had seen and taken for granted all these years and the uncertainty of what lay ahead did not make a full impression on them at the moment. It simply couldn't. So caught up in their departure, it moved beneath their consciousness like an undertow during a severe storm, unseen but there nevertheless. Ferries, tugs, and ships blew their whistles in salute. People lined the decks and waved, their cheers carried off in the din. A sleek motor launch, the *R. K. Fox,* Fox's private yacht, approached them.

"You'll be wanting a tow to the lower harbor," a crewman said. "No sense in rowing more than you've got to, eh?" He tossed a line to Frank, who was seated in the forward position closest to the bow. He made it fast, and the water soon churned white under the launch's transom. Swirls and eddies of disturbed brine surrounded the *Fox* as the line grew taut and the launch steamed south at a brisk pace. The forward motion caused enough of a breeze to flutter the American flag, which was attached to a varnished pole in the rowboat's stern as it headed toward the Narrows and out to sea.

As they reached the junction between Fort Wadsworth and Fort Hamilton, built as a first line of defense for the upper harbor, the curve of the shore obscured the Statue of Liberty and the island of Manhattan. The familiar skyline of the city vanished as if a door had closed. For a moment, they were caught between pincers of land, as if the shore wanted to close around them and cut them off from their journey. But the launch towed them through the Narrows, and the lower reaches of the bay opened up to reveal a sweeping expanse of shoal water dotted with lighthouses and unlit buoys, and beyond, the already darkened sea awaited them.

7

The *R. K. Fox* slowed to a stop off the shores of Brooklyn in Gravesend Bay, a mere curvature of land on Long Island north of Norton Point and the amusements at Coney Island, along the beaches on the southern shore. The sun hung low to the west, and a fitful south wind began to find its strength and build to a steady breeze. To the northeast, the thin wisps of high clouds that had turned the sky a bluish white earlier that afternoon thickened to cover the entire width of the heavens, creating a pale gray halo around the sun. George and Frank looked up at the many people lining the rails of Fox's private yacht. No doubt all of them, dressed in their city finery, would enjoy sumptuous dinners and a round of drinks once back in their safe, comfortable surroundings in Manhattan. Among them, they thought, was Richard Fox, though they couldn't make him out. He was an aloof man, they had found, not easy with a smile and short of words.

"It's time you're off," said the captain of the launch, nodding to the crewman in the stern to pull

in the line Frank had just cast off from the rowboat.
"Good luck and Godspeed," the captain cried. The
ladies waved their silk handkerchiefs; the men, their
black top hats and derbies. The launch moved forward, turning to give the rowboat plenty of sea room,
and steamed north back to the Narrows. The faces
of the passengers grew less distinct and finally faded
into the larger structure of the vessel as if they had
somehow evaporated into thin air. The two men
remained silent, each watching the last link to the
land slowly fade from sight. A long, gentle swell rolled
in from the east and humped up in the tidal currents
still streaming from the one-mile slot between Staten
Island and Long Island.

With the current to boost the *Fox* on her way, the
oars were put over, and the work began. The boat
moved easily through the water toward Staten Island
to pick up the main shipping channel leading to
Sandy Hook. Even a small boat like the *Fox* had to
avoid the shoals that extended outward from the
fringe of Staten Island and surrounded Hoffman
Island, where the tiny quarantine station for Ellis
Island perched on the shore, and Swinburn Island.
The cylinder of the West Bank Lighthouse, farther
south, jutted up from the water at the edge of the
flats. To the left, breakers surged white over the bar
to the north of Romer Shoal, the southernmost
extremity of which lay just off Sandy Hook. A small
boat, no matter how stout, could easily capsize if mis-
handled and caught in the currents and waves that
met the shallow depths, a visible turmoil of a force
that defied imagination.

As it often did in the month of June, the heat of
the day quickly dissipated with the setting sun. Despite
their work at the oars, the men began to shiver. First
Frank, then George, donned thick coarse oilskin
pants, which covered their woolen shirts in front and
back, much like the overalls farmers wore in the fields.

Next they put on their jackets, which hung down below the waist. The oilskin kept the dampness from their skins and broke the wind, which had remained steady but shifted gradually to the northeast.

The lighthouses marking the hazardous water throughout the lower harbor switched on almost all at once. The blinking red light on Norton Point was already faint in the distance, for it carried a much shorter distance than the white lamps that shined without blinking on the towers of the West Bank and, beyond it, Old Orchard Shoal. Together the lights created a baseline captains used to keep their ships from going farther west into the shallows; the red light on Romer Shoal warned them not to go too far eastward. The north beacon at the very tip of Sandy Hook and, behind it, Sandy Hook Lighthouse appeared as two white spots almost in line. Way down the beach, the two white lights atop the Atlantic Highlands, visible for twenty miles offshore, marked the presence of a headland and the approach to the large bay to the west of Sandy Hook. These lights were familiar and symbolic of home, safety, the day-to-day.

The steamers, packets, coastal schooners, and ferries bound for the Atlantic Highlands, also riding the fair tide, were already shining their running lights, the red and green illuminating either side of each vessel's forward section. The windows on the larger ships glowed an inviting yellow. One by one the vessels paraded down the main channel. Each overtook the *Fox* and left her behind with a speed that made the progress by oar seem painfully slow. The sun sank below the horizon, ushering in a penetrating cold.

George looked seaward and shook his head in disgust. "We've got a fog coming in, Frank. Looks like it'll be thick around us in a moment or two."

The fog bank, a darkness that hugged the surface of the ocean below the still deep blue of twilight above, flowed into the lower harbor and extinguished the comforting beams from the lighthouses. It erased all sign of land, and the night slammed down like a door to a dungeon. There is a strange silence in a dense fog at sea difficult for any to comprehend who haven't experienced it. A dull, muffled layer deadens the sharp slap of a wave against the hull, the splash of an oar, the moan of a ship's whistle. Everything becomes lost, all sense of sight, as well as the ability to accurately determine the direction from which a sound has come. The two men both knew the disorienting nature of fog; it didn't frighten them, though they strained their ears to hear the first signs of an oncoming steamer, its whistle, the wash of its bow wave. They listened for the sound of breakers on Romer Shoal and could just make out the staccato pings, three in quick succession every ten seconds, from the fog bell at the tip of Sandy Hook.

A light rain soon joined the fog. The droplets added to the condensation that covered everything. They rolled off the face of the little liquid compass screwed into the bottom of the boat under the aft seat, which allowed the man in the bow to steer a straight course. The soft yellow glow of the compass light flickered.

"Damn this weather. You'd think it would have held fair and warm from the way the morning made out. The clouds, though, they never lie, do they, Frank. Can't say they didn't warn us, eh?" George muttered, pulling rhythmically in time with each stroke of Frank's oars. He did not look over his shoulder at his friend, however.

"It's a good sign, this fog. An omen for our voyage. The sea is welcoming us in her own way, wishing us good luck and a safe passage," Frank said. "We're not to be lulled into thinking she'll not have her way with us all the way across."

"It's an unpleasant beginning."

The motion of the boat changed slightly and became increasingly rough as the water began to shoal, resisting the wash of the swells. The red smudge of Romer Shoal Light appeared out of the gloom a short distance away. To their right the shadow of an unlit buoy glided past.

"We're out of the main channel," George said. "Let's anchor here for the night. We'll stand a better chance of clearing any steamers in the morning. Make a fresh start after all the fuss today."

The anchor bit into the sand, the slack left the line, and the boat headed into the wind and the swell. Straining lightly on the anchor line, the bow of the boat lifted and fell, and every now and then a wave coming in from an angle on either side of the boat slapped against the hull, sending a little spray over the rail. The *Fox* was what sailors call "quick," which meant it rocked easily from side to side unless kept in perfect balance. This tenderness was exaggerated when not moving forward, the thrust through the water helping to add control and stability. Frank carefully leaned down out of the breeze to light the stove, mounted on a square wooden structure to support it, snug against the forward watertight compartment.

"It'll be good to have a hot cup of coffee," Frank said, shielding the flames from the drizzle with his hands. The warm yellow light, tinged with blue, seemed incredibly bright in the blackness. It failed to reach much beyond Frank, however, illuminating his large bulk in outline and dancing against the round door in the forward section. When Frank put the kettle on top of the wooden frame around the stove, the light dimmed considerably. His outline faded almost to nothing save for the subtle glow that grew more intense as he moved to one side and rested against the hull, his hands ready to protect the flames from any unexpected puff of wind.

"And something to eat," George said, yawning. "I'd forgotten how hungry I was till now, now that we've stopped."

While Frank prepared a little dinner, George removed the little spar that served as a mast for the flag, rolled the damp canvas around it, and stowed the pole under the thwarts. They would not need to show the colors once at sea. He unpacked the cover they had made to fit over the top of the boat from rail to rail in the fashion of a flattish tent. Under this he spread out canvas cushions stuffed with reindeer hair, which would serve as mattresses. If either man thought of how strange this routine was not six miles from a warm, comfortable bed in a cottage perched on the hills of the Atlantic Highlands to the south, neither of them said anything about it. The long days of planning, the hard work of getting everything purchased and stowed, the emotional stress, though not obvious to either of them yet, descended on them in the form of deep fatigue. Their small meal eaten, they snuggled close together under the cover for warmth, fully dressed in their oilskins and seaboots, and were soon fast asleep. The pings of the bronze fog bell at the tip of Sandy Hook a mile or so away and the dull red loom of the Romer Shoal Light made a comforting auditory and visual lullaby, a last shred of normalcy that soothed the mind into thinking all was well and that all would be well in the days to come.

8

A sloop under full sail and moving fast emerged out of a thick bank of fog in the predawn gloom, not far from the *Fox*, rolling and pitching in the waves stacked up on Romer Shoal. The sloop's large mainsail was let well off its right side to take full advantage of the northeast wind astern. The jib, set out on the end of the bowsprit, drew as well. With each puff the vessel heeled over, revealing the fouled growth of dark slime and white barnacles just below the waterline. Under sail, its progress through the water was almost silent except for the intermittent whoosh when the bow cut through a wave. Aboard the sloop, dressed in their dandy Sunday sporting clothes, were a bunch of well-to-do youths ready for a day of fishing on Shrewsbury Rocks.

"Look there! Off the port bow!" one of the young men shouted, and pointed at the rowboat almost directly in front of them. "Looks like a nice little boat has slipped its moorings."

"Bring her in close," another boy said to the mate at the helm. "Let's have a better look."

The mate turned the boat toward the wind, leaving the sails trimmed as they were to spill the air and slow the boat. The sails flapped as the boat moved forward under its own momentum and drifted to leeward, practically hitting the rowboat. The bowsprit passed over the *Fox*. All the boys ran forward and peered over the bow at this unexpected sight. The sound of sails flogging crackled in the near silence, startling George and Frank awake. Both of them pulled the cover off and sat bolt upright.

"What the devil?"

"People aboard!"

"Say, what are you two doing there?" cried several of the boys at once.

"Sheer off! You're going to run us down," yelled George.

"Sorry, there. We thought nobody was aboard," the mate replied. He put the helm over, turning the sloop away from the boat. "Sheet in the jib, boys. Now the main."

The sloop disappeared into the fog.

"That was a close call," Frank said, shaking his head.

"They were mighty surprised to see us. I guess they thought they might have caught themselves a boat from one of the resorts this day, as well as some fish." George laughed. "Can't blame them for taking a look."

"Can't say I do." Frank laughed along with his friend. "After all, the *Fox* is a mighty fine little boat."

"Day looks no better than last night, I'm thinking. But maybe this fog will burn off."

"It's done so often enough before. So why not today? It'll be gone, you wait and see," Frank said.

Anxious to get under way, they ate some bread and cheese, washed down with water, cool and sweetly pure, from far-off lakes in the mountains of upstate New York. The stove would only be lit once a day; it

would not do to run out of fuel in mid-ocean. Hot
food, a mug of steaming coffee—these ordinary comforts were to be guarded closely, like the treasures
they amounted to. A frying pan, a pot to cook in, a
kettle, the implements of daily life on the vast ocean,
where nothing in life meant much in terms of the
overwhelming indifference of the elements—these
humble and utilitarian implements took on an importance greater than any city dweller could imagine,
not only with regard to their use in sustaining the
body but in their simple ability, just the sight of them,
to offer a spiritual balm in an otherwise inhospitable
world.

With George at the oars, ready to guide the boat
once freed from the anchor, Frank moved forward
and slowly hauled in the line, coiling it deftly as he
worked. It was a job that came to both of them as
naturally as breathing. As soon as the anchor lifted
from the muck, blue and odiferous from the disinte-
grated shells of the mussel beds in the area, the bow
of the boat began to pay off, away from the wind
blowing over the expanse of Long Island, invisible
in the murk. George skillfully swung the *Fox*'s stern
around to bring the wind and waves at an angle
behind them as Frank finished coiling the anchor
line and firmly lashed both it and the anchor in the
bottom of the boat. "We won't need this anymore,"
he said, and he, too, manned the oars. The *Fox* picked
up speed.

"We'll steer east by south, Frank. Keep a weather
eye on the compass, okay?"

"She's making east by south. Steady at one hundred
degrees or so!"

They rowed with a will against the incoming tide,
each stroke of the oars clawing them farther out to
sea and away from the lee shore of Sandy Hook. As
the sun inched over the horizon directly off the port
bow, it made its first appearance as a band of white

light, with gradations of darker and darker gray, reaching skyward until it disappeared completely in the black dome above. Gradually, the wall of fog turned white throughout, and blue replaced the black above. On either side of the boat, and from the bow and stern, the face of the ocean looked deep black, its surface covered with small, steep waves which did not crest. The higher the sun rose, the thinner the fog became, until it all finally vanished on the wings of a warm southerly wind that came up the coast and brought with it a tangible lift in George and Frank's moods. The clouds remaining from the passing cold front lingered, however, but they, too, began to break up around noontime, revealing patches of blue that imparted the feeling of deep, cool distance in a limitless universe and the clarity of light one only senses after a weather system goes through and cleans house, chasing away the heavy, humid air for a short while.

The red hull of Sandy Hook Lightship at anchor in the outermost approaches to Gedney Channel gleamed in the sun. The two masts, each equipped with a lamp, were a very welcome sight for most sailors on their way in to New York, particularly at night. Upon sighting the light vessel, the pilot knew to start searching for the electric lamps mounted on poles, the first of their kind in the country, that marked each side of Gedney Channel. The lights atop the lightship's masts would appear over the horizon as a smudge and wouldn't become clear until long after the powerful beams of the twin towers on the Highlands hove into view. With the lightship, now west of the *Fox*, and the hills of the Highlands rising above the long, uninterrupted line of blue, both men, facing aft, greeted the open sea with their backs turned to it. The last glimpse of the lightship's tall spars represented a sense of closure. Soon the final signs of the land itself, a deep purple strip above the oceanic indigo, often with white puffy clouds above it, would sink ever deeper into the Atlantic.

From then on the ocean became all encompassing, a barren waste every bit as unforgiving as the Sahara. Yet, like the desert, the sea was never completely empty despite its harshness. Off the port of New York, the ships came and went. Pilot boats ranged far. Fishing smacks with clouds of seabirds dotted the horizon by day and scattered pricks of light across the inky blackness at night. The Sandy Hook Lightship gradually sank below the horizon. As both men rowed hard, they had a long time to watch it disappear. Around four o'clock, the last vestiges of New Jersey also faded away, and they were alone with themselves, their boat, and the sea.

Occasionally, a gannet dove from the sky and plunged into the ocean, its keen eyes fixed on an unlucky fish. Gulls winged overhead. Land birds sometimes flew near them, as if tired and looking for a place to rest. Eventually, these signs of life would become less common, until they finally vanished altogether far out in the icy reaches of the North Atlantic.

Each man rowed in silence and watched the sun sink slowly from the sky toward the rim of the earth almost directly behind them. The swell left over from the northeasterly wind made it difficult to row without catching air with each stroke of the oars. The south wind tried to drive them northward, back toward Long Island, which lay hidden but menacing astern. As experienced seamen, George and Frank knew the geography of the northeastern United States coast as well as the faces of their mothers. Their adopted home state of New Jersey ran south to north, but after that the land journeyed east up past Long Island, Cape Cod, and the Gulf of Maine, ever eastward through the Canadian Maritimes to the expanse of frozen seas of Baffin Bay and beyond. To clear the immense curve of the North American continent meant making significant progress southward to a latitude safe enough to carve out, day by day, a steady erosion of longitude, ticking off the miles ever closer to France.

The southerly wind, so prized among eastbound captains of coastal schooners heading down east to Maine or fishing schooners to the Grand Banks off Newfoundland, conspired to drive them from their careful plan. It kicked up an increasingly nasty cross sea, made all the worse from the unseen influence of an inshore current that battled against the elements in its flow to the south at a speed of approximately half a knot. Beyond the immediate grip of the coast, the tides began to flow in a circular pattern, rotating and oscillating in an ageless beat born from the spin of the earth; also unseen, it mingled with all else to make the sea come alive in its own unfathomable way.

The wind-borne waves married, or attempted to marry, with the longer, more defined waves that had received life from a wind now past but which had blown across hundreds, perhaps thousands, of miles from the point where the frontal system took shape and made its way to America. The water off New Jersey, notorious for its shallow depths, which tended to stack up the waves, made itself known in its customary fashion; choppy, dark, almost mean-spirited.

Along about sundown, the outline of something floating in the water a little way behind them caught their eye. Curious, they maneuvered the *Fox* over to it and found that it was an empty sea trunk, partly smashed, with crudely written letters on one side: G.S., New York, via Havre. They looked at the trunk, then at each other, both realizing the strangeness of it.

"I hope we fare better on our journey to Le Havre than that trunk did on its way from there," Frank said. "It's odd that we should meet this particular trunk on this particular day, don't you think?"

"It's not been in the water long, by the looks of it."

Neither of them speculated about how it got smashed and how it came to be floating in the sea. The probability that the trunk had floated, driven along by the northeasterly wind and easterly swells, from a ship that foundered in a storm seemed a distinct possibility. They pushed it away, sending it on its journey, and resumed their work. But the trunk had set off a somber frame of mind, and the darkness and cold that settled over the ocean did little to assuage it. Not even the canopy of stars, the vast wash of the Milky Way, the glimmer of the dippers, the green speck of Venus, could shake their sense of gloom.

The first steps in any great adventure bring a mix of emotions that cover a broad range, from euphoria that the envisioned dream has indeed become a reality to the innermost fears and self-doubts that the undertaking of it was in fact the right thing to do. The objective set, all plans made for its successful attainment, the matter became the doing rather than the thinking, and the putting into action of any great achievement requires a deep sense of courage and faith in one's own ability. That both men shared in the same desires, saw with the same vision, and worked together now in a tiny boat, each aware of the other's thoughts without voicing them, brought the wonder of their voyage and the danger of it to the surface. Neither man was given to carping or fretting and fussing. Each of them was endowed with a keen sense of honor and integrity, which weighed heavily on them as they thought of their respective loved ones, whom they had sentenced to months of uncertainty, pain, and worry, and whom they might never see again. The guilt of doing such a thing couldn't be lost on them, for they were sensitive, could appreciate the ways of the sea and its beauty, because they understood the meaning of love, family, and country and the very fragile aspects of these elements that go into being decent men. It would have been easier if they were dull-witted, selfish, and brusque. Such people aren't burdened with the kinds of thoughts that stir those with a kinder sensibility, and such men seldom accomplish anything great.

For the first time, they established their seagoing schedule and set the watches. One man would sleep, or try to, for a three-hour stretch while the other man kept the boat moving ever eastward from eight to eleven and eleven to two. The remaining hours of the night were broken into two watches of two and a half hours each. Frank took the eight to eleven watch, preferring to try his luck at sleep in the wee hours of the night. He strained to keep the boat moving into the head seas that foretold a shift of the wind to the southeast. With each wave that hit them, he felt the boat slow, then occasionally stop dead in the water. The waves weren't huge or terrifying, more a succession of bothersome obstacles that must be gotten over.

The red and green running lights and fixed white lights on the lofty spars of the liners steaming on toward New York passed the *Fox*, appearing from over the horizon and disappearing, all in the space of a half hour or less. Several times the man at the oars changed course to avoid getting too close to the ships. Seeing them reinforced the feeling of isolation and the vastness of the sea. As the night wore on, both men, each taking his turn at the oars, admitted that sleep had been an elusive blessing.

With dawn the fog returned. It enclosed them in a gray cocoon, wet and uncomfortable.

"Frank, wake up!" George said. It was seven o'clock, and the work at the oars had built up a fierce hunger. Frank grunted something unintelligible from under the canvas cover, but he soon emerged from "below," as they had already taken to calling the nook, rubbing the sleep from his eyes. He had had a hard time drifting off, yet the last thing he recalled was lying on his back in the dank darkness beneath the cover, drops of condensation raining on his face, listening to the steady beat of the oars and the water outside the hull, inches from his ears.

"The fog's back, I see," he said.

"Came in with the sun, what there is of it," George said. "At least the wind and the swell have let up some."

Frank took over the oars while George lit the stove. Neither had eaten much the day before, and both of them yearned for a piping hot cup of coffee and some warm food. The kettle was soon on, and the rich aroma of coffee swept over the boat as it brewed, slowly boiling a few eggs George put in for their breakfast. Since someone had to be at the oars at all times to keep the boat on course, they did not have the luxury of a leisurely breakfast together. Frank kept at it while George ate; then George took over while Frank ate. To get anywhere in a rowboat, that kind of military discipline was required, and they had more than three thousand miles of open ocean to cross.

By noon, the wind had all but died away, and the fog hung heavy over them. George carefully removed the paper and pencil and the chart, all still dry, from the watertight compartment in the stern. He quickly went through his figuring, estimating that with two men at the oars during the day the boat was probably moving through the water at around four knots, half that during the night, slightly slower than the ideal speed of five knots due to the head seas. They had run tests off the beaches of Nauvoo earlier in the year to gauge the boat's speed through the water. It was an essential component vital to even the vaguest methods of calculating a position based on dead reckoning. He took into account the drift downwind and down-sea, which sailors call leeway, but he had no real way of knowing exactly how far off their track the elements had pushed them; it was all a matter of educated guesswork. Adding up the number of hours rowed at the estimated speeds with one and two men rowing gave him a sense of their position, though nothing as definitive as a firm fix using his quadrant, impossible at the moment, since fog fully obscured the sun.

By his calculations, they had rowed about forty-five miles since leaving Sandy Hook, a respectable pace. But the nagging worry of not knowing their exact position began to take hold. George put it out of his mind, however, because there was nothing he could do to change the situation, and it was no use in dwelling on that which could not be controlled.

The fog remained with them all that afternoon and through the night, soaking everything in a cold layer of condensation. The south wind returned with a fury and brought with it heavy rain showers so intense that they flattened the seas, rounding off the steep slopes into long hills which reared up again as each cloudburst deluged them and moved off toward New England. The downpours drummed on the decks over the watertight compartments in the bow and stern and thrummed on the canvas cover. Brackish water collected in the bottom of the boat and sloshed fore and aft and from side to side. For the man off watch lying on the sodden cushions, which, when wet, gave off the unique pungence of reindeer, it was like trying to sleep in a bathtub. Bailing helped only a little.

Dawn on June 9 revealed a progression of heavy seas that rolled in from the south on the heels of the wind, which had shifted to the southeast and showed

no signs of abating. This was just the sort of weather
system George and Frank had worried about. The
little *Fox*, with only the brawn of both men to move
her through the water, was no match against the
elements, which seemed to conspire to put her back
ashore on the desolate beaches of Long Island.
Beyond the east end of Long Island lay still more
trouble, the shoals of Nantucket, a virtual thicket of
reefs, rock ledges, and snaking sandbars thirty miles
or more off Cape Cod. The *Fox* had to get far enough
offshore to avert these dangers for the very same
reason that they had carefully avoided the worst shoals
in the lower harbor of New York. But even though
they rowed with a will, the boat did not move quickly
east by south, as it so needed to do, but skittered and
rushed headlong against an immovable head sea. The
two men struggled just to keep position, bow headed
with the waves off the right side of the boat, pitching
and dunking into the crests. Their efforts, at the time,
smacked of pure futility. Both of them knew the sea
had the upper hand.

9

As the morning wore on, the gray and white scud whipping across the sky began to tear, as if the cloak that hung low all around the *Fox* had weakened under the stress of the wind. Streams of cloud opened, revealing long bands of blue. Beams of sunlight pushed through the atmosphere, creating patches of warm, glittering water, almost green in hue.

"Can you keep her to the wind, Frank? I'm thinking the sun may break out at any minute. We've got to get a rough fix if we can," George said.

"You'll have a hard time in this sea, George. But let's give it a try."

Frank felt the loss of George's efforts at the oars. With only one man rowing, the wind could more easily catch the bow as it rose up on a crest and push it off to one side, sending the boat rushing down the face of a wave. Seated facing the stern, he had to rely on the tingle the wind made on his skin to tell him when to react to a gust. That and the audible increase in the whir and whoosh; the louder the sound, the stronger the wind. He had to feel the boat, become almost one with her and the oars, which served as both propulsion and rudder as the hull responded to the massive force of the waves. He watched George struggling to get the quadrant, his paper and pencil, the nautical almanac which contained the numbers required to make sense of the measurements taken on the sun. The stern sank low as the boat headed uphill, then rose to the heavens, profiling George against a backdrop of blue and gray sky. The spray matted his hair and dripped from his mustache. A frown creased his tan face.

Bracing himself as best he could and as high as possible without tipping the boat, George gazed south in the earnest hope that the sun would break through the clouds. It was almost local noon, which meant that the sun would soon reach its highest point above the horizon in their own private stretch of ocean. To get a fix on their latitude using the sun, they had to sight it as close to local noon as possible. George checked his watch again. Yes, it was almost time.

"Here it comes, Frank!" George yelled as the bright white sphere broke through the tattered gray edges of the clouds. George lined up the sun in the mirror on the quadrant, then swung the reflected image of the sun down the arc of the quadrant so that the lowest rim just met the horizon. Reading the degrees on the arc gave him a measurement of the sun's altitude. He immediately repeated the process.

Next George ran through the calculations, based on the angles he had measured and the numbers listed in the nautical almanac for that time of year at local noon in their immediate vicinity. George smiled to himself as he went over his figures again, pleased that he had done them right. He had found their latitude. He had been a good student at the navigation school in Norway before his brief stint in the merchant marine, and his training had paid off well over the years. On this and the days to come, a

mastery of celestial navigation, an understanding of
ocean winds and currents, coastal piloting, and the
art and science of seamanship, meant life itself.

"You look happy," Frank said, his voice carried aft
on the wind.

"We've made a southing of roughly thirty miles
from Sandy Hook. We're off just a little north of
Squan Beach, at latitude forty degrees north and eight
minutes, about one hundred miles out."

Frank nodded. He, too, smiled. Evidently, the sea
didn't have as much of an upper hand on the little
boat as they had imagined. Through sheer muscle
and determination they had overcome the boat's tendency to drift northward before the south wind, a
feat they both felt boded well for their journey.

With the latitude known, George marked an X on
the chart to denote their approximate position. For
their exact location he would have had to determine
their longitude as well. But to do that required a
precise knowledge of the time down to the second.
Coordinates are measured in degrees, minutes, and
seconds—all based on increasingly smaller divisions
of a sphere. The precise time was crucial to arriving at
an accurate division of degrees, minutes, and seconds
both in latitude and longitude, which together give
a fix of one's position anyplace on earth.

Neither George nor Frank's watch was accurate
enough; it also wasn't imperative to get perfect fixes
for such a small vessel. Ships' navigators carried a
device called a chronometer that kept time to the
second. It was a prized instrument, extremely expensive. Even some of the smaller ships in the navy didn't
have them. Many a merchant vessel also lacked the
instrumentation necessary to compute with exacti-
tude one's longitude. Rather, the navigators used a
series of calculations and measurements from ob-
served celestial bodies known as the lunar-distance

method, a good enough way to get around the lack of a chronometer.

George and Frank couldn't afford a fancy time-piece, and they did not feel they really needed one. As long as either of their watches kept a fairly precise time, they would know the approximate arrival of local noon and could thus calculate their latitude with ease. Long ago, their ancestors traveled far from the North Sea using a very similar method. Once an estimated latitude was arrived at, the ship would keep on that track, following an invisible line across the ocean to its destination. Corrections of course kept the ship from straying too far off the desired latitude, enabling the captain to make a landfall thousands of miles away in an easterly or westerly direction. Traveling north or south posed far more difficulties, since at the time no method existed to determine one's longitude. Ships commonly stayed inshore, where landmarks could help determine position.

The crew of the *Fox* only had to maintain a grasp of latitude. It was a matter of finding the desired parallel, as they had done, and keep on the line until such time as the dead reckoning indicated it was prudent to shift the track to an increasingly more northerly latitude, all the while eating away at the thousands of miles they had to cross to the east and their ultimate destination, Le Havre, France, near the mouth of the Seine River, gateway to France's glittering city of Paris.

The navigation done, both men in turn enjoyed a noon repast of cold food, which had become their staple. Both longed for a cup of coffee, a boiled egg, some warmed corned beef or fried bacon, all of which they had with them but could not cook because of the wind and the work at the oars. They settled on slices of salty tomato, which seemed intent on rotting in quick order, some canned magnolia milk, and brown bread slathered with some of their precious supply of tinned butter.

Their moods uplifted with the news of their steady progress and the gnawing hunger eased, both men rowed hard. The combined strength of men who had worked the oars of a heavy clam boat for years, laden down with its daily cargo of gray shells, moved the nimble little *Fox* through the water like a minnow It darted from crest to trough to crest, leaving a vague impression of a wake, which the sea swallowed almost as soon as it broke from the stern. The boat, designed as a double-ender, meaning its stern was twin to its bow, only drew about eighteen inches of water. This was both an advantage and a curse. With no deep keel, she would skim across the surface of the water easily, whether pushed by the wind or the blades of the oars. Together, though, George and Frank held control. Three days out of New York, the routine of their lives at sea took over, and they were content, at least for the moment. The last of the clouds cleared off, and they dared to hope that they would enjoy a respite from the fog and rain.

The sea has often been compared to a cruel mistress capable of bestowing both pleasure of the rarest kind and punishment doled out on a whim. A spiteful bed companion can indeed bring one to the heights of ecstasy, then tease and disarm to enhance the power of the next blow to the heart and soul. In this way, the sea behaves similarly and thus has for centuries been hated and loved by sailors but never trusted.

The day ended uneventfully. The two men kept to their work together long into the night. The thermometer they had brought with them showed the temperature, around the time they had found their latitude with the quadrant, at about fifty-five degrees. With the sun behind the earth, leaving them cloaked in a damp blackness, the chill increased. From one watch to the next, both men watched the stars blink out one by one, and neither cared to comment. No need. The inevitable rain, soon to add to their discomfort, would not be willed or cursed away. It simply was part of life, of the world around them, and like all unpleasantness, it made itself at home most of the time.

Stroke after stroke, the *Fox* continued east by south, putting distance between the stern and the shoals many miles to the east. The succession of disturbed weather patterns, brought with the cold front that had settled in the first day of their voyage, showed no signs of abating all the next day, Wednesday, June 10. Thick fog surrounded them, but it did not stay in one place, as it so often does in the lush valleys and on the fertile fields of farms well away from the coast. There it is almost beautiful. Wisps of these landbound clouds come down to kiss the soil and linger for a while. They bead the windowpanes with crystal-like droplets, soak the hair and overcoats of landsmen, and dapple the pelts of animals and the feathers of birds. All is pleasingly silent, the world's harshness temporarily dulled. Out at sea, with a strong south wind and the hissing crests, the fog flew past the *Fox*, moving sideways at twenty knots and never seeming to diminish. It was not serene, peaceful, or beautiful, only uncomfortable and potentially dangerous.

The rain and fog came mostly from the weather systems marching off to the far north on the heels of that cold south wind. But making it worse was the *Fox*'s close proximity to the Gulf Stream. In the Gulf Stream the temperature of the water rises dramatically. It flows from the Sargasso Sea, with surface temperatures as high as seventy degrees, traveling from the Florida Straits northward toward Cape Hatteras at a rate topping four miles per hour, where it then slows and widens. Long, snakelike branches of the Gulf Stream work out from the main flow, and eddies develop—not the likes of which are seen on rivers, but enormous bends of warm-water currents so large they defy imagining. The water cools but never matches the cold, dense water of the northern Atlantic. When cold air flows over the warmer waters of the Gulf Stream, particularly in June, fog forms. Huge banks of it.

George had planned on encountering the Gulf Stream. In fact, he counted on finding it and staying with it for as long as possible. Although a wind blowing from the north would oppose the current, trying to make its way northeast across the Atlantic to warm the shores of Great Britain, southern Norway, and France, making for exceptionally steep seas, it made complete sense to take advantage of the mile- or at least the half-mile-per-hour push in the right direction. Off New York, the Gulf Stream abruptly turns northeastward, flowing up to the Grand Banks off Newfoundland, where it further dissipates. From there it is known as the North Atlantic Current.

The captains of sailing ships since the days of Ponce de León, a Spanish explorer who poked around the Caribbean Sea in 1513, have noted the presence of a current. They named it the Gulf Stream because of its similarity to a river. In 1769, Benjamin Franklin was the first to study the current, largely because this practical-minded man wanted to get to the bottom of complaints from colonists that mail carried aboard His Majesty's ships was much slower in arriving from England than getting there. Local fishermen knew about the current and accurately plotted its main course. The skippers of successive generations learned to use it in transatlantic crossings to the east and to avoid it in crossings to the west by ranging far north of its influence. A study of the rudiments of the Gulf Stream was part of any comprehensive navigational training, and George knew well of its importance to the crossing he and Frank had undertaken.

Still, it was bloody miserable out there, and fatigue

began to take its toll. To bolster themselves, they sang songs of their native land in their native tongue. The efforts were halfhearted, but to each the sound of a companion's voice rasping in time with his own lent a spiritual hand, reminding the two of them that without the will to persist the crossing would never be completed.

Again the cycle of the weather began to change. The wind softened at the surface of the sea, then dropped off altogether. The fog thinned out until they could see that the scud above them had shifted direction 180 degrees from its migration north, with the south wind to the opposite quarter.

"We'll be seeing a nor'wester soon," Frank said, leaning heavily on his oars for a moment, the blades dripping above the waves. "A north by wester, how I wish it were so."

"A land breeze from the big lakes'll bring an early summer warmth to Nauvoo, I suspect. But will it reach us out here? I'm thinking it may. What do you say to that?"

"I say it'd be as welcome as a cup of the wine we were given back at the wharf," Frank said. He dug his oars into the water and timed his strokes with his friend's. His oilskins began to dry in the sun, but the moisture locked beneath the outer waterproof layers mingled with his sweat. His woolen shirt itched his arms and torso; he ignored it.

"I know we'll be wanting a taste of it soon. Vino Kalafra. Vino Kalafra. Vino, Vino, Vino Kalafra. There's poetry in the sound of that. Poetry!"

George didn't usually put so much stock in the soothing effects of spirits, and neither did Frank. Both men were strongly religious Lutherans, as were most Norwegians in America and in their homeland, though some, of course, were more outspoken in their spiritual beliefs than others. George and Frank quietly kept their faith, never shouted it from rooftops. It just wasn't their way. But each man did believe in a higher being, that the world had in it more than the press of commerce, the business of love for one's family, the pursuit of personal happiness. There was a commitment to right, to a clearheaded, practical way of life that found grounding in the church and informed every other aspect of reality. It resulted in their habit of abstaining from smoking tobacco and drinking hard liquor.

Shortly after George arrived back in America with Anine, he had taken her to prayer meetings held at the New York Port Society's Mariners' Church, on the corner of Madison and Catherine streets in Brooklyn. The church served a large number of immigrants and sailors from off the ships that came to the port. Every Monday evening at seven-thirty, Swedes, Danes, Finns, and Norwegians gathered for a prayer meeting held in their native language. It became part of George and Anine's weekly routine to attend these meetings.

George sometimes thought about those early years with Anine in New York City, before they moved to the Atlantic Highlands, which was founded as a religious retreat and eventually grew into a bustling port. He found himself thinking of her and the children, especially Fritz, his youngest son, wondering how they were faring in Brevik. He recalled sailing his tiny sloop with Andrew. They would pack a lunch and sail up to the busy piers serving Fort Hancock on Sandy Hook and make their way down the peninsula past the old walls of the fort built during the Civil War, and anchor just off the beach. The boom of guns fired on the range a short distance away startled Andrew at first, but he soon lost his fear. He had written Andrew, promising to take him sailing again when the family was together back in America. At times, these thoughts weighed heavily on him as he rowed through the dark of night with little else to occupy his mind. However, memories of his family and his hopes for their future buoyed him more often than not.

Long before sunset, the wind sprang up from the north at the surface of the ocean, foretold with its advance guard of high scud moving south at a very good clip. It shifted round to the northwest, just as George and Frank hoped it would, a sure sign of a new frontal system, one that should usher in weather more to their liking.

10

When sailors come home safely from sea and find themselves on the beach between ships, a great many end up in the tavern and the brothel, in that order. They sleep in seaport missions set up for men with nothing but the silver coins in their pockets and for those who spend them and have not even the slight comfort of money. These men experience no more of a connection to the land than as a temporary stop, a place where life doesn't seem real. Ashore, petty concerns about things that aren't really important clog the thoughts of almost everyone, but it's not like that on the ocean. Out there the world is strikingly simple and harsh. Being on the beach held little for them besides the pleasures of the body. Their souls, empty of the love of others, looked to the empty sea to fill the void. It often did, until it took them one day to Fiddlers Green, a netherworld where old and young sailors, released from their earthly ties, gathered to drink and whore in perpetuity, as the legend goes.

But the more fortunate sailors with a home and a

family sat snug and warm in front of a roaring fire in cottages perched along the shore and told stories of adventure. The children listened in rapt attention to the tales of exotic ports, strange people from the other side of the world, and storms—the storms off the Cape of Good Hope and Cape Horn, deep in the roaring forties and the screaming fifties, where the wind blows unobstructed around the globe. In those latitudes the storms could frighten the most hardened mariner and sink the best of ships, and hearing stories of the sailors who lived through them instilled fear and respect in the landsmen. The widows pacing in cupolas atop the homes in New England found little solace in the knowledge that these storms killed with regularity as they watched the distant horizon in vain for the ships carrying their husbands, who would never return home again. But that was the way of the sea and the way of life for any whose loved ones set off upon it.

The storm at sea, in the eye of a landsman, usually amounts to a vision of hell: black clouds, sheets of lightning, wind that whips the ocean to a white froth, and waves the size of small mountains cascading in on themselves like waterfalls. The image is reinforced every time a sailor tells his story. But if pressed, he'll admit that another kind of storm exists, the clear-weather gale. These, he'll say, can be just as terrible, even more so because while all appears blue and clear above, the sea down below turns to a hell every bit as dangerous as the storm one unfamiliar with the sea immediately thinks of when the conversation turns to talk of a blow.

On the morning of June 11, the thermometer aboard the *Fox* registered a jump from fifty-five degrees to sixty-five. The frontal system that both men had wished for arrived, and with it came clear skies the likes of which bring joy to any who see the sun after days of missing it. They peeled off their oilskins and rowed in their shirts, which dried in the brisk wind, blowing ever more in a westerly direction. The waves began to build, but since they were dead astern and the *Fox*'s design provided plenty of buoyancy fore and aft, the boat picked up speed and surged forward. Every passing hour ticked the miles away, bringing the coast of France closer.

It was almost like the famed Nantucket sleigh ride. When a longboat put off from a whaling vessel, the crew rowed quietly up to the great beast as it either slept or rested on the surface. Closer and closer the crew rowed till the harpoon found its target. The terrified and mortally wounded whale naturally tried to swim away, and that's when the sleigh ride began. The line attached to the end of the harpoon yanked bar tight, and the crew let it out to give the whale room. The bow lifted, and the longboat seemed to fly across the waves, until the whale tired. The *Fox*, built lighter and with better curves than a ship's longboat, seemed especially suited for this west wind. George and Frank took advantage of their blessing and rowed harder than ever before, making sure not to let the stern get pushed off to the side of a wave as it caught up to them and passed under the boat. Such a ride posed a danger of capsizing. However, the boat's design accounted for the risk in a couple of ingenious ways.

Back in the wood shop at William Seaman's place in Branchport, the boatbuilder had talked at great length about what might be done to make the *Fox* unsinkable. Boatbuilders in New England had been experimenting with cork as floatation in small rowboats, but that wasn't acceptable, since so much of it would be needed and every inch of space counted aboard the *Fox*. The watertight compartments fore and aft seemed the answer. They were sheathed in galvanized iron inside to provide a good seal from the elements. The doors required a delicate hand at the tinsmith's to ensure that the seal would not leak. When they had taken the boat off the beach and capsized her, the doors leaked and had to be redone. Neither George nor Frank had tempers swift to ignite. The leaking compartments caused them great concern, though. If they were to fill during a capsize or the routine, partial filling of the open boat when a rogue wave boarded her, the vessel would no doubt swamp and possibly sink like a stone.

Later trials found the repaired watertight compartments satisfactory. Seven men standing on the upturned hull of the *Fox* couldn't push her under. She did, however, remain very stable upside down. This, too, caused the voyagers great concern. An unsinkable boat turned wrong side up would do no good at all. William Seaman fastened two rails along the underside of the keel to help them right the boat in case it capsized. When the Harbos and the Samuelsens heard about these precautions, they became further convinced that their loved ones had lost their wits. Why plan for disaster? Just avoid it by staying home. But for George and Frank these design features comforted them as they winged their way east at the heels of the mounting west wind.

As for William Seaman, he had built many a fine boat for the fishermen off Nauvoo and Galilee. He had leaned back against the workbench in his shop, fragrant with the tangy odor of cedar and woodsmoke from the potbellied stove, and kicked at the carpet of wood shavings on the roughly hewn plank floor. He looked the two Norwegians up and down for a while, taking in the full import of their words and his measure of the men. Cross the ocean in a rowboat. Seemed crazy. But the men, oddly mismatched in size, with one of medium height and stocky build, the other as big as a house and as lean as a post, didn't appear insane. Rather the opposite. In the end, he didn't quibble over why these fellows wanted a skiff. If they had the money to pay him, he and his son, Harold, would build the best boat on the East Coast for the purpose, and that's exactly what they did.

The boat was just over eighteen feet long and five feet wide. He selected the best Atlantic white cedar for the planking, which was laid up over the oak timbers used for the ribs and stem in the old way, with one plank slightly overlapping the next. Seaman and other builders of boats had learned the fashion of lapstrake construction from their elders, who, in turn, had learned the technique from theirs. The clinker, or lapstrake, method originated with the Norse more than one thousand years earlier, but that wasn't common knowledge. Empty, the boat weighed about 250 pounds. He had built her to ride high, counting on the weight of the two men and all their provisions to put her in proper trim, balanced like a dancer in the fullness of grace.

The noon observation with the quadrant showed they were still holding course to latitude forty degrees, eight minutes north. With the west wind behind them, George altered course to due east, no longer needing to compensate for the northward push from the south wind. As the wind continued to increase during the afternoon, the seas grew higher and higher. The ride became more dangerous. Yet the *Fox* made great headway, and not wanting to lose a good opportunity to shave miles off their voyage, George and Frank kept pushing on through an ocean that began to take on an almost alpine look. Hills of water a hundred yards long rolled under the boat. Atop these hills, nasty breaking waves formed, their crests collapsing and blowing off toward Europe in sheets of spray. All the while the sun shone brightly, and not a cloud scooted across the deep blue sky.

The men worked the oars till their muscles screamed for rest. Each stroke demanded concentration. They shouted to each other to time their pull on the blades, left or right, to keep the boat from sliding sideways down the face of the waves. The sky slowly turned to crimson in the west, and they watched the reds turn to a dark purple. The warmth of high noon departed little by little, and at sunset the wind turned the chill of twilight into a deep, bone-numbing cold. It pierced the layer of their oilskins and wool shirts. They shivered despite the hard labor at the oars.

"We'll have no sleep tonight, George," Frank called to his friend in the stern. He had to yell to make himself heard above the wind and the noise of the sea. The waves that rose up behind them and broke sounded like surf on a beach.

"I think you're right," George shouted over his shoulder. "I don't think it safe for only one man to stay on the oars, not with this sea running."

"We'll keep on, then. That's the way of it, I guess," Frank said. "At least we're making fine headway. There's that to be thankful for."

All through the night they rowed like demons. In the blackness, they could not see the monster seas heading for them. They maneuvered the *Fox* by feel instead. As she rose to the summit of the crests, the two men eased off on the oars to slow the boat and let the wave pass, then renewed their efforts to keep her moving, down the smooth back of the wave into the trough and up the face of the next sea.

Each man strained at the oars and fought the growing fatigue that made every movement a chore. The pitching and rolling motion of the rowboat bruised their muscles as they were thrown about. Their hands went numb with the cold and stiffened further whenever they took turns with the bailer. The prolonged exposure to the salt water softened the deep calluses on their palms and fingers, causing them to bleed. Despite their efforts, the reindeer cushions and their blankets were thoroughly soaked, wringing wet. It seemed that nothing aboard the *Fox* would ever be dry again.

Dawn broke ever so slowly, and when it got light enough to see, the world around them seemed strangely out of sync. The beauty of the sunrise, the soft pink appearing first as a slight rim in the white edge of the earth, emerged rapidly into a band and finally filled the cloudless sky in a shimmering tapestry. On the sea, the fury of the waves belied the serenity aloft, and the contrast contributed to the ordeal of the mind. Surely a storm in the usual sense was easier to take, since the mind could accept it more readily than this marriage of opposing sights. Adding to their low spirits was the certainty that this was only a small gale, nothing like what the sea could dish out in a true survival storm.

As so often occurs offshore, the ocean's mood changed almost instantly. The west wind dropped off as the morning progressed. It no longer shrieked in their ears and drove spray into their faces, though it still had quite a bit of muscle. In turn, without the influence of the high wind, the waves grew tamer, though, like the wind, they, too, still retained much of their punch. But the conditions had improved enough for the men to consider lighting their stove to heat some coffee. They had longed for something warm to drink for almost twenty-four hours and would have given just about anything for the simple pleasure. Neither had eaten anything during that time, and they felt completely drained of energy as a consequence of their fast and the hard work keeping the boat moving.

"Some coffee'll warm us up," Frank said. "I think I can get the stove lit with a little luck."

"I'll get you some matches," George said. He carefully laid his oars inboard, knelt in front of the watertight compartment, and retrieved some matches. He was pleased to see that everything inside the compart-

ment had remained dry despite the amount of water
that had been sloshing around their ankles all night.
He pivoted around to face Frank, who was working
the oars, and slid the matches into the pocket of his
friend's oilskins, which he'd taken off and laid across
the thwart, hoping to dry out the inside of the jacket.

"I'll take over now, Frank. I'll try to keep her as
steady as I can for you," George said, pulling hard
to compensate as the boat yawed to the left.

Frank carefully laid his oars inboard and turned
around on the seat. He drew water from the forward
water tank and filled the kettle with just enough to
make two cups. Hunched over the stove, he lit a
match; it promptly blew out. After several more
attempts, flames flickered up in the little burner, and
only Frank's efforts to block the wind with his hands
and body allowed them to gain strength. He put the
kettle on to boil.

"We'll have our coffee soon!" Frank said, turning
aft to face George, the cheer evident in his voice.

He turned back toward the bow, anxious to keep
the wind from blowing the fire out, and gasped in
surprise. Billows of black smoke hid the stove, its
housing, and the kettle. Before he could react, flames
erupted. Fanned by the wind, they exploded into a
full-fledged fire, licking the wooden frame that supported the stove and blowing forward toward the
watertight compartment in the bow.

11

Long tongues of yellow-and-orange flames leaped from the stove housing. The paint along the rail and the front of the forward watertight compartment bubbled and burned away. A trail of black smoke rode the wind close to the boat. For a moment both men stared at the fire, scarcely believing what they saw. A fire in a small wooden boat more than three hundred miles from land . . . If it continued to burn. . . .

Frank quickly took his oilskin coat and covered the kettle and stove with it, hoping to smother the flames. The coat began to smoke, and it looked as if it were about to catch on fire. Seeing that this remedy wouldn't work, he removed the coat before he lost it. They had no spare clothing, and its loss would have been serious. Exposure to the elements meant a long descent to death. If a strong northeast wind bore down on them, bringing with it the teeth of the icebound wastelands of Greenland, death would come fast.

Both men grabbed bailers and proceeded to splash the fire. The flames sputtered and hissed. Steam rose from the sides of the kettle. The smoke blew off as the last of the fire fizzled out.

"That was looking pretty dangerous there for a moment," George said as he began to bail the water out of the boat. He found himself starting to laugh, not a typical reaction to a near disaster, he told himself, but he couldn't help seeing the irony. "You know we just finished bailing the boat, and now we put the sea back in only to take it out one more time. It's like it can't make up its mind where it wants to be."

Frank said nothing. He examined the stove and the forward section of the boat. Satisfied there was no damage other than to the stove housing, he felt the kettle. Still hot.

"It almost got away from us, George. That blasted stove!"

"The damned thing will sink us yet."

"After all this, we may as well see if the coffee's hot enough," Frank said. He poured a cup for George and sat back with his. The coffee was lukewarm and had the distinct taste of brine.

"This is the worst cup of coffee I've ever had," Frank said. "But you know, I still wouldn't think of tossing it overboard."

While they nursed their coffee, they broke out some of their bread and the last of the tomatoes and cheese, along with some tinned beef. The warm liquid and the food revived their spirits. They ate together, leaving the *Fox* to tend to herself.

The west wind, apparently tired of blowing them across the Atlantic, continued to drop off during the afternoon until it barely made itself known to the two men in the form of dark patches atop the waves, which had stopped cresting much earlier. They were long black rollers with a silky skin. The occasional puff of wind created ripples on the surface that came and went, keeping the *Fox* and her crew company for a little while longer before finally vanishing altogether.

The thermometer registered seventy glorious degrees. Without the wind, the sun's warmth returned.
Both men took off their shirts and spread their oilskins open to dry. The reindeer cushions, stinking
horribly, were taken up to air, as were the blankets.

The work at the oars seemed a little less arduous,
their spirits a lot higher than they had been the previous night. That salty coffee, a little bit of food, and
a break in the weather were all the men needed to
renew themselves and find the strength to go on. For
the first time, George set a course that put the bow
of the *Fox* slightly north of east to begin their long
track to the cold latitudes well above the upper
reaches of the Maine coast and the lower Maritimes
of Canada. The needle of the little compass read
eighty-four degrees, east by one-half north. Although
they had no idea of their longitude, they estimated
that the previous twenty-four hours' rowing with the
west wind had hurtled the Fox an additional ninety
miles, very good progress indeed given the state of
the weather and the size of their craft.

Throughout the afternoon the ocean flattened into
a sheet of glass, broken only with the low swells left
over from the west wind. They washed slowly past the
Fox in a gentle way, almost as a mother rocks a child
in a cradle. A pair of offshore seabirds, storm swallows,
flew above the *Fox*, riding the long, invisible wash of
the wind sweeping across the empty sea. These black
little birds often accompanied the *Fox*, as did gulls,
flying high in good weather and low across the wave
tops in bad weather. Unlike the gulls, however, the
storm swallows held a special meaning for sailors. It
is said that these birds are home to the souls of dead
sailors and to hurt or kill one will bring bad luck.
They are said to carry their eggs under their wings and
that they never seek shore. The swallows occasionally
landed near the boat and pecked at the remains of
food the men had thrown overboard. They, too, were

solitary members of the world offshore, and seeing them made the men feel less alone.

With such calm conditions, George and Frank celebrated with a dinner of sea biscuits and butter and a tin of baked beans and cold ham. They did without their much-loved coffee, thinking better of the idea of trying to light the stove, even though the opportunity to do so was ideal from a weather standpoint. Instead, they opened a can of condensed milk mixed with water from the tanks.

"The night looks fine," Frank said. "As fine as any soul could ask for."

"That it does. No one can say we don't deserve it. I'm looking forward to some sleep. 'Bout dead to the world."

Frank offered to take the first watch. He was himself partial to the later hours of the night. He liked the dog watch, the midnight hours, those wee times before the first gray of dawn ushered in a new day. He settled in to the solitary labor while George, exhausted yet content, made himself as comfortable as possible on the reindeer cushions, since the boat was packed full of provisions, lashed everywhere about the thwarts and stuffed under the seats. Soon Frank heard George's breath slow into the deep, steady cycle of sleep.

Frank gazed around, his eyes searching for any sign of a ship. Although their watches were set mostly to keep at least one man at the oars at all times, thus ensuring that the *Fox* inched her way ever eastward, the threat of being run down by a ship was quite real. The ocean may have appeared empty, a vast waste devoid of life, but it was not. The North Atlantic had been a busy place since the mid-1500s, when voyagers from Portugal, France, Great Britain, and even earlier, Scandinavia, had ventured across the waters to find new lands and profit from the rich fishery off the coast of the New World. The flood of transatlantic shipping had grown steadily over the last four centuries, and it seemed that the twentieth century would see no end to the lines of ships traversing the waves.

No navigation lamps twinkled on the horizon, however, after the last vestige of daylight dwindled into nothingness, leaving the *Fox* and her sole rower afloat in an inky world in which the sky and the sea merged into one. The only source of light came from the stars—faint sparkles billions of years old. The welcome noises of peace—the swish of the blades dipping into the smooth sea, George's muffled breaths, the gentle rub of wood against the leather wrapped around the oars where they moved against the rail and between the tholepins—all shattered in an instant.

A sharp crack that sounded as if the *Fox* had struck a log or some other debris startled Frank and jolted George awake. The sea was littered with debris that floated and could sink the boat: hatch covers, lumber, boxes, and crates washed from the decks of overladened ships; weed and barnacle-covered logs and branches from the depths of interior woodlands down rivers and out to sea on the tides; and all manner of spars—yardarms, hoists, booms, even the stumps of masts—set adrift after a ship foundered. All these varied but no less deadly forms of battering rams could be encountered by chance at any time. If the *Fox* came down hard on wreckage in a heavy sea, odds were fair that the boat might well be holed and quickly sink as the weight of the water overpowered the buoyancy of the watertight compartments. Both men knew about this danger but could do nothing to avoid the objects in the dark.

"What in the world was that?" George said, sitting upright.

Both men peered into the blackness astern but could see nothing in the water.

"I wonder what we hit," George said.

A flash of phosphorescence, green like the tail of a firefly, caught their attention. They had watched the oars stir up the tiny organisms in the sea, which, when disturbed at night, emit a faint light. The blades dipped into the smooth surface of the water, and for a moment a pool of phosphorescence marked the spot where the oar had pushed the *Fox* forward. But neither of them was rowing now, and it became apparent that there was something swimming in the water near them—something big. They leaned over the side of the boat and saw an enormous fish, roughly nine or ten feet long. It circled the boat and rubbed along the keel, then hit the side of the hull with its tail hard enough to kick up spray.

"He's trying to find a way into the boat," Frank said.

"I'd like to send that monster to another world," George said. "And I would if we had a gun."

As the fish scraped against the boat several more times, George tied the hatchet they had with them to one of the oars. He tried to whack the fish. However, the creature refused to stay still long enough for him to hit it. Since there was nothing that could be done to kill the fish and it didn't seem intent on capsizing the boat, George went back to sleep while Frank rowed on through the hours of his watch. The phosphorescence glimmered and disappeared, providing Frank with a fix on the position of the fish relative to the boat. It stayed nearby, so close that Frank almost hit it with the oars as he rowed. The thought that it was a hungry shark entered his mind but brought no fear. As long as they stayed in the boat and the fish stayed in the water, all would be well.

At eleven o'clock, Frank awoke George to take his turn at the oars.

"Have we got the big fellow with us yet?" George asked, looking around the boat.

"Oh, yes. He's around, though I can't see him just now."

"Well, get some sleep. It's a good night for sleeping."

The next morning, Frank's suspicions were proven correct. The fish turned out to be a hammerhead shark, which have been known to attack humans on occasion. The gray back and white underbelly looked distorted under the surface of the water, and its eyes on either side of its long, rectangular head were black as basalt and every bit as hard. It stayed with the boat through the rest of the morning. Then, just as George and Frank were getting used to seeing it, the shark simply vanished into the deep.

The weather continued fair, with the wind blowing lightly from the south and shifting to the east by noon. Again the temperature reached seventy degrees. For a little while at least, the ocean appeared tamed and in its present state even beautiful. It stretched out in a seemingly infinite expanse of dark blue to blend with the azure above the horizon, tinged white with the first streams of cirrus clouds.

The triangular topsails of a schooner appeared over the horizon later that afternoon. The two men watched with increasing excitement as the lower portion of the sails and finally the hull of the ship slowly came into view. On its present course, it would sail close to the *Fox*. They waited patiently, and when it became obvious that the two craft would pass near enough to merit the effort, they rowed toward the schooner.

It was one of thousands of small, independently owned sailing vessels working the coastal trade routes off North America. Similar ships carried granite from Maine to New York City for use in building skyscrapers. Great blocks of ice, stored in sawdust as insulation and cut in the wintertime from freshwater ponds and lakes that created splashes of blue in an evergreen sea during the warm summer months, also came from Maine. Crammed with spirits and sugarcane from the

Caribbean, the cargo of ships returning from the tropics found its way to the cities along the East Coast. Tobacco and cotton flowed from the rich fields of the South. The decks of this little schooner were piled high with poles bound for New York City. They would be offloaded there and be added to the vast number that supported miles of telegraph wires and wove a black web over the crowded streets. Looking skyward, city dwellers viewed elevated trains, linemen tending the wires not only for the telegraphs but for electric lights as well, and skywalkers, those workmen erecting the steel frames, the skeletons of office towers and apartments.

The sight of the ship brought back the reality of life ashore. Its cargo, too, so indicative of a young nation racing forward into the next century with all of its wonders, acted as a catalyst that further galvanized their desire to succeed in the crossing. To do the impossible seemed somehow appropriate. It symbolized a new way of life, a coming of age just as important to individuals as it was for the country in which they resided. The ship's bow passed them, with the barest wave pushed outward as it moved through the water at the heels of the light east wind, its sails spread out to catch its every breath. The stern passed, and George and Frank could see that her name was *Jessie* and that she hailed from Nova Scotia. A large man, whom they identified as the captain, leaned over the taffrail and shouted to them, asking if they needed help.

"We are the rowboat *Fox* out of New York. We're bound for Le Havre, France. Please report us to the newspapers. Can you give us our longitude?" George cried, keeping his voice loud and his words short to make certain that the skipper heard him correctly.

The man seemed to understand. He said something to the fellow next to him, and the mate disappeared belowdecks. Meanwhile, every member of the crew lined the rails. Those men off watch must have been there because not so many souls at one time were needed to run the schooner. The *Fox* rode the easy swells a short distance from the ship, which began to pull away.

The captain's voice boomed over the increasing expanse of water between the two vessels. "Your longitude is sixty-eight degrees, forty minutes west. We've had nice weather the last couple days. Very easy sailing. Godspeed, little *Fox!*"

"Thank you," both men yelled together.

The *Jessie* sailed on toward New York harbor. Five days later, after tugs towed her safely to the docks of lower Manhattan, true to his word, the captain reported sighting the two "mad" Norwegians and their little rowboat. He also noted that they were in good health and spirits. A few daily papers carried the story, and many readers regarded the voyage with interest, though it wasn't the talk of the town, as it had been on Saturday, June 6, when they had first set off. Out of sight, out of mind. The attention span of the average reader seldom lasted for long, but the brief mention of the crossing's progress still registered on the public's consciousness.

For Richard Kyle Fox, the publicity already had contributed in a small way to furthering the popularity of the *Police Gazette* and increasing its already wide national circulation. These were the types of stories he knew collectively made his paper what it was. He had long ago figured out that tales of little people doing big things had a way of capturing the imagination of all the other little people, the ones who worked in the sweatshops and factories, in lumberyards and bakeries, in the fields, and on the waterfronts. This audience was most inclined to read about the outlandish, the base, the violent, the sexually provocative, and the heroic. He had taken to publishing news of inventors trying out flying machines, since these

attempts had started to become more numerous and
many of them ended up ending the lives of would-
be aeronauts. Fox hoped that more ships would report the progress of the two immigrants; he didn't
much care whether they died or not as long as they
didn't do it too soon. Every time word came in about
them, the interest in their endeavor would grow.

As Frank rowed toward France, George worked out
their position on the chart. In eight days they had
covered 365 miles to the east, roughly as far out in
a direct line to the north as Penobscot Bay in Maine.
They had actually rowed more miles than that, however, to make up for drift. They had also increased
their latitude in keeping with their plans. When
George gave Frank the news, they both felt cheerful.
Their average of 45 miles per day meant that the
3,250-mile trip to Le Havre would run to approximately seventy-two days. They had provisioned for
sixty days, but they thought it quite possible that additional stores could be begged off passing ships if necessary. Besides, with a little luck they would soon find
favorable west winds to speed them on their way all
the faster.

They settled back to their work at the oars. As the
day wore on, the clouds thickened. The altocumulus,
mid-level clouds that give the sky a mottled look some
equate with the scales of a mackerel, choked off the
cirrus. Soon the wind began to increase in velocity
from the east. Both men knew the signs. Another
frontal system had swung in to pay them a visit, and
this time it threatened to undo all the progress they
had made with the rough but fast-pushing west wind.
By six o'clock, the sea had lost all evidence of its
former tameness.

Stoic by nature and hardened through years of work
on the water, the two Norwegians struggled on. They
were resigned to row against the east wind and hold
their position. Every hour they strained meant less

headway lost. A mile won by sweat and muscle is a mile any man will fight tenaciously not to lose.

The rain swept in on them after dusk. The temperature dropped rapidly. Everything was soaked again. To keep up their strength, they decided to try to adhere to their watch schedule, which would allow the man off watch at least a slim chance of catching a few moments of shut-eye. At around eleven o'clock that night, George, who was at the oars, noticed the loom of a white light directly astern of the *Fox*. In the poor visibility he could not tell where the ship was heading relative to the boat, but as he continued to peer at it, he was sure it was closing. Out of the rain two more lights appeared, one red, the other green. These were the ship's running lights, each located on either side of the vessel. Seeing both at once meant one thing: It was steaming straight for them on a direct collision course at upwards of fifteen knots.

12

The dark and rain obscured the massive bow of the steamship and any lights showing from the bridge. Only the navigation lamps, dimly visible in the murk, revealed the approaching danger. For any mariner, an impending collision at sea represents one of their worst nightmares. It is one of the few eventualities that can strike fear into a hardened seaman and turn the hair of the most seasoned captain prematurely gray. Collisions mean almost certain death to the crew of the smaller vessel involved. That had been proved repeatedly throughout the ages, from the days of sail and wooden hulls to the time of steam engines and steel ships that became floating cities.

Ships up and down the coast sank regularly as a result of collision. On Georges Bank and the Grand Banks, liners sliced through the Gloucester schooners and crushed dories. Entire crews of a dozen men or more disappeared without a trace in the thick, damp fog, even on calm nights. Once immersed in the near-freezing water, death came in minutes. For this reason many sailors never learned how to swim. They simply didn't want to prolong the agony. The lightships off ports such as New York and Nantucket Shoal routinely got run down in poor visibility. And the liners sometimes hit each other or collided with icebergs.

Without a light shining aboard the *Fox*, there was no chance that the watch aboard the steamer would spot the boat in time to change course. Even if they could, it takes several miles for a large ship to stop or turn, and George knew it. He also knew that at the speed of an average liner it would take less than ten minutes for the vessel to travel the two miles to the point of impact. On a clear night, the running lights of ships could be seen for many miles, but on a night like this one George doubted the ship was more than two or three miles away. Of course, it was possible the bow wave would toss them to either side of the ship; it had happened before in cases where a small boat encountered a large ship. But the odds were better than even that the boat would either be crushed to splinters in seconds or sucked under as it got caught in the wash of the ship's propellers.

He immediately changed course by ninety degrees, heading north, and called out to Frank that he needed his muscle fast. The *Fox* had been facing the seas, pointing almost due east. However, turning off the wind to avoid the ship forced them to take the seas on the right-hand side of the boat. As Frank groped his way to his seat and positioned the oars in place between the tholepins, cascades of green, solid water poured over the rails and began to fill the boat. The weight of it slowed the *Fox* further. For a few moments she lay stationary in the path of the oncoming steamer.

To die this way, not from the hand of nature but in a seagoing traffic accident, would have been an insult to these men. Death at sea never is noble, nor is it particularly so in most other instances save, perhaps, on the battlefield or in bravely facing a serious

illness. But for reasons that run deep, it appears more
honorable to go down fighting something far more
intangible and powerful than a hunk of steel. No one
would know how they died if the ship hit them; but
they would. The lights grew more distinct in the rain
and dark. They knew they had only a few minutes of
life left if they failed to get the *Fox* moving.

"Row with a will, George," Frank yelled above the
wind. "She's coming fast!"

George needed no encouragement from his friend,
who was by far the stronger of the two. Each man
rowed harder than they thought possible. It proved
difficult to keep the blades from catching air as the
boat pitched from rail to rail, sending the oars on
one side high and the others deep into the troughs.
They could not hear the thrum of the engines or the
wash of the bow wave as the ship drew closer. Inside
the liner, the passengers slept snugly in their berths.
The night owls danced to the harmonious notes of
a grand piano and sipped cocktails in the elegant
ballroom. The ship's officers stood on the bridge and
looked out through the rivulets of rain running down
the windows into the blackness, searching for the
telltale loom of navigation lamps. But they saw nothing except the Atlantic in a sour mood. The building
seas sent sheets of spray up the hull of the ship, and
the wind carried it several more stories into the air,
then shot it aft into the night.

Below, out of sight, the *Fox* rolled and pitched. The
red and green running lights shone with a clarity
neither man wished to see. They were high above
them now and very close. They redoubled their
efforts, and at last the green light on the right-hand
side of the ship suddenly vanished.

"We're almost free of her," George shouted.

The red light grew closer and came even with the
stern of the *Fox*. They could see a vague outline of
the ship towering above them and a few splotches of

yellow light from the windows of the upper decks. Then the ship was gone, proceeding on to Hamburg, Liverpool, Southampton, Le Havre, or some other European port. Its last farewell was the wake churned up from the propellers deep below the surface of the water. The near vertical waves roared across the westward moving seas, hit the *Fox*, and eventually died some distance off.

Alone again, George and Frank lost no time in putting the *Fox* back on course, head to the seas. They did not have the luxury of sitting about reflecting on their close call. No time to go through the mental shock that sets in accompanied by shivers and a cold sweat, when an individual realizes that he almost died. It was not that these two men were superhuman; each reacted to the incident in his own very human way. It had happened, and that was that. If they had died, no one would have known their fate. But as it stood, their fate was still very much in their hands, quite literally, as they pitted the strength of their arms, shoulders, and backs against the most powerful force on earth.

The wind howled throughout the night, increasing to thirty to forty knots with higher gusts by eight o'clock on the morning of Sunday, June 14. This was the men's first true gale, and both of them felt a deep-seated anxiety about how the *Fox* would hold up as they rowed through the night, too wet and cold to sleep. They could guess that the boat's design and its crew could handle these conditions, but so far no hard proof existed. The men rowed till every ounce of energy drained away. They rowed on and on, desperately fighting the weather and knowing they were losing ground every minute.

The waves built to twenty to twenty-five feet. The crests began to break apart into long, sinewy strands of spindrift that blew toward them across the faces and backs of the seas from east to west. The water itself seemed alive, like a gray shapeless animal, a creature with an ill temper most landsmen never witness except when perched on the jetties or on the shore, staring in awe at the power of nature. Yet as humbling and amazing a spectacle it is to see what a big wind does to the ocean from shore, it cannot possibly imbue the beholder with anything but an inkling of what it is like far away across the water, where no land lies for hundreds or thousands of miles.

The largest waves came in groups of three or four. These sometimes broke, the crest unable to stand up to the force of the wind. When one of these giants boarded the *Fox*, and many did, one man would have to stop rowing to bail. It was a task much like that of Sisyphus, who had tried to cheat the boatman whose duty it was to transport the recently departed across the River Styx. For his misdeeds he was doomed to a life of senseless labor rolling a rock up a hill in Hades every day, only to repeat the process for eternity.

Bailing wave after wave out of the boat imparted a similar sense of futility, a resignation to the fact that as soon as the task was completed it surely would have to be repeated again and again to prevent the *Fox* from swamping and floating dead in the water, beam to the seas. In that position, she would roll over and over like a water-soaked log. Provisions would be lost even if she stayed afloat, buoyed up from the air trapped in the watertight compartments. Worse, one or both men could be washed away from the boat. It would take just moments for the man to lose sight of the *Fox* in the pelting rain and the gray, white-crested hills of water.

For the first time, the violent motion of the boat alarmed George and Frank. The gusty wind created sea conditions that both knew were far more threatening than would be the case had the wind blown at a steady rate. The unsteady wind velocities made for seas of varying sizes in the extreme. Fearing for their safety, exhausted, hungry, cold, and wet, they gave up trying to fight the ocean.

Back in the Atlantic Highlands, when they had fitted out the boat, they had talked about what to do in a case like this. As experienced seamen, they knew eventually that there would come a time when proceeding on course might mean capsizing or being thrown end over end down the face of a wave. Together they designed a device called a floating anchor, often known as a sea anchor. Constructed of heavy canvas in the shape of an open-ended cone, it functioned as a kind of brake. It was attached to a long, stout line lashed to the bow of the boat. The cone grabbed the water, thus keeping the bow into the wind and waves. Neither man, however, had been out in conditions bad enough to test its abilities, and as Frank deployed it, their hearts raced.

Almost as soon as the sea anchor was put over the side, the *Fox*'s bow rose up on the face of a wave. The boat wavered, as if deciding whether to surge backwards into the trough. The line went bar tight for an instant, and the wave passed harmlessly under the boat.

"It's good we planned for this," George said. "Very good indeed."

Realizing there was still a significant chance that the boat might fall off the face of a wave and capsize, sending them both over the side at once, they donned their life belts. They hadn't deemed them necessary until now. Both men hurriedly strapped on an eight-inch-wide belt stuffed with reindeer hair and covered with waterproofed canvas to keep the hair dry. Reindeer hair, when dry, has far more buoyancy than cork, a subject they had explored at length prior to setting out. Attached to the life belt was a thin, strong line about twenty feet in length which was tied fast to the rail. Having done everything possible to ensure that their little boat weathered the storm, George and Frank sat in its bottom, out of the full force of the wind and the flying spray it kicked up. Frank checked the thermometer at noon; it registered forty-five degrees. The gale reached its height at about this time.

When conditions are bad enough to lay to a sea anchor, the passage of every minute seems to take hours. Time literally stands still, its meaning lost in every sense. The world becomes alien, unreal. It is as if the soul has been transported into hell with no hope of returning. At such times, sailors have been known to go insane, particularly down in the roaring forties, when storms can rage for weeks. The cold penetrates the marrow and numbs the mind. The violent motion of the vessel bruises and lacerates when the body is thrown against the hull and decks. George and Frank had experienced storms before, and both knew of the psychological and physical demands. They knew that riding out a gale in an eighteen-foot rowboat would tax them, push their limits perhaps beyond the point of endurance. Neither of them said anything to the other as the hours dragged on. They simply endured what nature had dealt them and longed for the front to pass by and for conditions to improve.

And slowly, as the afternoon progressed, the front did pass them by. The crests on the larger groups of waves stopped breaking. The wind no longer screamed, nor did it try to snatch their breath away when they faced eastward. The motion of the boat remained violent, but just a little less so. It is these signs, almost indiscernible at first, that mark the beginning of the end of a gale. Weak from hunger and their exertion, both mental and physical, George and Frank felt at last that it was safe to open one of the watertight compartments to retrieve some sea biscuits, a can of roast beef, and a bottle of the Vino Kalafra.

Eating proved difficult. As the bow of the *Fox* rode
up to the summit of a wave, occasionally it met a layer
of disturbed water with an inordinate amount of air
in it. The boat sank to the heavier water, sending a
white froth over the forward deck that instantly blew
back on them. They each huddled with their backs
to the sea, cradling the sea biscuit and beef in their
hands to keep it as dry as possible while they wolfed
it down. Then they passed the bottle of wine back
and forth. The warmth of the alcohol deep inside
their stomachs fanned outward, traveling to their
extremities to spread a feeling of well-being.

"She did well this day, eh, George?" Frank said.
He patted the rail next to him.

"That she did. Seems our thinking was right about
the floating anchor. At least with that we haven't
drifted too far back."

"Are you thinking it's safe to go on?"

George looked over the rail of the boat. The wind
had dropped off quickly. Without its power to drive
them, the waves began to tumble down. They lost
their shape, and the pattern became even more confused. Nature strives for order, and without the east
wind, all order disappeared as the waves struggled to
find a new direction. The *Fox* pitched and jumped,
rearing up and slamming down.

"We won't make any headway in this. We'll wait a
little longer," he said.

They lay down till evening, passing Sunday away in
a forced observance of the day of rest, celebrated less
often in the traditional way as the new century loomed
close at hand. As the hours ticked on, they were aware
of the miles they lost. But each man knew that to row
against such a confused sea would prove nothing. To
succeed in this adventure meant having the sense to
quit when doing so made sense and to preserve their
strength and dole it out wisely.

At around six o'clock, they ate another meal consisting of more beef, buttered bread, and eggs, which they drank raw from the shell after tapping a hole in the top. As they ate, they noted a shift in the wind to a southerly direction, and with it came a light fog. The sea continued to subside. They hauled in their sea anchor and set the night watch so that each of them could try to get as much sleep as possible while the ocean let them. That night, as each man slept in turn, the other at the oars worked to regain all the miles they had lost.

13

About three o'clock in the morning, the wind veered around to the west. The fog blew off toward Europe. A new wave pattern began to develop as the wind picked up. Three- to four-foot rollers rode across the long easterly swell left behind from the gale. Its effect created a series of undulations on the horizon that became visible as the sun rose almost directly ahead of, but still to the south of, the *Fox*'s bow. The sea is never still, even in a dead calm. Some far-off storm somewhere always sends in a swell. The wind in the local area makes waves. The water responds in many ways, and is seldom the same from day to day, hour to hour.

The *Fox* moved forward, regaining the twenty to thirty miles lost during the gale. The temperature remained cold, still hovering around forty-five degrees. Back on land, with its tendency to hold the heat of the sun, the people in New York City and the surrounding countryside enjoyed the warmth from the west wind blowing from the Ohio Valley across the Appalachian Mountains to the coast. It was a pleasant day in mid-June, nothing out of the ordinary. Very few thought of what it was like hundreds of miles to the east, where the same wind brought no warmth, where the world appeared altogether different ... barren, hostile, unforgiving. One's own perspective on a day derives from where one happens to be both in terms of physical location and feeling ill or good about the way life appears. Out at sea it is difficult not to think about the people on land, comfortable and safe worrying about things that really don't matter when measured against more cosmic concerns. It's hard to come to grips with one's own fragility, one's insignificance in the wider world. The sea brings all this to the fore; it never lets a sailor forget.

The wind increased in strength all through Monday, June 15. A high sea erased the last vestiges of the easterly swell. The ocean had achieved order once again. The long lines of waves marching toward Europe sped the *Fox* along. Both men were cold but happy. They worked the oars hard, and by Tuesday at noon George estimated that they had traveled 130 miles to the east since Sunday night. Adding to their good cheer, the wind dropped off and the thermometer registered sixty-five degrees. It was still damp, their clothing and bedding sodden. As the sun shined down on them through a cloudless sky, a white film of dried salt, left behind as the water evaporated, covered the boat and everything in it. Far off on the horizon, they spotted a sailing ship. It crossed the curve of the earth, its hull never coming into view, and gradually faded away. Tuesday passed uneventfully.

Life became a series of trials interspersed with respites. It was as if the sea were testing them. It pushed them harder each time, threw another obstacle or danger in their path, then let up to give them the strength to try the next test and the next. Of course, the sea isn't a living thing; it's incapable of being cruel. It can only be indifferent. But to the men who set out to challenge it, it did seem alive, cruel, and yet benevolent. To the sailor the sea is seldom an it. It is a she.

The *Fox* pushed on, with a light west wind and smooth water all night Tuesday and into Wednesday morning. The men were solidly in their rowing routine now. Their hands had developed thick calluses, as had their buttocks. Their skin was tanned a deep brown. Salt crystals clung to George's mustache. The calm conditions induced them to risk lighting the stove for the first time since it set fire to the boat six days earlier. No coffee for six days! That had been hard to bear, and both of the men yearned for a drink of it.

Carefully, and ever so slowly, Frank lit the stove. He didn't take his eyes off it once. He just sat watching, waiting for it to flare up. It didn't, though, and as he passed George a hot cup of coffee and an egg he had put in to boil with the brew, he smiled.

"Ah, this is heaven," George said, sipping deeply. "I hope the stove gives us no more trouble. The crossing will be all the harder without it."

Frank agreed, admitting that the coffee and boiled egg made him feel better than he had in a couple of days.

The day looked as if it would be as uneventful as the last, but at around nine o'clock, they sighted the long, columnar spout of a whale several miles ahead of the boat. As they scanned the horizon, more spouts appeared. Dozens of them. Soon it became apparent that the school of whales was on the move, heading straight for them. Within minutes the *Fox* was surrounded.

The creatures ranged from sixty to eighty feet in length. The men watched their black backs emerge from the deep, revealing much of the whales' shapes for several minutes; the rush of air from their blowholes sent spouts twenty feet skyward. Far back from the heads of the whales, high, triangular dorsal fins sliced through the water. The white undersides of the whales seemed to split them in two, creating a contrast of light and dark shapes as the whales swam nearer. They did not seem curious about the object floating among them, though the men could clearly see the massive heads of the whales. Their eyes—set just beyond their huge jaws, white on the right side and black on the left—looked almost human. Frank recognized these whales as the baleen type, as opposed to the toothed whales.

Fearful of what the whales might do, George and Frank changed course to avoid the school. But as they did so they came dangerously close to some of them. Although the whales appeared indifferent to the *Fox*, the men had the distinct feeling that their presence was known, that they were tolerated and allowed passage only so long as the whales saw fit to grant it.

"If we touch one of these big fellows, it'll all be up for us," George said quietly. He remembered an old saying among sailors that was meant to comfort but provided little at the moment: If you don't touch the whale, he won't touch you. The likelihood of touching one seemed quite strong, and both men felt their palms go sweaty and their heart rate increase. At least fifty whales surrounded them, many larger than either had seen before. All around them they sounded and surfaced, blowing the sea to heaven as they exhaled.

The men rowed as hard as they could to extricate themselves from the danger. As the blades hit the water, the men watched, ready to pull the oars up if it looked as if they might hit a whale. One large whale surfaced right next to the boat and blew. They felt its hot breath, smelled a peculiar odor, not quite fishy, and a mist of vapor from the whale's lungs moistened their skins. It was a strange but appropriate sort of baptism. The presence of the whales, the largest mam-

mals on the planet, humbled the men. They were
prey to the whaling vessels, but in all their days at sea
the men had never experienced being so close to so
many of them in such a small boat.

After a short while, they had gotten the *Fox* clear
of the whales, which, at any rate, had simply passed
by without paying their human observers the slightest
attention. The whales followed the same path every
year, migrating from the warm Caribbean Sea in the
spring to the cold northern waters during the summer. Once there, they feasted on herring and other
small fish, and krill, a tiny shrimplike crustacean
between two and three inches long. The krill produce
a form of plankton. Whales feed on it, as well as small
fish that eat it. The whales that had just passed the
Fox no doubt were on the hunt for food, playing their
part in an ageless cycle.

And at the top of the food chain stood man. Near
Sandefjord, where George was born, one of his countrymen had invented a very effective type of harpoon
gun that revolutionized whaling. The old wooden
whalers, with their longboats, had become obsolete.
Killing whales was far more efficient—another sign
of the times. Technological advances had changed
everything, and whaling was certainly no exception.
In Farsund, near Frank's parents' little farm in
Elunde, the port bustled as well. Whaling was an inte-
gral part of life in Norway, perhaps more so than it
was even in New England.

The two Norwegians, far out in the ocean in a little
craft, had seen the whales in a different light for the
first time. They had seen them in their natural state,
without the fear of pursuit, and had found them
graceful, if not fearful, in their size and ability to
destroy. Yet they had not destroyed. Unlike the hammerhead, they had neither attacked nor tried to.
Instead, they appeared, then went in peace. It is easy
to ascribe human characteristics to an animal that

seems intelligent and that so dwarfs the human fo m
that its sheer size demands the respect only inte li-
gence can afford. The whales were the equivalent of
the king; of the sea; like the lion, their most dange:-
ous enemy was the human beings that entered their
world and challenged their place in it.

With the school of whales behind them, the men
turned the *Fox* back on course. The compass still
pointed at around eighty-four degrees. Their long
track to the higher latitudes had begun in earnest.
The thermometer registered seventy degrees. The
sun warmed their skin and continued to dry their
belongings, and the sea remained mercifully calm.
They kept to their schedule, rowing together throughout the day to get the most speed out of the *Fox* and
rowing in turns during the night. Although a light
rain fell and a dank chill filled the wee hours, the
sea remained smooth. The exertion was almost pleasant, as if they were rowing around Sandy Hook Bay
to tend their clam beds. The ocean, it seemed, had
decided to give them time to relax and make progress
across.

Dawn on Thursday, June 18, saw the rain clear off
and a return to fair weather. The spirits of both men
were higher than ever, and they sang songs together
as they rowed. They told each other jokes, though
they had each heard the other's many times before.
If anything, the bond between them had grown
stronger. Many people ashore in the fishing commu-
nities on Sandy Hook Bay and the beach on the Atlantic side had warned them that friction might develop,
that their close proximity to one another would test
the bounds of their friendship. Thus far, though, all
was well. The crossing appeared more possible than
before.

Frank glanced over his shoulder toward the east
and noted a ship steaming fast in their direction,
black trails of smoke belching from her three tall

funnels. He and George watched for a while to determine if there was any danger of collision, but it looked safe enough. The liner would pass about a quarter of a mile away. Her plumb bows sliced through the waves, kicking up a white curl of water that contrasted against the black hull. As she drew closer, George unfurled the American flag. He inserted the pole, now weathered, its varnish starting to peel, into the fitting on the aft deck. The Stars and Stripes fluttered in the light easterly wind.

"This way maybe they'll report us and they won't think us in trouble," George said.

"She's one of the Hamburg-American line," Frank said. "She's bound to be carrying mail to New York. I hope she doesn't stop for us."

Neither man thought it appropriate to delay a liner like this, particularly one carrying the mail. Every hour made a difference to the recipients and even more so to the owners of the ships, who competed fiercely for the contracts from the U.S. government which went to the fastest, most reliable vessels. At the time, twelve major shipping companies ran a total of eighty-five transatlantic steamers. The German companies outpaced much of the competition with a growing fleet of sleek vessels, the envy of not a few shipping magnates and the bane of many.

"She's hoisting her colors," Frank said.

The German flag rode up the aft mast behind the main body of the superstructure and snapped in the wind created by the forward movement of the ship as it passed them. Painted on the fine curve of the transom was its name, the *Fürst Bismark*, one of the finest ships afloat, a true greyhound of the sea. Built in 1890, it had completed its maiden voyage from Southampton to New York in six days and fourteen hours, at an average speed of twenty knots. First-class passengers enjoyed commodious accommodations and promenades along her decks. Polished vents protruded skyward from the top cabin, standing almost half as high as her funnels, which were canted aft in a rakish appeal and a visual pronouncement of her speed.

"Why, she's coming about. They don't know who we are, I'm thinking," George said, irritated that he had now delayed the ship.

Both of them waved as the ship executed its turn to the left and came close by about twenty minutes later. A man dressed in the resplendent uniform typical of the German shipping lines peered over the rail high above them and shouted, "Are you shipwrecked?"

"No, we're rowing to Le Havre, France," George called.

"You're what?" the officer asked, thinking he had heard the scruffy, red-haired man below incorrectly.

George repeated: "We're the rowboat *Fox* out of New York bound for Le Havre, France."

"To France in that boat? You'll never get there. Let me take you back to New York. You'll be fine there," he said. His tone of voice indicated that he thought these men were just this side of crazy. He spoke to them almost as if they were children. The sun had gotten to them.

"No, thank you," Frank cried. "We're fine right here."

"All we want is for you to report us to the newspapers when you get to New York," George said.

As this exchange of words was going on, there was a great commotion on the deck of the liner. Passengers lined the decks two and three deep, and still more streamed out the cabin doors and tried to catch a glimpse of the two men in their rowboat. The ship actually began to list to the left. The weight of hundreds of people along the port-side rail put the vessel out of trim. The captain was well aware of the list, but he didn't consider it too dangerous in the calm seas. However, skippers of the smaller imm ships had to forcibly keep the passengers below upon entering upper New York harbor. If left t the passengers would inevitably crowd the left-hand side of the ship to get a look at the Statue of Liberty. A severe list in either direction was very dangerous because it could capsize a small vessel, which would quickly lose its stability if the ballast shifted. Whether human or cargo, it made no difference.

"Well, I'm sorry, then," the officer said. "We'll have to leave you."

The passengers cheered and waved as the *Fürst Bismark* powered up her engines and slowly pulled away. The sound of so many voices moved both men. It brought back vivid memories of watching the faces of the passengers aboard the *R. K. Fox* as it left them and proceeded back to the Narrows the night of June 6. It recalled to their minds the throngs lining the Battery. Frank thought of Caroline, his sister, and wondered what his father, Emanuel, and his mother, Elizabeth, were going through. Worried about him, no doubt about that. But at least word would reach them when Caroline wrote with news that they had been reported safe once again. Seated at the kitchen table in the little cottage, they would tear open the letter not knowing if it contained good or bad news, and at least for a short time they would feel relief.

Thoughts of family invaded George's mind as well. Anine and his children would fare well with her parents in Brevik until he made it across. He would hold Fritz in his arms, high above his head, to make him laugh. Annie Louisa and Andrew, older, would be no less overjoyed. It would be a fine time. He vowed never to be separated from them again. They would, at last, be together back in America, their future more certain than it had ever been before. Once he and Frank had set a world record and earned a handsome sum from the lectures and exhibits, they would settle down to lead a life not devoid of work but one much less difficult.

They watched the *Fürst Bismark* steam away, each lost in his own thoughts. The ship disappeared over the horizon in less than a half hour. They were alone once again, and this time they both felt it keenly. They could not possibly have escaped these feelings even if they had wanted to. To deny the desire to be with family and to have them not worry would be to deny their humanity. They were hard men, but they were sensitive. Out on the empty sea, such thoughts were more easily put to rest. But seeing a ship like the *Fürst Bismark* so close, with all of its passengers, the comforts, the ease with which they could have given up the crossing and come home, made an impression, however temporary.

The rowing commenced. As they pulled at the oars, which had become appendages, wooden extensions of their arms that they simultaneously loathed and loved, they watched the little wake of the *Fox* swirl behind them. Every stroke put them closer to the end of the voyage, and they rowed steadily on, ticking off the miles one by one, each a step in the right direction, one that led to closure and a new beginning.

14

With any great effort, there must for its success come a good deal of luck. Had the wind continued to blow strongly from the east, nothing the two men did would have prevented the *Fox* from an unwanted return to the United States. Had a violent storm of true survival proportions arisen, the might of the sea easily could have overpowered the vessel. The men themselves required a command of their bodies and minds few of their countrymen possessed and were fortunate in their ability to work as one. To keep rowing day after day, no matter what, demanded a level of endurance most people would consider impossible to achieve.

The men became automatons, blinded by their own sweat, the salt from their bodies and the sea stinging their eyes. Muscular pains plagued them, particularly in their hands, arms, backs, and legs. The quick motion of the *Fox* made it risky to stand up in calm weather and unthinkable at all other times. Since they were unable to stretch their legs except on their off-watch hours, their muscles cramped. Frank, with his six-foot frame, longed to stride free on land. The skin on the upper side of their hands, constantly exposed to the elements, burned and peeled and often bled. Their noses chapped, became painful to touch, and never seemed to tan like the rest of their faces. The skin under their clothing seldom dried and took on a pasty white wrinkled appearance. Yet they continued to row, and for a time the sea granted them easy passage, making the physical discomfort a little more bearable.

After the first thirteen days, filled with a series of adventures and misadventures, life aboard the *Fox* actually became dull. The weather continued fair for nine more days, with one exception, on Tuesday, June 23. Southerly and westerly winds for the most part brought intermittent fog and sunshine. The sea kicked up now and then but soon settled down again to near calm. The temperature within this stable weather system remained between sixty and seventy degrees—conditions ideal for making good progress, and the *Fox* did. Between Thursday, June 18, and Saturday, June 26, the little ship clicked off approximately 455 miles. With their good luck, the crew of the *Fox* maintained an average of forty to fifty miles per day, with several days somewhat better than that.

As George went through his noon sun sights and calculated their position, he became concerned that they were making too much of a northing. They had moved nearly a full degree of latitude to the north of their original course from Sandy Hook by June 20, to roughly forty-one degrees, five minutes north.

The Grand Banks, with some of the most treacherous and rough waters of the North Atlantic, lay to the north of them. The deep ocean shoals rapidly there, hence, the name Grand Banks. During the Ice Age, sea level dropped by as much as 330 feet. Surf broke on the edge of the continental shelf. The Banks were bone-dry. The coast of present-day Maine sat hundreds of miles inland. On a scale difficult to imagine, the climatic changes that ended the Ice Age caused a rise in sea level which took place quickly in geologic time. The ocean reclaimed ridges and valleys and turned them into havens for fish. More than 90 percent of all the fish in the sea live in the relative shallows created as the sea rose; the abysmal deep is a veritable desert, devoid of most life down in the frigid blackness of the depths.

The Grand Banks form a huge dam of sorts. Wind-driven and ocean currents pile into them and blend into unseen rivers marked only at the surface by the ubiquitous presence of confused, steep seas. The currents churn up nutrients in the water, creating a life-sustaining concoction for the continuation of the food chain. Link by link, it all falls into place on the Grand Banks. It is a place of life—fertile, rich, and plentiful. But it is also one of death, both for the hunters and the hunted. One of the most fearsome areas for the fishermen centered around Sable Island, a ridge of sand that rose above the waves, with long protrusions far out on either side. The bones of many ships are buried there. Fog shrouds the whole region much of the time. With all the schooner traffic and the liners that frequently cut across the banks, George didn't want to get anywhere near it. He corrected his compass course to more south of east, about ninety-five to one-hundred degrees.

For several days, the *Fox* maintained its course and stayed at just about forty-one degrees north, which placed them essentially in line with Cape Cod, far to the west. The southerly winds pushed them to the north, but the course changes compensated for the drift. On Tuesday, June 25, George estimated that they had inched little by little more than a full eighteen degrees of longitude since encountering the *Jessie*. If his calculations were correct, they were now at fifty degrees, twenty minutes west. That would put them in a direct line of longitude right smack on line

with the Grand Banks. But they were well to the south
of the fishing grounds and their attendant dangers
and south of the steamship lanes as well. They had
seen very few vessels of late. George changed course
again, steering north of east, thinking he would clear
the Grand Banks easily and pick up the lift of the
Gulf Stream. All told, they were nearly one third of
the way across the Atlantic Ocean.

The only ship they sighted during this fair-weather
period of great progress was a bark that came within
two miles of the *Fox* on Tuesday, June 21. The wind
blew freshly from the west at about twenty knots, with
a moderate sea running. On its northwesterly course,
under a full spread of canvas, the sailing ship heeled
to the wind and kicked up white water around the
bow. As sailors say, it clamped a prodigious bone in
its teeth. Three headsails flew from the foremast to
the bowsprit. All the staysails, triangular cuts of canvas
rigged between the three masts of the bark, were
sheeted flat to catch the wind, as was the broad
expanse of canvas on the aftermost mast. The square
sails, flown from the yardarms, remained furled, since
they could not draw with the ship pointed so close
to the direction from which the wind came. It was a
grand sight to see such a large ship bounding across
the waves, especially for Frank, who harbored a deep
love of any sailing vessel.

It was common knowledge among many sailors like
Frank that the days were indeed short for these
square-rigged ships, and many of the men who had
worked aboard them abandoned the sea altogether.
They found jobs in the ports or headed inland. There
is a saying among some seamen whose love of the
sea fades, for whatever reason. They say they'll walk
inland with an oar on their shoulder till someone
asks what it is they are carrying, and that is the place
they'll put down roots.

The watch keepers aboard the sailing ship, if they

had seen the *Fox*, had not considered it necessary to find out if the occupants of the rowboat needed help. Both men wished that they had stopped, if only for a moment, to give them a firm fix on their longitude. All the figuring that went into finding their position, based on dead reckoning, was suspect, and George readily admitted this to Frank. In reality, they had no way of telling exactly where they were. However, they both had confidence in their latitude and that served them well enough for the time being. For a number of days they had seen patches of brown-and-yellow seaweed floating in the water, indicating that they had in fact been receiving a push from the Gulf Stream. Borne on the now-weak current, the weed had traveled thousands of miles, from the Sargasso Sea, deep in the tropics.

The monotony of each day became difficult for them. The noon sights broke up the day for George, but all Frank had to look forward to was rowing and more rowing. They had used the stove very little, fearing an accident. They were also short of kerosene. Eating cold, canned meats, the fat white and solidified, drinking eggs from their shells, washing it all down with condensed milk diluted with water, did little to boost morale. The occasional drink of their Vino Kalafra helped a bit and reminded them of the civilization that somehow seemed less real; it had become an intangible element, as elusive as a wisp of fog. When they spotted a black object floating in the sea on Thursday, June 25, they took full advantage of the sighting to divert themselves for a few minutes.

They maneuvered the *Fox* over to it and discovered that the object was nothing more interesting than an old log. Their imaginations had run wild for a time as they rowed to it; in the sea, finding anything is possible. They poked the log and rolled it over. A thick coat of barnacles covered the entire stretch of rotted wood below the waterline. They guessed at where it had come from. It was huge and looked as though it had been shorn of branches in preparation for the mill. Probably it hailed from Canada, carried almost one thousand miles by the vagaries of current, wind, and wave. A message in a bottle, it is said, can travel the world over if dropped in the sea off Cape Horn; only no one would be likely to find it in those harsh latitudes.

A school of tiny striped fish swam under the log. They darted about, frightened at the approach of the *Fox*.

"They must think us a giant fish out to eat them," Frank said, laughing.

"I think these are pilot fish," George said.

Both of them peered over the rail at the little creatures. Ordinarily, the sight of a school of fish wouldn't have interested them much at all, save as potential bait for a fishing expedition. But they had seen few signs of life for days, at least not up close like this. They watched the fish like little children.

Finally, they pushed the log away and started rowing again.

"Look at this." George laughed. "We've got company!"

About half the fish stayed with the log. The others joined the *Fox* in her journey. The men stopped rowing and leaned way over the rail to get a look at their new companions.

"They're hiding under us," Frank said.

The fish stayed with the *Fox* for a day or so. Every now and then the men stopped rowing to watch them. They formed flashes of light in the shadow of the boat. Then, like the hammerhead shark which had grown disinterested in the *Fox*, the fish disappeared without a trace.

On Friday, June 26, the weather continued fair, but the wind began to box the compass, which produced some anxiety. First it blew from the east and began to increase markedly around noontime. As George shot the sun with the quadrant, he muttered about the headwind.

"We don't need another easterly, Frank. It'll be bad for us if it blows up again from that quarter," he said.

Frank saw no need to comment on statements of the obvious. He waited till George finished and marked the chart before asking their position.

"We've made another half degree north or so. Nothing to worry about."

The wind slacked off, then switched to the south. It briefly swung to the north and, as if it couldn't make up its mind whence to blow, abruptly swung west back to south. When the wind behaves this way out at sea, it's a sure sign that a more defined weather pattern will develop soon. The question in both their minds was where will the wind blow next? Their preoccupation with such matters took over, weighing heavily on their minds as they rowed. Wind was the most important element in the overall equation of failure or success. If it blew against them long enough, they would run out of provisions long before they could reach land. It had to favor them; they were very much in the hands of nature. No will was strong enough to influence the sea, and they resigned themselves to whatever hand they were dealt.

Sure enough, the weather began to change during the night. One minute, Frank was rowing easily along in a sea almost as smooth as glass. The next, he felt a puff of wind on his cheek from the southwest. It slacked off, and the soft caress of the south wind returned, but only briefly before it vanished on the heels of a stronger whoosh of wind from the southwest. The pattern continued for a short time, and the southwest wind finally overrode its weaker cousin. By morning, it blew steadily at roughly twenty to twenty-five knots, bringing with it a building sea.

"Seems we have our new front," George said, as he took over for Frank so that he could eat a breakfast of milk and sea biscuits.

Between bites Frank looked over the left-hand side of the stern at the clouds on the horizon. "It's going to rain, George. I can smell it."

"I can see it."

Earlier in the voyage, having everything soaked from the rain had not made them happy. But they accepted it as one of the hardships they would have to endure. Now they dreaded rain, foul winds, currents, and the rogue waves that necessitated bailing. The psychological stress still didn't show itself in the form of arguments, though. Each man kept the little annoying things the other did to himself. To succeed in the crossing, they needed each other. Aboard the *Fox* there was no room for quarrelsome behavior, petty concerns, or ego.

The rain started falling shortly after noon. The sun had long since departed behind the layer of clouds, making it impossible for George to take a sight with the quadrant. The patches of Sargasso weed became less numerous. They were at the edge of an eddy of the Gulf Stream and might even encounter one of the reverse currents known to branch off and head southward. If they found themselves in one of these countercurrents, their work would be all the harder. They tried not to think about these negative aspects of the day; it took a lot of willpower. Their unspoken frustration mounted.

The southwesterly picked up its heels and ran throughout the night of June 27. Rain pelted the men, blowing across the waves in sheets into their faces and down their necks. The moisture softened the calluses on their palms and fingers and their muscles stiffened as it began to grow cold. Morning dawned gray and miserable, with winds gusting to thirty knots and waves building to ten to fifteen feet.

"Check the thermometer. It can't be as cold as it feels," George said.

Frank looked for the little box that housed the thermometer, but it wasn't tucked away in its usual spot. He let out a groan as he picked it up from the bottom of the boat and opened it. The tiny glass tube had fractured. Silver blots of mercury dotted the felt lining.

"What is it?"

"The blasted thing is broken, George. It must have shaken loose and one of us crushed it last night."

The two of them stared at the box in silence for a few minutes. It was a small thing to lose the thermometer. Certainly it was nice to know how warm or cold it was; it gave them a proper perspective on how they really were, as opposed to how they felt, which was often far colder than the true temperature. They glared at each other for a moment.

Frank sighed and threw the box overboard. "That's the end of that."

"I wonder how it got broken. Careless of both of us. But these things happen."

"We're getting tired, that's all," Frank said.

"No small wonder of it, either, having rowed one thousand miles or so."

"One thousand miles."

"And we've got two thousand more to go."

"Thanks for the cheer, George."

They sat looking at each other, each halfheartedly working the oars. They started to laugh.

"Look at us sitting out in the middle of the ocean broken up about a little thermometer!" George said. "You'd think it was worth its weight in gold."

The truth was that the thermometer represented normalcy. It was a link to life ashore, one they missed dearly. With two thousand miles to go, they had to keep their spirits up. To drift into depression resulting from a feeling of disconnectedness meant failure, and failure, quite possibly, would mean a situation far worse than losing a mercury-filled glass tube.

The wind continued to blow strongly from the southwest, with no letup in the rain for the rest of the morning on into early afternoon. The *Fox* surged through the waves, with a fair wind almost directly off the stern. They noticed a long swath of nearly white water near them that seemed to indicate the presence of a tide race. Other races where the waves practically stood end to end appeared. George began to get very uneasy. The presence of such strong currents meant that he may have miscalculated their latitude. They could be on the outer fringe of the Grand Banks, after all, and this worried him. He shared his thoughts with Frank, who voiced concern as well.

Later in the afternoon, the wind backed quickly to the southeast and began to howl. With no rigging to set to humming, it didn't rise from a low moan to a low-pitched scream as it would on a sailing ship. Nevertheless, the increasing fury made a sound George and Frank found all too familiar.

Darkness came early that day. At around seven o'clock, both men had grown too tired and hungry to keep the *Fox* safely on course. An angry cross sea had replaced the relatively consistent pattern of waves built up on the southwest wind. Instead of marching on in well-defined rows, with the larger groups in good order, the southwesterly progressing waves collided with the newer ones coming from the southeast. They sometimes merged together to create waves twice the size of the usual height. Sailors call these freak, or rogue, waves, and they are extremely dangerous, because they come from nowhere and often from an entirely different direction than their smaller kin. They live for a short time and die, but they can inspire terror during the minutes they rear up above all the other waves and break for hundreds of yards, turning the surface of the ocean to a frothy white.

"I don't want to meet one of these big fellows after dark, not tonight, not ever," George yelled. "We'll ride to the floating anchor till this blows over."

In the fading light they peered astern at the waves, waiting for the larger group to pass before pulling for all they were worth on the oars to turn the *Fox* head to the seas. A series of much larger breaking seas swept over them, partially filling the boat. But they got the *Fox* turned around. Frank deployed the sea anchor before the next monsters bore down on them. As before, the *Fox* faced the crests. She pitched and yawed violently, but they were safe, at least for the moment. As they lay cramped together in the bottom of the boat, they wondered just how long the gale would last this time.

(*Above*) George Harbo, born in 1864 in Sandefjord, a Norwegian fishing port that was home to fleets of vessels that hunted whales in the Norwegian Sea. *Courtesy Joan B. Minnis*

(*Right*) Frank Samuelsen, born in 1870 on a dairy farm outside of Farsund, a thriving port in southwestern Norway in the mid-1800s. *Courtesy Spencer Samuelsen*

The rowboat *Fox*. Shortly before setting out, Harbo and Samuelsen exhibited the boat at several rowing clubs in Manhattan along the Harlem River. Only eighteen feet long, the *Fox* was patterned after the fishing boats used along the Jersey shore, which were launched and landed in heavy surf. For the ocean voyage, the rowboat was equipped with two water tight compartments to keep key items dry and provide added buoyancy in the event of a capsize. *Courtesy Spencer Samuelsen*

In 1996, members of the Long Branch Ice Boat and Yacht Club tried to row the replica of the *Fox* from their boatyard on the Shrewsbury River to the Statue of Liberty on the centennial anniversary of George Harbo and Frank Samuelsons' voyage. After exhausting ten rowing teams, and fighting poor weather and a foul tide, they had to turn back at the Verrazano Bridge. *Courtesy Long Branch Ice Boat and Yacht Club*

Samuelsen (*left*) and Harbo on Saturday, August 1, 1896, when they landed in the Scilly Isles after fifty-five days at sea. *Courtesy Spencer Samuelsen*

The *Fox*, tied to a schooner in the harbor at Le Havre on Friday, August 7, 1896, the day Harbo and Samuelsen successfully completed their voyage. *Courtesy Long Branch Ice Boat and Yacht Club*

(*Above*) After two days in Le Havre, Harbo and Samuelsen rowed up the River Seine to Paris, where they planned to exhibit the *Fox*. Although they drew crowds, the rowboat failed to capture the imagination of the Parisians. *Courtesy Spencer Samuelsen*

(*Right*) Frank Samuelsen back on the family farm outside Farsund. He returned to Norway after George Harbo died of pneumonia in 1908, and he remained there until his death in 1946. *Courtesy Spencer Samuelsen*

(*Above and opposite*) A member of the Long Branch Ice Boat and Yacht Club in New Jersey, working on a replica of the *Fox* in 1975. It was built with the help of Harold Seaman, who, along with his father, constructed the original *Fox* in 1896. *Courtesy Long Branch Ice Boat and Yacht Club*

Shown here outside their Brooklyn home are Anine Harbo (*seated, center*) and her ten children in 1908, shortly after George Harbo's death. Georganna, seated in Anine's lap, died of pneumonia a year after this photo was taken. Anine also died of pneumonia in 1911. Fridtjof (*standing, right*) fought with the American Yankee Division and was killed in action in France during World War I. Grace Almira (*lower left foreground, seated*) became a famous model. She and her infant died in 1920 in a natural gas explosion in their home. The other children lived into their seventies and eighties. *Courtesy Joan B. Minnis*

15

"I think the wind is going down some," Frank yelled to George.

Neither man could sleep. Water sloshed onto their faces and their oilskins. It filled their seaboots and flooded out over the tops. The wind sent a shower of spray across the rails into the boat, and every once in a while, the bow dipped low to scoop up green water.

"I think so, too. It doesn't sound as menacing."

"We won't be sleeping tonight. Let's try to keep going, okay, George?"

After a few minutes, they resolved to row all night and make the best of an unpleasant situation. If a freak wave found them, they would deal with it as best they could. The idea of sitting still in the midst of the foul weather nagged at them. All they wanted to do was get across, and they would never do it huddled in the bottom of the boat, the cold and wet sapping their strength little by little. Slowly, each man dragged himself to his seat.

"Ready, George?" Frank called.

"Ready!"

George unshipped his oars and started rowing hard as Frank pulled in the sea anchor. They couldn't see the waves in the pitch-black. Only their white crests scratched the night where ocean and sky were one and the same. Frank waited till a particularly large wave passed under the boat and rapidly pulled in the sea anchor. Together they turned the *Fox* around and sped off toward Europe. As hard as it was to row, making even a little forward progress improved their state of mind. Inaction was the enemy; each man began to realize that. They had to press on. They had no other choice.

The wind again shifted back to the southwest, and this time it brought a heavy fog with it. They felt the dank mist swirl around them. It filled their lungs with a deep chill. The frequent wind shifts further aggravated the sea. It was as nasty as any they had hitherto encountered, even in the big easterly gale. The steepness of the waves convinced George that they had blundered onto the Grand Banks, and he was glad they were racing east as fast as they could to get off the shallows. The Banks, like an island in the middle of the sea, offered no comfort to any save those headed away from them with fish packed on ice in deep holds.

The next day passed much as the previous one had, with no diminishment of wind and sea. The fog obscured everything from sight. Occasionally, though, it tore apart and revealed a wider picture of the ocean's fury. Angry waves raged around them and faded into the gloom, where the walls of fog thickened. Then all but the seas directly behind them vanished as the fog closed in again. It was as if they were actors in some awful play and a gray curtain rose and fell for an invisible audience of sadists. Once, when a gust parted the fog immediately around them, both men were startled to see a schooner racing toward them out of the murk. The little ship carried only a storm jib; its giant mainsail was shortened in a deep reef. It buried its bow deeply into a wave, and green water covered it from the bow halfway to the aft deck. Fully ladened, it labored heavily in the stormy conditions. In winter, thick with the ice that collected on the hull, spars, and rigging, schooners sometimes dove deep and never rose to meet the next sea.

"She looks like she's having a harder time of it than we are," George yelled above the wind.

"With luck she'll be home soon. A lot sooner than we will," Frank replied, never missing a stroke of the oars.

The weather remained the same—bad and cold, with southwest winds at thirty to forty knots that gradually worked around to the west. The waves built to twenty feet, and many soared higher than that. They were not the same type the *Fox* had encountered before. Their uneven, steeper nature appeared more coastal in shape and therefore more dangerous. It was impossible to eat, sleep, or drink. Every time one of them eased off the oars, the *Fox* careened down the face of a wave and threatened to send them overboard. It took the strength of both men to keep the boat moving and on course. They kept rowing, not wanting to stop with the wind pushing them quickly eastward, not unless the weather got worse. The risk involved in keeping on struck them both as well worthwhile.

At last, on Wednesday, July 1, the wind eased slowly back to more reasonable levels, and the waves responded in kind. The relationship between wind and wave never ceases to fascinate sailor and nonsailor alike. To blow in one's coffee cup to cool the liquid creates waves. To slosh the coffee around and around in a half-full cup creates surges. The breath of wind grown to a tempest metamorphoses the sea. It is always the same but never the same, always the waves come, but they are never identical to those born from another wind at another time. The one certainty was that when the wind dropped, so would the waves; if given a long enough time between the coming and going of the oceanic winds. For this George and Frank were grateful and hopeful that they might get some much-needed rest and a hearty meal.

They ate and rested in shifts. Both felt much better. The seas continued to roar down on them, but the wind moderated, and the sun broke from the clouds, stretching in a gray mantle from horizon to horizon. All signs of the silvery fog vanished. The man off watch lay in the bottom of the boat and stared up at the sun. The wind eliminated most of the warmth, but not all of it. Out of the wind, away from the oars, and freed of the cramped position at the seat, each man let his mind wander. Like prisoners, they found it important to induce their minds to carry them away to another place, another time, whether in the past or in the future. Their thoughts temporarily allowed them to escape the harsh environment they had chosen to challenge, to live in as long as it took to get across. The respite in the weather aided them in their cerebral flight.

"George, I see a fishing schooner off the bow. About four miles off, I'd say. She's heading south."

George pulled himself up to take a look, then laid himself down again.

About a half hour later, Frank sighted another schooner. It also sailed southward. Still another schooner hove into view about an hour later, and this time its course favored a chance for the two men to hail the crew. It sailed toward them under full canvas and soon came within shouting distance. Four days had elapsed since George took a sun sight. He and Frank desperately wanted a firm fix on their position and for the ship's crew to report them when the ship arrived at port. By now they suspected they were on the Grand Banks.

"Surely they must see us," Frank said. "They're not a half mile off."

"She looks empty. Almost like a ghost ship."

They rowed the *Fox* closer to intercept the schooner as it passed them on its way to the distant coast to the west.

"Hello, aboard the schooner!" George yelled. "Hello, aboard the schooner!"

By this time one lone man could be seen. He stood at the helm, seemingly frozen into stone. Startled back into reality, however, the man ran to the rail and stared at them. It was not unusual to see men in a small boat out on the Banks. The schooners dispatched fleets of dories with crews of two or three men to work the trawls, the long lines sometimes a mile in length, with a thousand baited hooks attached to shorter lengths of lines. The dory crews baited the hooks aboard the mother ship and carefully coiled the trawl in such a way as to facilitate its setting. Long after the backbreaking work of pulling it into the dory, weighed down with nearly a ton of cod, the crews aboard the mother ship took to cleaning and packing the fish in ice. Clouds of fat seagulls, possibly the best fed in the entire North Atlantic, hovered around the schooners and feasted on the heads and entrails tossed overboard. But although small boats rode the big seas of the Grand Banks, the *Fox* did not resemble a dory; it looked more like a ship's lifeboat. In fact, the Sea Bright skiffs originating along the beaches of Nauvoo and Galilee served as the basis for lifeboat designs because of their sea-keeping ability. In this the sight of them off the schooner caused the man to stare.

"Hello!" he cried, and ran to the companionway. A few moments later, twenty-three fishermen, who had presumably been belowdecks eating their dinner, mustered on deck and stared at the *Fox*. Plowing through the heavy seas, the schooner passed the *Fox*. George and Frank turned and rowed behind it, fearing to get too close lest the stern smash down on the boat. The ship was the *Leader* out of Lunenburg, part of a fleet from that Canadian port presently fishing the banks.

George cupped both hands to his lips and shouted, "What is your latitude and longitude?"

The westerly wind snatched George's words away. The captain of the schooner heard only a garbled, far-off voice.

"Tell us where we are!" George cried again. The schooner was slowly pulling away from the *Fox*.

The captain hurried below and emerged on deck a few minutes later. "You're at forty-five degrees, thirty minutes north. Fifty degrees, twenty-five minutes west," he said.

This surprised George a bit. They had made a northing of at least four degrees of latitude in the last four days. It seemed unlikely, but with the influence of wind and current, together with any miscalculations he may have made, it was possible. At any rate, he had no reason to doubt the skipper or his own feeling that the *Fox* was indeed where the schooner's captain said it was. George fished the stub of a pencil out of the pocket of his oilskins and wrote the coordinates down on the rail, which was painted a light oak color.

"What are you doing?" Frank asked.

"I don't want any chance of forgetting these figures. They'll keep there till I can get into the compartment for some dry paper."

"Are you astray?" the captain called. He had headed his vessel closer to the wind to spill air from the sails, slowing it down.

"Not exactly," George replied. "We're the rowboat *Fox* bound from New York to Le Havre, France."

The skipper's response was almost identical to that

of the officer aboard the *Fürst Bismark*. The exception, however, was that the captain of the schooner expressed a high degree of curiosity about the *Fox*, and how it was able to live in the very rough seas they had been experiencing over the last couple days.

"It's been so rough, we've not done any fishing," he said. "Yesterday was as bad as we've had in a long time."

"We've had our troubles, too," George said.

"And you have come all this way with no sail aboard?"

"Nothing but oars," Frank said.

The captain shook his head in disbelief. "Come in closer so we can get a good look at the boat!"

"No, thank you. It is too rough and getting dark. Please report us to the newspapers when you get to port," George asked.

"I will. We wish you a safe voyage!"

"Thank you," George and Frank called together.

The two vessels parted, each set on a course opposite from the other. Soon only the sails of the schooner were visible in the gathering gloom. Exchanging a few words with other sailors did the spirits of both men good. The disconnectedness that had settled over them dissipated somewhat. Yet another schooner, several miles distant, hove into view off the left side of the *Fox*.

"This is a very busy place," George said. "And the work—I don't envy them. I think we're safer than the dorymen, since we've got plenty of supplies and a boat that will take a capsize."

"They're a tough lot, that's certain," Frank said. "We feel the cold now. Imagine what it is like in winter when they're out in their dories in a snowstorm. And what it must be like to go astray. The merchant marine seems an easy way compared to this."

The fate of many a Grand Banks fisherman resulted in getting separated from the mother ship, which is

called "going astray." One of the most celebrated
stories from New England to the mid-Atlantic states,
told and retold in fishing-village taverns, on the piers,
and in the parlors was the tale of Howard Blackburn,
perhaps one of the toughest, most famous dorymen
of all. Few fishermen on the coast had never heard
of him. He had crossed the Atlantic twice in two small
sailboats and had lost all of his fingers and toes in a
bad winter storm in January 1883, when he and his
dorymate became separated from the Gloucester
schooner *Grace L. Fears*. The two transatlantic crossings, which had brought Blackburn considerable
acclaim, were nothing compared to the dangers of
working the Grand Banks in winter.

The ship was off Burgeo Bank, a sail of several days
from Newfoundland. Blackburn and his crewmate,
Thomas Welch, set out from the schooner to retrieve
their trawl. They located the flag buoys marking their
line and proceeded to haul it in but found the catch
disappointing. The schooner tacked back and forth
a half mile away in a gathering fog and a mounting
southeast wind. The two men were not alone, but the
moan of the foghorns all around them imparted a
feeling of desolation. A snow squall blew in from the
northeast, and the *Grace L. Fears* vanished as visibility
closed to zero and the waves began to build.

Although they tried, the two men could not row
back to their ship. The squall turned into a sustained
storm, and the seas poured into the boat. The men
began to freeze to death as they bailed and bailed,
rowed and rowed, and pounded the ice that formed
all over the dory, threatening to sink it. Welch became
delirious and ultimately froze to death. Blackburn,
who had lost his mittens, deliberately froze his hands
to the oars and rowed on toward Newfoundland
through the storm. If he could not row, he would
die, and he knew it. For five days Blackburn rowed;
every stroke of the oars scraped the flesh from his

dead hands. He finally did make it to a little port on
Little River, Newfoundland, but the harsh winter cold
had taken his friend and crippled him.

The long, cold row tested the mettle of those brave
men. But it was only because Blackburn survived to
tell the tale that word of his heroism spread. Many
others had fought hard and failed and were never
heard from again. As George and Frank rowed eastward across the Banks, they were following in Blackburn's footsteps in many ways. They, too, were setting
out to challenge the sea and take what it dealt. If they
succeeded in the challenge, the sea would reward
them. Like Blackburn, they, too, were ready to pay
the price if necessary.

The *Fox* rode up and down the crests. From the
summits, the view was almost panoramic. Frank
caught sight of a dory ahead of them. He shouted to
George, but when George looked, he couldn't see it.
When both craft were in the trough simultaneously,
neither crew could see the other. In a somewhat social
mood, the two men decided to row up to the dory
if they could and talk to its crew before night fell.
Watching for the dory as it topped a crest, they rowed
over to it.

"Good evening," George said as the *Fox* moved
close to the other boat.

The three men in the dory were dressed in heavy
peacoats. The two at the oars wore thick wool mittens
to protect their hands. George and Frank had nothing
more than their oilskins to combat the weather. They
had only one pair of mittens between them, and they
took care to ensure that each one got to wear them
for equal lengths of time. Aside from being friends,
it was in the interests of both that each man stayed
healthy. Neither had the strength to make landfall
alone.

"What do you think of the weather today?" George
asked.

"Well," one of the men said, "it looks pretty fair this night."

"It's cold out here, even though it is supposed to be summer," Frank said. "Is it always this cold in July?"

"The Banks are cool most all the time," another man said. "They know no summer."

The men asked how George and Frank came to be on the Banks if they weren't there to fish. When they finished their story once again, the men invited them to come aboard their schooner, the *Volunteer*, also of Lunenburg, Canada.

"You'll have a warm supper," they said. "Your last one must be a long time past."

But they declined the offer, though they were sorely tempted. To give up hours for the warmth belowdecks and a good meal would perhaps induce them to reconsider heading eastward. It would further drive home just how much at the mercy of the sea they were, how far they were from the most basic of comforts, and how many days and weeks of bare existence lay ahead. They reluctantly declined the offer.

The two small boats parted and soon lost sight of each other in the darkness that swept in rapidly as the wan sun slid below the horizon. With sunset well after ten o'clock, nights in these high latitudes in July were mercifully short. But when the darkness did come, it was like stepping into a cave. The cold was almost unbearable as they ate a little food, in shifts, as usual. Too uncomfortable to sleep, they rowed through the night at the heels of the southwest wind on a compass course south of east to keep from being blown northward.

The next day, with a light west wind at their backs, the crew of the *Fox* rowed off the Grand Banks into a sea they knew would probably remain empty of vessels, save for the occasional fast steamer, for many days to come. They had emerged from a world, though desolate and harsh on the Banks, that still remained obliquely connected to humanity. Now the sea beneath extended downward for miles to the dense primordial ooze on the bottom. The color of the ocean changed to black or the depressing color of weathered lead. They had reached a place few people ever saw except from the protection and comfort of the great liners. The *Fox*, a mere speck in the timeless wash of the North Atlantic, had never been so far from the grasp of civilization.

16

All through Friday, July 3, the *Fox* battled waves of fifteen to twenty feet high with winds from the south at close to thirty knots. Along the coast, sailors would call them a strong breeze, a near gale. Out beyond the Grand Banks, these were the usual conditions. Only when the winds began to hit fifty knots and the waves climbed to heights of thirty feet or more did captains begin to consider the day a rough one. Aboard the rowboat, however, the many days of high seas, cold, and wind, combined with little sleep and food for the crew, created a dangerous situation. Fatigue clouds judgment and frays tempers. It leads to immobility and deep depression. George and Frank had far more than an indifferent North Atlantic to conquer. They began to realize they had to face the weakness within themselves. Ashore, one's self can hide in the frenetic pace of daily life, and weakness can be ignored—an impossibility at sea.

They turned the bow of the *Fox* toward the southeast to confront the wind and waves. On the present heading, the waves approached at an angle about forty degrees off the bow, give or take the ten-to-fifteen-degree swings required to zigzag through the worst of them. It remained imperative to keep the *Fox* moving because for every mile they rowed in a southeasterly direction they drifted northward. They intended to reach Le Havre, and to do so meant passing to the south of Ireland and Great Britain. Neither man relished the notion of fetching up on the Irish coast and having to row south against the prevailing winds around the islands before crossing the English Channel.

That night, a north wind came up strong with lots of rain. They were so tired, though, that when their turn came to lie down on the soaked cushions, they thanked the heavens for the break from rowing and were grateful that the man at the oars still had the strength to keep the *Fox* on course. They pulled the wet blankets over their bodies and faces and briefly found escape while the rain and spray drummed on the canvas, buttoned tight over their heads. Sleep never fully settled on them. It hovered elusively around the rim of consciousness.

With the arrival of the new frontal system, the bracing north wind brought clear cobalt-blue skies. The quality of light took on that clarity so familiar to sailors, when everything—the waves, the deep darkness of the troughs in shadow, the weathered paint of the boat, the undulating line along the horizon—appears in sharp detail. There is no blur, no indistinct hues. Just hard, cold contrasts of color. The wind dropped down to a mere whisper of ten knots from the northeast by mid- to late-afternoon, and both men took it as a gift from the sea.

"It's the Fourth of July, and we deserve a celebration," George said. He unfurled the flag and wrung it out. He spread it over the aft deck and tied it in place. Saturated in salt, it would never dry, nor was that his intention. He and Frank wanted to pay tribute to the day, a holiday they held dear. Although America had failed to grant them the lives they had envisioned before their arrival, it did offer opportunity, seemingly limitless in scope. It offered a chance, at least, to carve out something special. They had assimilated and embraced the new land with all the enthusiasm possible to muster. They thought about the festivities going on in the cities and towns and farms all over America. The picnics, the cold ices topped with maple syrup, glasses of tangy lemonade, and thick, juicy steaks broiled over open fires. Fireworks displays would illuminate the sky, and the country would ring with the sound of church bells and cheers. There would be dancing and singing in the streets this night.

"It's not much of a party, Frank. But let's clean up and have a nice dinner."

"You think we can spare the fresh water?"

"A pint or so, I think. To use a pint won't do any harm."

Both men stripped off their oilskins and their shirts and got a good lather going from one of the bars of soap they had brought with them. They carefully washed their faces and upper bodies. Burned almost black by the sun, their faces and hands looked as if they could have been wearing the blackface paint performers sometimes wore in carnivals. The fresh water removed the thick film of dried salt from their skin. It afforded a level of comfort that reminded them that it was the simple things in life that really gave one great pleasure. Simple and undeniable well-being, basic physical comfort, and the touch of a loved one were what mattered most.

The fair weather on July 4 boosted their spirits considerably. It lulled them into a false hope that the Atlantic had tested them and found them deserving of a respite similar to the long period of relatively smooth rowing that marked almost a third of the previous month. The wind held in the northeast and continued light throughout the night. For the first time in days, George and Frank slept soundly during their off-watch hours. Their belongings even dried out a little. Dawn on Sunday, July 5, broke in a spectacular tapestry of reds, pinks, and purples. The sea rolled on as usual, but the wind remained light. The *Fox* had made good headway. All seemed right with the world.

The noon sun sight indicated that the *Fox* had kept a good course. They had made no appreciable northing. George's calculations put them right on the forty-fifth parallel. He estimated that they had made 115 miles to the east in the last thirty-six hours, with averages of forty to fifty miles per day, even during the stormy weather on the Grand Banks.

As the sun began to dip low over the stern of the *Fox*, the northeast wind dropped off and shifted abruptly to the southeast. Their present course brought the wind hard on the bow. Rowing against it would only tire the men again. The frustration returned and rumbled within each man's heart. When would the sea give them safe passage? It seemed to conspire to build their hopes, only to dash them once they had taken root. It was easy to impart human characteristics to the sea at such times, and they both considered it with the disdain they would show a spiteful woman.

By dusk ragged clumps of scud pranced across the sky. The fading sun painted the edges a silky white, while the interior of the clouds resembled coal. A dark, menacing bank of clouds formed along the southern horizon, and the wind awakened and swept the sea. Neither man found it surprising. They resigned themselves to their latest trial but found their patience fast on the ebb. All one man at the oars could do was keep station. No headway was possible till the wind shifted to another quarter.

The wind and waves gathered strength throughout the night. But perhaps the sea had noted the *Fox* and granted it a reprieve, for the wind, as it came on strong, gradually shifted to the southwest, then all the way to the west come noontime. Another gift! the men thought. George and Frank rowed with renewed vigor. The *Fox* galloped over the waves, speeding on her way toward France. The only disturbing sign was the swell. They had remarked on its presence during the fitful period of northeast winds. Even the stronger southeasterly hadn't erased it. A huge, rolling swell from the west had been their companion now for over twenty-four hours. The evidence was clear. Only a violent storm could produce a swell like that, and it was headed for them, on its way at the heels of the west wind they had at first found cause to rejoice in.

"She's going to roll mountain high, I'm thinking," George said.

Seated in the bow position, Frank looked beyond his friend and the stern of the *Fox* at the swells marching toward them. The hills of water lifted the boat gently up and stretched on either side of the boat for more than a hundred yards. From the top, the seas building on the backs of the swells foamed and hissed. It was, for all its desolation, an incredible sight. The *Fox* teetered on the summit among the wind-driven waves and rolled and pitched down the back side of the slope deep into a trough, where the wind barely blew, blocked as it was behind the next little mountain.

"We'll have the devil himself to pay if these big fellows start breaking. They must be running over thirty feet," Frank said, more to himself than in response to George. He had seen swells such as these before aboard the square-rigged sailing ships he had served on in the merchant marine. These weren't the usual swells. They were the harbingers of some really bad weather still beyond the horizon. If the weather system stalled, perhaps they could row the *Fox* out of its reach. It was that hope both men kept close to heart, and they rowed as fast as they could, ever eastward. When the *Fox* came down the faces of the waves, she practically surfed. Spray flew off the bows, and a well-defined stern wave followed her. It required great skill at the oars to keep her stern pointed into the seas.

Two steamers appeared not a mile off the *Fox*'s bow. With their backs to the east, neither man had noticed them. But they caught sight of them as the rowboat reached a particularly high summit. The ships disappeared for a full five minutes before becoming visible again when the *Fox* ascended the heights once more. The bow of one of the steamers impaled itself in the face of one of the swells. A full third of the vessel vanished in the black water. Spray as thick and white as a waterfall inundated the bridge.

"Pity the passengers aboard those ships. They're having a hard time of it, that's a certainty," George yelled. "Look at them plunge!"

It was an incredible sight. To see a ship several hundred feet long nearly engulfed in the waves proved that might isn't always the winner at sea. The ships, so large, could not ride over the swells and their accompanying waves. They had to punch through them. The storm had not yet arrived, but the steamers labored. The passengers, seasick in their berths, must surely think the end of the world had come. The captains by this time must be nervous. The engines would be set to provide steerage way but little more. If conditions rapidly deteriorated, the steamers would turn tail and run before the storm. But now was not the time. They pushed doggedly on because they had schedules to keep. They were soon lost from sight.

As the day progressed, George and Frank became increasingly alarmed at the state of the sea. The swells weren't breaking yet. But they had grown in size and

gradually joined company with the waves. The sea
had reached an order of sorts, and it was truly awe
inspiring. The *Fox* was actually moving too fast
through the water. Each time she went down the
waves toward the trough, she threatened to roll over
and over downward, like a log, her beam to the crests.
For the first time in their long journey, the men
turned the *Fox* bow to the onslaught and kept on
rowing. They let the wind and waves propel them;
they used their muscle and skill to ride eastward stern
first. In this way they could slow the boat and better
steer her.

The quick maneuvering with the oars became much
more difficult after nightfall. But still the men crab-
bed backward, bow to the seas, summoning every
ounce of energy they had, all of their collective years
of experience, to keep going. Around midnight,
though, the first breakers began to appear. They were
unseen in the blackness. The men knew of them
nevertheless. When a wave thirty to forty feet high
breaks, it makes a sound often compared to a thunder-
storm or a passing freight train. The possibility of
being in the path of one of these breakers bore down
on the men, and they wisely acquiesced, having the
confidence that they had made stupendous progress
this day.

"I do believe it is time to heave to," George said,
almost matter-of-factly.

The understatement didn't surprise Frank. He
almost laughed, but the situation stifled the brief
impulse. He deployed the sea anchor. As usual, the
little *Fox* settled down a little. The two men began to
relax.

Out of the general roar of the wind and sea came
a sound that sent chills up the spines of both men.
The unmistakable tumult of tons of water collapsing
on itself grew louder and louder. A moment later,
solid water buried the bow of the *Fox* and flung her

sharply off to the left. A sharp snap, like a branch breaking, occurred simultaneously, and the *Fox* swung quickly over on its side, filling with water as the sea took her.

17

"The cable's parted! The sea anchor is gone!" Frank yelled.

George and Frank responded instantly. They had only seconds before the *Fox* capsized. As fast as they possibly could, they unshipped their oars and rowed furiously, pulling hard on the left-hand side to push the bow up the face of another mammoth wave. They had found themselves in the middle of one of those larger groups of seas. The second sea seemed intent on finishing the business its predecessor had begun.

The *Fox* wavered. The weight of the water trapped inside lowered her sides almost level with the sea. The bow began to rise. High above the men the crest overhung the rest of the wave and started to break. Again, the sea granted the *Fox* a reprieve. The boat shot up over the top and down the back of the wave before it broke. The third wave passed harmlessly under the keel.

The loss of the sea anchor gnawed at the two men as they rowed together into the storm. They had come to depend on it. When they were too tired to continue their work, it allowed them rest without suffering too much drift in a contrary direction. In heavy weather, it let them take whatever shelter they could from the elements. With it gone, the *Fox* relied entirely on the men for her safety, and if the men let her down. . . . It was this that flitted around their minds like a wisp of evil smoke. If we let her down, then what?

The seas broke all around them now, though they could not see just how huge they were. Not one star shined through the thick layer of clouds above them; the darkness was unfathomable. Torrents of rain beat down on them but did nothing to mitigate the seas.

The two men rowed on as best as they could, lashed to the *Fox* in their reindeer life belts in case a wave swept them away or the boat turned bottom up. They had no choice but to call on their strength when strength appeared nonexistent. They had to fight, or the sea would take them. It was only a matter of time, though, before it would become impossible to handle the boat in the breakers. The water would take hold of the *Fox* and toss her over on her beam ends and swamp her. The men cursed the weather, the waves, the wind, and most of all, the need to bail. Bail, bail, bail, constantly bail. When the waves filled the *Fox*, she sat upright, with the sea boiling over the top of the rails. To empty a swamped boat in these conditions required stamina and an indomitable will to survive. One man tried to steer the bow of the boat into the wind with the oars while the other bailed in a frenzy. Often, when the task was half done, another wave came along and filled the boat again and again. The force of the water snatched the oars from the oarsman's hands and lashed them overboard. Only the stout lines tethering the oars to the boat prevented their loss.

By daybreak on Tuesday, July 7, more than thirty breakers had completely inundated the *Fox*. The men were battered and bruised, hungry, and cold down to the marrow. Their tongues swelled up, and their lips split. The work at the oars had partially worn through the calluses on their palms. The tips of their noses were devoid of skin and extremely painful to the touch. As they gathered their wits in the gloom of dawn, the sight of the waves inspired a profound silence between them. The ocean looked more broken and angry than either man could recall during the entire length of the voyage so far and very few times during their tenure at sea. The waves still broke, but to the boundless relief of the men, not quite so often.

"We were lucky to get through last night without much more loss," George said. Two of the extra water cans they had brought to augment the supply in the galvanized tanks had broken out of the lashings and washed away. The force of the water against the cans must have been terrific to snap the lines used to keep them in place. The loss of the water, while not serious yet, did imbue the morning with a touch more misery.

At eight o'clock, George felt it safe enough to open the watertight compartment in the stern. It had been twenty-four hours since he had been able to write in the log. He also took out some sea biscuits, and the two men ate like wolves. The wind decreased and shifted back to the northeast, but the seas from the west kept coming almost as large as before. The men slept in shifts during the day and tried to recover their strength.

The following day, the wind shifted back to the west. The waves remained high, and by the looks of the weather the gale had not blown itself out at all. It had merely regrouped. Or perhaps another even stronger westerly storm remained hidden over the horizon. The swells running so high indicated that the turmoil beyond their immediate area continued to reign free, as it does in those latitudes. Fearing the worst, George and Frank worked on a new sea anchor, which they knew would be indispensable in the event the gale returned more angry than ever. That it had let up meant much to their safety. If it blew at a high rate for days, both of them admitted, the boat might well be overcome.

"We'll be too tired to do anything," Frank said. "She'll go bottom up or end over end, and that will be the end of us."

"I'm not sure if we've got enough material to make an effective sea anchor. But you're right, we've got to try before the wind blows in again."

They had kept some of the canvas they used to construct the first sea anchor. All they had were three or four pieces, each the size of a handkerchief, but it would have to do. They sewed them together into a misshapen cone open at the wide end and bound a long line to it. They also rigged up additional lines to secure the oars. During the repeated swampings, the extra oars had tried their best to escape the *Fox*. The water floated them up out of the boat, and only good fortune kept them from being torn free. The leather wraps had begun to wear through on several pairs of oars, and splits appeared at the border of the metal ribbons affixed to the blades expressly to keep them from splitting.

During the rest of the afternoon, the wind shifted to the southwest and finally came in like a runaway locomotive from the south. George's noon sun sight put the *Fox* almost at forty-two degrees north. He didn't want to risk the wind sending them farther to the north, so they tested their new sea anchor, hoping to reduce the drift as much as possible. The little anchor held the *Fox*'s bow to the wind, but only just. Occasionally, gusts sent the bow careening into the confused seas.

Just as it looked as though their fears about the return of the westerly gale appeared unjustified, the wind shifted again, this time back to the west. By dusk on Thursday, July 9, the men experienced a strange feeling of déjà vu. They rowed into the waves and wind and continued to race eastward stern first, just as they had earlier in the week.

As they pressed on into the night, the air suddenly turned cold, far more so than usual. A thick mist blew over them. It wasn't fog; at least it didn't feel like the ordinary fog they had long since become used to during the voyage. The mist seemed filled with tiny ice crystals that stung their faces and hands. It swirled around them and darkened the already black night. They peered all around them, fearing the unknown. Had they been more superstitious, they might have guessed that they had encountered the angel of death.

"What is this?" they said to each other.

The mist vanished, and the sea went immediately still. The wind no longer howled. The low rumble of surf reached them. Hearing that familiar sound more than one thousand miles out to sea unnerved both of them.

"It sounds like breakers on a shoal," George said.

"It does. But there are no shoals here. Nothing at all. I'd say we were under a spell of our minds, except why is the sea so smooth?"

The icy mist still surrounded them. They shivered, for both had stopped rowing, and without the exertion, the cold penetrated deeply.

"It's an iceberg! God, we're in the lee of it!" George said all at once.

The sharpness of his voice in the near silence startled Frank. It was eerie, hearing surf, the mist, the smooth water. It didn't add up, and the contrast between where they had been minutes before compared to the present could not have been more acute. They stared into the darkness, trying in vain to see what was happening. Not more than one hundred yards away, invisible in the blackness, an enormous iceberg calved from a glacier far to the north rode the west wind toward them. It loomed high above the *Fox*, so high it created its own weather in its lee.

How far away the berg was they did not know, and they were thankful not to know. Each found it sufficiently close to cause fear, and as the minutes ticked on, they wondered when it would emerge from the depths of the gloom and ride over the *Fox*. In seconds, it could have turned the boat into so many splinters and sucked the men down its steep submerged walls. Fog joined the mist. Still the water did not heave. The men's hearts raced. They had confronted many dangers; this one, the not seeing, the knowledge that a massive structure of ice could be bearing down on them, projected them into a netherworld in which even the sea itself had been robbed of its power.

"Bring her round to the north, Frank. We'll get clear of it, I'm sure."

The little lamp near the compass flickered a dull yellow. The needle of the compass swung from the east toward magnetic north. Still time dragged on, and the gale failed to rematerialize, until it suddenly rushed back with all of its previous fury. The contrast was remarkable. It was as though the men were adrift on a mystical sea and had been forced back out of a curtain of fog into the reality that had continued to spin forward all around them.

In the morning, George and Frank half expected to see the ocean dotted with the white and deep blue islands of ice so common in the northern reaches of their homeland. But the gray dawn revealed nothing except dark, blackish waves topped with white and bearded with spindrift, the leaden sky, and clouds as somber as the wings of crows.

18

The presence of pack ice in the high latitudes has never remained altogether consistent. In some eras there is more of it and in others less. The packs always push south and break apart, creating large, flattish islands of drift ice. But the key question is . . . how far south? Glaciers on Greenland calve icebergs of prodigious size that can float south of Newfoundland to below the fortieth parallel during the summer months. Over the centuries the pack ice, and to a lesser extent icebergs, have blocked and opened transatlantic routes and as a consequence greatly influenced the timing and success of the great voyages of discovery.

In 325 B.C., a Greek mathematician named Pytheas sailed from the Mediterranean Sea out through the Straits of Gibraltar. He was determined to explore the vast unknown seas to the west. He and his crew sailed far to the northwest, discovering Iceland. According to ancient records, he almost made it as far west as Greenland before pack ice blocked his passage. At that time, the climate in the Northern

Hemisphere had cooled dramatically. It was as much
as several degrees cooler on average than it had been
for thousands of years, enough to spur the growth of
the ice sheets in the high northern latitudes, which
in turn created huge expanses of ice in the North
Atlantic. Voyages to the west across the ocean in the
high latitudes became virtually impossible until the
climate began to warm again at around A.D. 200,
peaking in balminess between A.D. 800 and 1200.

As the average temperatures increased, the ice
retreated back to the north, and the western ocean
became more hospitable for voyaging. The warmer
climate also acted as an impetus to the overpopulation
of the northlands, where the Norse had developed a
thriving maritime culture. Known to Europeans as
Vikings, which means sons of the fjords in old Norse,
the adventurers explored and often looted cities such
as Paris, Kiev, Hamburg, London, Lisbon, and Cadiz.
They set sail westward as well in beamy, round-
bottomed ships of lapstrake construction, not the
dragon-festooned warships that have come down
through the ages as the Viking's vessels of exploration.

When Eric the Red, born in A.D. 950, was banished
from Iceland due to unsavory behavior, including
murder, he sailed west and encountered none of the
ice that Pytheas reported centuries earlier. He established the first Norse colony on Greenland in the
closing decades of the first millennium. The settlers
found forests and a rich fishery. They raised crops
and led austere, though not unpleasant, lives. A trader
called Bjarni Herjulfsson reported sighting lands farther to the west that led Leif Ericson, son of Eric the
Red, to Vinland, which is thought to be present-day
Newfoundland.

All of this occurred in large part due to the more
hospitable climatic conditions prevailing during these
centuries. However, as it had previously, the climate

changed yet again, and the ice slowly extended its reach southward. Eventually, Greenland became a wasteland, devoid of any of its former hospitality. In the early days of the settlement, graves for the dead were dug deep in the rich soil. Over time the permafrost made this practice impossible. Graves became shallower and shallower until finally, as the Norse population dwindled almost away, the bodies of the dead were buried above ground under piles of stone. The last known corpse of a Norse Greenlander was discovered in 1540.

By this time, the climate in the Northern Hemisphere had plunged into a period of markedly colder temperatures, even more severe than those which had set in motion the demise of the Norse on Greenland some three to four centuries earlier. At around 1450 there began a four-century period of colder climate called the Little Ice Age. Glaciers advanced over farmland in Scandinavia and Canada. Winters were more harsh and ended later, with some recorded cases of frost on the ground in June in the vicinity of New York City. It was far worse in the higher latitudes.

The Little Ice Age lingered on until 1850, and in the higher latitudes it lasted well into the late 1890s. The icebergs that clogged the sea in the high northern latitudes traveled far to the south, borne on the currents and eddies of the sea and the vagaries of wind. The iceberg the *Fox* encountered was not so unusual. Nor was the wicked weather. Neither man could know that they were trying to row across the ocean at a particularly dangerous time, that their ancestors before them had encountered weather far less destructive. In fact, the series of westerly storms was actually working in their favor by speeding the *Fox* on her way, if they could only survive them. Such workings on a scale exceeding the imaginations of most people would not have influenced them much, anyway. As they continued their long, tired fight with the gale, their reality came down to the most simple elements of human existence. There was no room for profundity, the grand schemes of science, or the climatic change that had influenced the development of civilization and, on a smaller scale, might well determine the outcome of a voyage undertaken in a rowboat.

It had been over twenty-four hours since either man had slept or eaten. The *Fox* demanded much to keep her from capsizing in the seas. They ran before the gale at a breakneck pace as long as they could, then turned the *Fox* head to the sea and went stern first. Good sense would have prompted almost any sailor to heave to under the sea anchor and ride out the storm. But the men aboard the *Fox* had become obsessed. Worn down by their long ordeal, they pushed on, ever eastward at the heels of the west wind. They paid for their speed with the occasional breaker that swamped the boat and forced them to bail. Each time, the *Fox* came close to capsizing. Their luck held, and she did not.

The night passed much as the previous one, with breakers chasing them like monsters in the dark. The morning of Friday, July 10, brought more of the same; except the waves, which had not seemed to grow much beyond their already enormous size in the last fifteen hours, apparently had received a new influx of energy. Their growth in size from twenty-five feet to thirty and thirty-five feet on average meant that the wind had increased to the west and the newly enhanced force of the storm had not yet reached the *Fox*'s immediate locale. Waves, no matter how much ocean exists for them to build upon, only reach a maximum height based on the speed of the wind. Increases in wind will make them grow higher, as will meeting shoal water. George and Frank looked westward with mounting anxiety. A really bad wind, the worst they had encountered so far, was on its way.

It arrived at around noon. The wind shrieked like witches at the stake and sent shivers through the men. The sea boiled white with foam that flew over the rails of the *Fox* into their faces. Facing the wind, they lost their breath. Its force was like a wall; it was even difficult to sit up. Gusts of sixty to seventy knots roared across the mountainous waves and ripped their crests off. Breakers were everywhere now. When the men saw a particularly dangerous wave coming, they tried to row out of its way. This was sometimes possible, sometimes not. Both of them felt the stress, physical and emotional. It had been two days since either of them had slept; they had eaten practically nothing. The motion of the boat, the need for both of them to man the oars, made food a luxury they could not afford. But they were heading east, and that at least gave them some small degree of comfort. George estimated that they had made an easting of over two hundred miles during the most recent onslaught of these west winds, fine progress, a momentum they held on to as if it were gold.

The storm increased all through the day. Briefly during the late afternoon it appeared that the blow might have finally lost some steam, and the men hoped and longed for the end of their latest ordeal. But after the short lull the wind increased even further. These teasing respites the sea provided did the men no good. The false hope of relief, dashed once again, made it still more difficult to endure what lay ahead. It sharpened the degree of cerebral torture as keen as the blade of a razor, which in many ways affected the men more than the physical hardship. Better that a storm blow on and on unabated till it was finished than to have it sway back and forth, undecided as to what path it wanted to take and how badly it wanted to blow.

Not long before dusk, the seas ran higher than ever before on the voyage, and although both of them had seen truly horrific waves in their long years at sea, from the low vantage point of the rowboat each wave took on an almost unreal proportion. Neither man could hear the other's shouts above the wind and the noise of cascading water despite the fact that only a few feet separated them in the boat. They rowed on and on, dodging the larger groups of waves. They only just managed to keep the bow facing into the fury of the storm.

Off the port bow, still in the distance, a mighty wave towered above all the rest. It seemed to grow in size exponentially, rising higher and higher until it totally blocked out the broken horizon even while the *Fox* rode the crests. The wave gathered speed and power. Created by the marriage of several large waves, it somehow came to life in that strange combination that occurs when several seas suddenly come together and move forward in the same step. Like soldiers marching in line, their legs moving as one, so, too, did the merging of several waves tap an engine of nature endowed with unimaginable strength. The face of the wave looked as deep and black and impenetrable as outer space. The nearly vertical wall steepened, and the top became unstable and gradually outpaced the lower reaches of the hill below. A white line of foam boiled at the summit as the shoulder of the wave broadened to well over a quarter mile. Steadily, it approached the *Fox*, ready to break at any moment.

Frank looked over his shoulder at his friend seated in the stern seat. Their eyes met, and they nodded to each other in silent communication. Each knew the wave would soon strike, that its size and shape meant that no hope existed. They could neither get out of its way nor go over the top. The very real possibility that the *Fox* would rise up the face and flip end over end surfaced in their minds with remarkable clarity. It is every mariner's nightmare to get caught in such a situation; the preparation for the worst can

never ease the fear of facing it. It settles over the
soul and mind and body like a heavy cloak, dulling
responses and slowing time to a standstill.

The men felt the *Fox* trying to rise up the wave,
and seconds later the world went black. The noise of
the breaking water drowned out the sound of the
wind. The violent motion of the boat suddenly
stopped as the men were lifted bodily out of the little
vessel into the very heart of the wave. They felt the
lines on their life belts snap tight, the cold water flow
into their mouths, noses, eyes, and ears. They each
struggled for life in a separate world, kicking their
feet, which were weighted down with seaboots, flailing
their arms and legs, encumbered in heavy clothes and
their oilskins. Only a matter of yards spanned the distance between them, but it could have been an eternal
space, one that was as unreachable as the stars.

Coughing and choking, they rose to the surface of
the ocean downwind of the *Fox*, their heads almost
submerged in a layer of foam that carpeted the denser
water just a foot or so below. Strong swimmers washed
overboard in fierce storms where the air and sea mix
on the surface have drowned in the layer of foam. The
water below keeps the swimmer's head and shoulders
high, but never high enough to catch a breath.
George gazed at the *Fox* floating upside down as he
swam toward it. He noticed how free the bottom was
of barnacles and weed, a strange thought to have at
the time. The human mind when faced with shock
often leaps to thoughts of a routine nature that diminish the severity of the event. A good clean bottom.
The *Fox* is in good shape, he thought.

The waves continued to break over them as they
finally managed to pull themselves back to the *Fox*,
using their lifelines. Tethered to the boat, their oars
floated alongside. They hung on to one of the rails
the boatbuilder had constructed along the center of
the boat's stem. With both men on one side of the

Fox, they pulled. She didn't want to come back rightside up. Fighting back their fear, they pulled harder, and at last, with the help of the seas, the boat rolled over. Frank swam around the *Fox*. They both clambered back in from opposite sides to keep their weight evenly distributed and prevent the little ship from turning back over. The airtight compartments kept her rails just above the surface of the water, though foam and spray flew. It stung their faces like bees, except the sensation was not of hot, searing pain; rather, the prick of cold as deep as the touch of death.

Panting for breath, the men vomited up sea water as one bailed and the other kept the boat pointing in the general direction of the storm. Every effort, every movement, inflicted additional pain on their bruised and bleeding bodies. Slowly, the bailing reduced the volume of water inside the *Fox*, and she rode better. She was far easier and quicker to move. Deft steering and some hard pulls on the oars kept her from being capsized yet again.

With some control regained over the craft, George and Frank surveyed the chaos the wave had created. Their hearts sank. More than half their remaining provisions were gone. The snapped ends of lashings hung everywhere. The sea claimed their cooking pot, frying pan, dishes, one can of water, one of the rattan seats, which helped lessen the pain of prolonged sitting while at the oars, and their newly made floating anchor, along with its cable. Other things were missing as well, which they discovered later when looking for them. The dire circumstances they faced hit them hard. More than halfway across the North Atlantic, exhausted beyond any limits they had yet encountered, they lacked food and water to make it to the other side. Now they were no longer voyagers out to set a record; they were castaways completely at the mercy of the sea.

19

Neither man could bear to speak to the other. The effort to shout above the storm was futile. Silently, each alone in his despair, the men took up the oars and rowed the *Fox* into the raging storm. Hope winged away into the gathering night, and when the blackness surrounded them, they shivered convulsively in their soaked clothes. Every minute brought more and more pain as their traumatized muscles stiffened. Their hands, curled around the oars, went numb and threatened to retain the clawlike shape. The waves broke over the boat from time to time; it was all they could do to keep bailing and rowing. The urge to quit, to let the sea take the *Fox* if it pleased, passed through their minds, as it does when any human being faces something as all-powerful and unrelenting as nature. It strips off the layers of humanity one by one, leaving only the bare connection of flesh that refuses to die. Thoughts disappear in the haze of fatigue; the body moves as if it is mechanically driven.

The mountain climber ascending peaks far above

the thick layer of oxygen on the ground knows the tests that nature can muster. The cold, sharp beauty of the blue ice and gray rock, the clarity of the sky, the sunbeam robbed of all its warmth, transcend the tremendous pressure to take flight back down the slopes to safety. The experience of entering a world within the world at large, a tiny piece of the earth that resembles nothing the common man ever sees, compels the climber. It drives him onward to seek the highest peaks. The dance with danger becomes an addiction, and it is a difficult one to break. The desert traveler also enters a world within the larger world. The rolling dunes of certain sections of the Sahara, like the waves of the sea, cut through all the trappings of humanity and reduce the traveler to the most basic level of existence. The polar regions hold the same kind of magic. The hardship is unbearable, but the time out in the wasteland remains unforgettable.

So, too, the sea, with all of its power and beauty, plays upon the mind and body. It is a place that draws people to the shores along coasts and compels them to sit and stare wistfully at the distant horizon and imagine what it is like out of sight of land. It is a world within the larger world, filled with mystery and the unknown. To cross it is not to diminish it or even to know it more than on a superficial level. But like the highest mountains and the hottest deserts, it does offer a strange kind of gift, humility, to any who open their hearts to it and let the force of natural power work and shape one's character. To descend to that last floor in the gallery of one's mind and soul and find that the strength, though gone, still flickers, the will, though defeated, still burns like the deep red of an ember inspired by a bellows is the truest test any individual can live through. It is life changing, usually in a quiet way. George and Frank had reached that final floor, and they were not found wanting.

The *Fox* pounded and pitched through the interminable night. The men still kept the bow headed to the seas. They could look directly east as they rowed and search for the first signs of dawn. It would break gray and cold, but at least the light might bring a sense of place and relief. Slowly the darkness peeled away in layers almost indiscernible at first. The eastern horizon became visible. The clouds and waves took shape. The new day revealed an ocean gone mad.

As the hours passed, the men cursed the sea and the wind. Go down! they shouted to themselves. Go down, down, down! Each of them had now gone without sleep for three days. Their bodies cried out for relief. They were nearly beyond the point of caring what happened to the *Fox*, and by extension, themselves. The gale swept onward toward Europe, and at around noontime the wind began to pay heed to the wishes of the men. It slowly diminished. The waves, in turn, slowly stopped breaking as much as they had during the night.

Unable to stand their discomfort any longer, George and Frank took turns at the oars while the other removed his clothes. Every movement hurt, so it was a slow process. First the oilskins were laid down in the bottom of the boat lest they blow away. The shirt came off and was wrung out, then put back on. Pants, undergarments, and socks next. The routine provided little comfort, but at least the clothing wasn't soaking wet after the wringing out. They shivered less, though only to a small degree.

"This gale these past three days feels like six weeks onshore," George said. "It seemed like we'd never get through it there for a while."

"I counted every minute of it like a week. I hope we've seen the last of this fearsome weather," Frank said. "It's about taken all we've got, hasn't it."

"I've got to sleep. We both have to sleep."

Seeing his friend grimace with pain as the boat

pitched, the haggard, gaunt lines in his face, the hollow eyes, Frank offered to take the first watch. "I can hang on longer. You get some sleep, George."

Grateful, George collapsed in a heap at the bottom of the boat and within seconds sank into an exhausted sleep. Alone at the oars, Frank looked about him at the sea, humbled by what he saw, how close they had come to losing their fight. Had either of their lifelines parted, the outcome of the voyage would have been sealed; neither man had the strength to row on alone. As it was, without provisions to last till they reached land, the trip had taken on an uncertainty that gnawed at Frank and caused him to fear the days to come. No doubt, he thought, George shared similar concerns.

Frank checked his watch to see how long he had before calling George to take over for him. The hands had stopped at approximately nine o'clock. That's when the wave hit us, he thought. He stopped rowing for a moment and shook the watch, tried to wind it. Water filled the inside of the face. By the looks of it, the timepiece was finished. He sighed and kept rowing as long as he could, and when he felt a sufficient amount of time had passed, he called George.

George lurched out of a dreamless sleep at the sound of Frank's voice. Shivering violently, he opened his eyes and found he could ba-ely see. The tissue around his eye sockets had swollen up to such an extent that the skin nearly sealed the lids closed. His muscles ached enough to make him cry out. He tried to move but couldn't, at least not on the first try.

"God, I'm stiff as a board," he said.

"We got plenty mashed up when the boat went over. This cold and wet hasn't helped any, either," Frank said. "My legs feel like they're logs."

George willed his legs and arms to move. He actually had to crawl into the rowing seat while Frank kept the boat as steady as possible. He bent his hands around the oars and tried to pull. Searing pain shot through every nerve.

"Can you hold her?" Frank asked. His voice was low and far-off.

"I can, I think. You get some sleep. Everything will be all right."

Frank looked at his friend. Never before had he seen George looking so awful. He clamped his mouth shut tight to bite back the pain as he rowed. His red hair, now longish and unkempt, was plastered against his skull. His bushy mustache looked like a red gash across his face, pallid despite the deep tan.

"My watch stopped last night when we went over," Frank said.

George checked his watch and found it had also stopped. Without their timepieces, life would be more difficult. Timing the noon sun sights, if the sun ever shined again, would require more effort. Running accurate watch schedules would require some careful work to ensure that each man rowed his fair share. Too tired to think beyond these thoughts, George set to the oars, ignoring the pain as best as he could. Shivering now that the work at the oars was done, Frank had no choice but to trust that George could in fact keep going. He lay down in the bottom of the boat and slept, his life in the hands of his friend.

The rest of the day, the men slept in turns. The man on watch kept the *Fox* heading eastward. In addition to his duty at the oars, the imperative of sighting a ship close enough to intercept meant keeping a close eye on the horizon. The men feared that the storm had blown them out of the transatlantic shipping routes, and if that was the case, they had little or no chance of resupplying. No sign of life, not even a seabird. Hour after hour, their only companion was the sea. As the sun sank below the horizon, the blackness that followed mirrored the state of their spirits.

The following day, Sunday, July 12, yet another gale from the west blew in from its breeding grounds a thousand miles away over the gloomy waters of Nova Scotia. It began raining around noon. It seemed to both men that misery knew no bounds. How long could they keep this up? The question remained unasked; there was no answer. The sea still ran high, but not nearly as high as it had during the storm. It all came down to a matter of relative size. A sea which would have appeared large early in the voyage now appeared average. As they rowed, though, they noticed that the waves began behaving in an unusual way. They grew steep and adopted the shape of pyramids, a positive indication of an adverse current.

"It looks as though we have a current running against us," Frank said, frustration evident in his voice.

George nodded. "But maybe it runs with us. We've got to hope it does, anyway. I can hardly think about being set back now, not now."

Clinging at straws, wishing for the best—it was all they could do.

Late that afternoon, the crew of the *Fox* received the first sign that there was yet still hope to embrace, that their forced sense of optimism in fact had at least a small basis. To the south of the rowboat the superstructure of a steamer plowing westward through the head sea emerged over the horizon. The wind whipped the black smoke from the stacks and blew it to oblivion. The bow plunged deep into the waves and poked out the backs. She was too far for them to intercept, but seeing the ship instilled hope that others might steam closer. The storm, it seemed, had not blown them out of the shipping lanes, after all. It was small comfort. The men clung to it, though.

George's optimism, such as it was, remained guarded. He thought to himself, What are the odds that a ship will pass us by close enough for us to speak it? In

these seas, a watch officer would never see the *Fox*.
The odds of stopping a ship, he thought, were about
equal to those of shooting a bear in the eye at long
range. His spirits sagged through Monday. Even the
winds, which dropped off significantly and shifted to
north, and a diminishing sea didn't cheer him up
much. Frank, always the quiet one, took on a sphinx-
like demeanor; his features hardened into a counte-
nance of sheer determination as he rowed. He glared
at the sea, sick of its constant bombardment. Neither
he nor George trusted the moderating conditions.

On Tuesday afternoon, Frank watched George, who
was on the off watch, carefully remove the logbook
from the aft watertight compartment. He tore a blank
piece of paper out and started writing. When he had
finished, he placed the paper in one of the envelopes
they had brought with them, miraculously still dry in
its place inside the watertight compartment. Writing
letters in the middle of the Atlantic? Had George
begun to lose his mind? Where did he think he could
post a letter out here? Then George started writing
another letter. Frank rowed on, observing his friend
almost as carefully as he watched the horizon for any
evidence of a ship. But he said nothing about the
odd ritual. If jotting down some private words, whatever the motive, brought comfort, he was welcome
to write as many as he thought necessary.

The wind continued light and shifted to the south.
Without the sustained gales to drive the waves into
towers, the sea calmed down considerably. The long
westerly swell smoothed out into mounds with
choppy, wind-driven waves on top. The men slowly
regained some of their strength because of the
respite. While off watch, sleep came easily and was
seldom interrupted. Their muscles ached less, though
they felt the afterpains of the pummeling they had
received when they were ripped out of the boat. It
must have struck them as it rolled over. The whiplash

effect of their lifelines being yanked taut also contributed to their bashing.

Their lack of food and water occupied their minds. A deep hunger was their constant companion. Their tongues swelled and stuck to the roofs of their mouths. Their lips split and bled. It took every bit of discipline they had to ration their supplies. When the body demands food, when the hunger reaches down and twists the stomach into agony, it is extremely difficult not to try to assuage the pain with an extra gulp of fresh water, an extra sea biscuit or can of meat.

By Wednesday morning on July 15, five days after they had capsized, they felt more rested. With their renewed strength came the ability to face up to their situation and determine exactly how long they had left if they rationed their provisions to survival portions still large enough to allow them the needed calories to row closer to Europe. They could stretch the food and water out for many days if they drifted and conserved their energy, but both agreed that would be unwise. The sea would likely take them that way. If they kept rowing and got closer to Europe, there was a better chance of intercepting a ship or an offshore fishing smack. It was a calculated gamble, but then the entire voyage had been based on such risks. That this decision more tangibly represented a life-or-death issue really didn't strike them as momentous. It was simply decided what was best between them, and they felt their best chance was to keep on rowing while consuming as little food or water as possible.

To figure out the true range of the *Fox* with its present supplies required a pretty fair assessment of their position, which they did not have. Their last sun sight was taken on July 8 and placed the *Fox* nearly on the forty-sixth parallel, a latitude just below Newfoundland and just about in line with Bordeaux, France, and the Bay of Biscay. Their last firm fix on the *Fox*'s position was more than two weeks old, when they had met the Canadian schooner *Leader* on July 1. The captain had placed them at latitude forty-five degrees, thirty minutes north, longitude fifty degrees, twenty-five minutes west. Or on the eastern edge of the Grand Banks off Newfoundland, approximately 160 miles southeast of Cape Race.

Based on George's calculations, he placed the *Fox* between the forty-sixth and forty-seventh parallels. But without a sun sight he couldn't pin it down to more than a guess. It was safe to say, he thought, that they were somewhere between the sixty nautical miles that equal one degree of latitude. His dead reckoning as far as their longitude went was far more suspect. The westerly gales had pushed them along at speeds exceeding any possible under oars alone. In fact, on the days when the wind fell light, few as they were, their progress to the east slowed dramatically. By his best figuring he estimated that the *Fox* had traveled east from the Grand Banks at least seven hundred miles in the last two weeks, a safe bet, since it kept within the projected fifty-mile-per-day average.

Looking at his chart, George quickly ticked off the distance the *Fox* had to travel to reach Le Havre. "We've got twelve hundred or more miles yet, Frank. But less than that to the Cornwall coast of England."

"If only we knew for sure. I'd like to think we've made it two-thirds of the way across. I would very much like that."

Two-thirds across. Two-thirds across! If George's figures were correct or even nearly so, they had come nearly two thousand miles in thirty-nine days. Taking stock of their position tempted the men to hope for a good outcome for the journey. Nearly one thousand

miles of rough North Atlantic still lay ahead. They
had not enough food and water to make it that far,
but if luck held and they kept going, perhaps they
would spy a ship. Perhaps it would be close enough
to see them. Perhaps, perhaps. . . .

20

George thought about the letters he had written the previous day. One he had addressed to Harold, his brother, who had carved out a life for himself and his wife in Jersey City. He had described the journey so far, its trials and travails, including the capsize and his hopes for ample reward when they got across safely. Like Frank's family, George's had not seen fit to encourage him in the venture. The letter might shed some light on why he had felt compelled to go. The other letter he addressed to the *New York World*. It, too, gave a firsthand report of their progress.

"You know, I don't know what made me write those letters yesterday."

Frank smiled. "You had something to say to Harold. Why not write him a letter. I have to say I thought it strange to see a man out in the middle of an ocean writing away as if he was in his living room, though." He laughed.

George laughed, too. "I think I did it because I wanted to believe we'd see a ship soon. I still think we'll see one. I really do."

George laid his oars inboard and gingerly stood up. His legs felt very shaky. The sea was calm and the wind light, so he took a chance and stood up on the seat to gain even a little extra height. He scanned the horizon all around but saw no ships. He sat down, a little disappointed.

"You won't see far in this haze," Frank said.

"It still doesn't hurt to look."

"So, how long do you think we can go if we don't speak a ship?" Frank asked.

"A week, maybe a little more."

They turned the subject over again, poking and repeating, as if going over it and over it might turn up a new angle. No solution presented itself. Their situation rested on simple terms. Either they would find a ship and obtain the provisions they needed, or they wouldn't, and the sea would win. At the moment, though, their spirits were much higher than they had been during and just after the storm. They had eaten enough for breakfast to take the edge off their hunger. They rowed on, nursing their hopes for the best.

The ocean in many ways can alter one's senses. As with the desert or polar regions, the solitary traveler may hallucinate. With the lack of visual stimulation from the flat nothingness of these locales, mirages appear out of nowhere. The strange impression of sailing or walking uphill when the surface of the sea or land is in fact level; the sudden appearance of apparitions; the sight of buildings or natural forms, such as mountains or lakes or islands, emerge not from reality but from the deep recesses of the mind. The traveler knows what he sees isn't real and yet clings tenaciously to the hope that it is. Frank thought he saw something off the port quarter masked in the haze. He blinked and tried to focus more clearly.

"I see something!" he shouted.

George followed his gaze. "Where? I don't see anything."

Whatever it was disappeared. "Now I've lost it," Frank said.

Had he been seeing things? Did his sheer will to see a ship conjure one up out of thin air? It was a distinct possibility. George kept rowing while Frank concentrated on the smooth, oily-looking water, the white glare of the haze off the boat's left side. To the north of them a dark smudge blotted the horizon. It seemed to hang suspended in the air.

"I see it again!" Frank said. "There." He pointed at the dark spot. "It's a sailing vessel."

Containing his excitement, George stood up very carefully on the seat and squinted through the spy glass, which fortunately hadn't been washed away during the capsize. Slowly, the masts and sails of a ship sailing eastward became visible. Relief flooded over him. He almost shouted with happiness. "I think it's coming our way!"

"I hope we can hail it. I hope they see us."

"It'll be a gift of providence," George said. He kept staring at the ship. "I'm sure it's coming closer. But she'll pass to the north of us."

The men immediately changed course to intercept the ship, loafing along in the light westerly breeze, with every stitch of canvas spread on its yardarms. The headsails and the large mainsail boomed way out to the left side of the ship's aftermost mast, kept the ship moving slowly. George and Frank rowed as hard as they could to get close enough to the bark, but it glided well through the calm seas and looked as though it would pass too far away for anyone on deck to see the rowboat in the haze. They had steered well to the front of the bark, much as would a duck hunter who fires not at the duck itself but in the air beyond its bill. In this way, the men hoped to gain on the ship as it sailed past. Its bow closed quickly with their course, and soon the ship would come abreast of them, still too far off.

"She's going to pass us by. We're going to miss her!" Frank growled. He pulled mightily on the oars. His muscles bulged beneath his clothing. A wake swirled off behind the *Fox*, which was near enough for the men to see the details of the ship's standing rigging. They noticed the weathered look of its hull, green with slime and speckled white with barnacles along the waterline. Yet it could have been a mirage, a visitation from an unreal world, as long as it remained too far distant to offer them the help they so desperately needed.

"God, I wish the wind would die out!" George muttered. "We'd catch her then."

Both of them knew better than that. The wind would not die out just because they needed it to. In fact, it would probably blow up strong and steady in the next few minutes just to spite them. The elements had taken on an almost human nature. They were more than all-powerful. They toyed with the men, beat them, and reluctantly gave solace in the respites between storms, as though sparing them for more agony later. Certainly the wind would pick up. Why should it not?

The ship was now almost abreast of the *Fox*. Still, no one aboard had seen them. George grabbed one of the blankets rumpled up on the bottom of the boat and tied it to one of their sweeps, the longest oars aboard. He stood up, careful not to shift his weight too quickly, and began to wave the oar back and forth. The blanket caught the wind and spread out. It collapsed and filled.

The ship passed them. The men fought off the despair that threatened to overcome them. George frantically waved the blanket, holding the oar as high above his head as he could. The *Fox* rocked from rail to rail.

"She's coming around! She's seen us!" Frank yelled.

George smiled broadly as he quickly took his seat and added his strength to Frank's at the oars. The little *Fox* leaped forward through the water. The ship drew closer, and the men could make out her name. She was the *Cito*.

"Her rig looks Norwegian. But that's not a Norwegian name," George said.

"We'll soon find out where she's from."

Two men stood at the main-topsail yard, well above the main-topsail and the mainsail below it. The billowing canvas obscured all but their upper torsos. Behind the sail, their legs extended below the yardarm, their feet braced securely on the footropes. One of the men, the first mate, scanned the little boat with a glass and could scarcely believe his eyes. "Two Negroes in the rowboat, sir!" he called down to the captain, a small, thin man wearing a fine coat of tanned rawhide open to the moderately balmy air. The captain raised an eyebrow. Two Negroes in a rowboat?

"No, sir," the mate called. "No, I think they're Indians!"

The captain signaled the crew, all of whom had gathered on deck to take in this odd sight, to brace the yards. The deck watch pulled the lines running up to the ends of the spars to swing the yardarms so that the square sails backed. The wind now pushed from the front of the sails and stopped the ship. The headsails still drew, however. Two opposing forces—the square sails pushing backward and the headsails pushing forward—neatly parked the ship in mid-ocean. She rolled in the gentle swells.

"What nationality are you?" George cried.

"We are Norwegian," the captain answered.

"We are from there, too."

"What are you doing in that little boat?"

As with the ships they had met before, the men repeated their story.

"You're welcome to come aboard."

"Thank you," George said.

George and Frank rowed close to the side of the ship. Close to the hull it became obvious that the swells, gentle as they were, posed a danger to the *Fox*. The water whooshed and sucked around the rounded sides of the ship. The men made several passes to get a feel for the timing they would need to bring the *Fox* safely alongside. They rowed quickly to get some speed up, then shipped the oars before they struck the hull. The *Fox* ground and bumped along. One of the crew dropped a rope to them, which Frank made fast on the bow. They tried to climb aboard but found their legs too stiff. Finally, they hauled themselves up the side of the ship hand over hand, relying on the brute strength of their upper bodies and arms.

Once over the bulwarks, they dropped helplessly on deck as two of the crew walked the *Fox* around to the stern of the ship and hoisted it up out of the water to prevent damage. A man stayed to keep an eye on it for them. In the meantime, George and Frank staggered to their feet but fell down again. The muscles in their legs had cramped so badly in the boat over the weeks at sea that walking seemed unnatural. They struggled to their feet several more times, rejecting the offers of assistance from the crew, and wobbled down the length of the ship to the aft deck, where the captain stood watching them with a look of pity mixed with admiration.

"You are the most daring fellows I've ever met," the captain said, and thrust out his hand. "We took you for castaways, you know."

"I mistook you for Negroes," the mate said. "Then I thought you were Indians. Now we find out you hail from Norway!"

George and Frank looked at each other. It was as if they had seen the other for the first time. Their

faces were deeply tanned and blackened from grime.
They smiled. Negroes. Indians. It wasn't surprising
that the mate had been mistaken. "We do need a
wash," George said.

The captain was in the process of taking a sun sight.
He lifted a battered sextant to his eye, and as he
worked, he said, "Are you hungry?"

"Not very," George said. "But food would go down
good."

Frank grinned at his friend, always a man of understatement. True, they weren't as hungry as they would
have been had they not eaten anything earlier in the
morning. But their stomachs growled for a good meal.

"Dinner will be in a few minutes," the captain said.

"Where are we?" Frank asked.

"We're more interested in our location than dinner," George said. "We've been two weeks without
a firm fix and no sun sight for more than a week.
How far have we come?"

"Now, if you'll wait a few minutes, I can tell you,"
the captain said.

"Just estimate. You surely have an idea," George
said. It suddenly became more important than anything else to know their position. He seldom exhibited impatience, but he had to know, now.

"Well, by my reckoning, we're between thirty-one
and thirty-two degrees west of Greenwich."

Longitude is marked off east or west from the prime
meridian, which runs directly through Greenwich,
England, at zero degrees. As the *Fox* progressed, she
would actually pass the prime meridian and have to
measure her progress east of Greenwich, though not
for long. Only when the *Fox* reached the vicinity of
Le Havre and the River Seine would their longitude
switch from west to east, and by then they would no
longer need to know their exact position because all
navigation on the river would be line of sight. But
those days were long ahead. George guessed that the

Cito and the *Fox* were about nine hundred miles from the Scilly Islands, the southernmost lands of Great Britain. He said as much to Frank.

"Well, well. That west wind did push us along, eh, George? Two-thirds across the North Atlantic!"

"It was a rough spot of weather we've had," the captain said. "You'll be fine the rest of the way if you could live through these last weeks at sea. A wicked west wind kept us under shortened sail till we thought we'd never see full canvas on the yards again."

The cook came on deck and told the captain that his dinner was served. The off-watch crew scurried belowdecks for their meal as well.

"Come, you should enjoy a good hot dinner and, after that, a good washing," the captain said. He showed the men down below to his cabin.

The men ate hungrily, and in between bites they told the captain and his mates more about the voyage, their encounter with the giant wave, and why they had undertaken to cross the Atlantic in a rowboat. The captain at first did not understand the venture. The *Cito* had sailed with a cargo of lumber from the St. Lawrence River, east across the Gulf of St. Lawrence, and out across the sea, bound for England, which had a need for the fine, sturdy Canadian wood as it continued to burst at the seams. England, like America and many other European countries, had seen remarkable growth as industrialization fanned the fires of commerce and spurred the growth of cities. The voyage across thus far had been a hard and dangerous one. The risks, though, were small compared to those two men aboard the *Fox*. Why risk life and limb to set a record? Why indeed. The concept of exhibiting the boat and giving lectures at the great theaters of Europe seemed unusual, but upon reflection, the logic appeared sound. At times, a man has to break off the course most followed and set one that takes his ship to less traveled places. It is safe to

chart paths through the known, much more dangerous to push off on one's own to see what that may
bring.

"I would like to ask a favor of you, Captain
Clausen," George said, as they finished their meal.

"What might that be?"

"Would you spare us enough provisions to take us
the rest of the way? We'll be glad to pay you for them.
We have some money with us."

"You'll have all the provisions you need, and more!
And I'll not take any of your money. It's the least I
can do for a fellow Norwegian."

Both men thanked him profusely.

"And there is one other thing," George said.
"Would you come look at our boat and verify that
we have no sail, mast, or rudder? There will be some
who may not believe we achieved the crossing without
deception. Some will claim we were given a mast and
sail once we left sight of New York."

The captain agreed. "Yes, there will always be people like that. It's easier to mistrust than it is to believe
in the impossible, eh?"

After they washed themselves from head to toe, the
men felt better than they had since leaving New York.
The weight of the last weeks lifted from their shoulders. No longer did despair linger nearby, beating its
wings in their ears and threatening to settle on them.
The captain's kindness chased the bird away. Looking
at the pile of provisions on deck, the men knew they
now had a fighting chance to reach land on their
own. But many miles still lay ahead of them and anything could happen.

Before they loaded the boat and lashed the supplies
with great care, Captain Clausen climbed down into
the *Fox* and looked around. "I see you have told the
truth. I admit I wondered myself how it could be
possible for such a little boat to get out here with just

oars. You must make it all the way to Havre. The world must see what two Norwegians can do!''

Captain Clausen wrote the following in their logbook:

> This is to certify that I met the rowboat *Fox* of New York in latitude forty-seven degrees, ten minutes, and longitude thirty-one degrees, twenty minutes on this day July 15, 1896, and that the boat contained no mast, sail, or rudder.

> Bark *Cito* of Laurvik
> N. E. Clausen, Master

After George and Frank finished loading and securing the supplies, they were ready to cast off from the *Cito*. In a few minutes both vessels would part company and would again move on alone, each with its own destiny determined by the sea.

"Have a safe crossing," the captain called down to them. "And may your hopes for a good financial return come true."

"And a safe voyage for you, too, sir," George and Frank said. "Thank you for everything you have done for us."

"Tell me, men!" the captain shouted to his crew. "Would any of you want to trade places with these fellows?"

Heads shook no all around. Everyone laughed.

"It seems only you two are mad enough to tempt the sea in that little boat." The captain chuckled.

George and Frank waved good-bye, cast off the lines, and pushed off the hull of the ship. When the *Fox* cleared away enough, they dipped their oars into the water and pulled hard. The *Cito* turned, and the wind filled her square sails with a slap and a bang of canvas. A froth of white appeared at her prow, and soon she grew small on the distant horizon. As dusk approached, bathing the Atlantic in orange and pink, the sails turned almost bronze in the soft light before merging into the blues at the edge of night advancing from the east.

21

With the darkness came a damp shroud of fog. But the wind remained light from the west, and the sea behaved itself. The loss of their watches troubled George and Frank, for they had no way to determine how long either man had been at the oars or asleep in the relative comfort beneath the canvas cover. Since the capsize, the nights had remained black under layers of storm clouds or fog. With the nautical almanac, it would have been possible to ascertain the time. The hours of the moon's rising and setting were listed there, and with some figuring the task of estimating the duration of each watch would have been easy. The book also listed the rising and setting of stars in the major constellations as well as the planets. Rowing hour after hour in the darkness, the minutes dragged, with no means of marking the passage of time. It cast them into a sort of limbo, a kind of physical and mental purgatory in which the world at large represented nothing but oars, the rap of a wave against the hull, and the impenetrable tar of a starless North Atlantic sky.

The slicing up of hours shared at the oars was a niggling problem compared to what they had been through. However, aboard the tiny ship it meant much to share in the chore of rowing equally. Neither man wanted to cheat his friend out of even a minute of precious sleep. George devised a method that, while it certainly lacked precision, helped ensure, at least on a psychological level, that no friction would arise between them.

When he took over the oars from Frank, George rowed for what he thought was a half hour. He retrieved the kettle from its place up forward and set it on the stern seat. He rowed for another estimated half hour and stuck his jackknife in the seat next to the kettle; he repeated the process once again, this time using the spy glass, a can of meat, or even a short length of line. He then reversed the procedure. When he finished his watch the objects were all back in their places. It ultimately came down to trust, though. Each man had to take the other's word that he had completed the entire three-hour watch.

"It's time to get up, Frank," George said.

He could barely see the outline of Frank's form. The tiny light of the lamp next to the compass cast strange shadows, silhouetting George's feet, the seat, and the looming shape of his friend.

"The kettle has made its rounds, eh," Frank mumbled, shaking the sleep off. He pulled on his oilskins, and the men switched spots in the boat.

From then on neither the moon nor the stars shined at night. Each man accepted the goodwill of the other, trusting that even if one of them misjudged the time it was not out of selfishness. The need to work as a team obviated the tendency to argue about small details, which might have mattered much at the moment but really didn't in a larger sense.

The following morning, Thursday, July 16, the fog remained, as did the light west wind. The men feasted on raw eggs, some fresh bread, and condensed milk. They craved a cup of hot coffee. The weather was calm enough to light the stove, but they decided against it. They only had enough kerosene to boil three or four full pots. They thought it wise to husband their resources.

The two rowed together after taking turns to eat. They were back to their fair-weather routine. There was comfort in it, though in an odd manner. It is not comfortable to row day after day, but the repeated routine did manifest a degree of stability. As long as they worked together and moved ever eastward, as long as the sea continued to let them pass without kicking up a storm, they were as happy and content as they could be under the circumstances. Both of them missed their lives ashore, and their families. They longed to see their homeland once again, and most of all, they longed to be free of the *Fox*. They both hated and loved the boat. This, too, was natural. Their emotions drove them onward, always onward.

"Looks like we have a companion," Frank said, pointing at the dorsal fin of a shark off the stern.

George leaned over the side for a better look. "He's a big fellow, there."

The men looked at each other, then back at the shark.

"I'm glad he wasn't in the neighborhood when we took our unexpected bath. Otherwise we wouldn't have been eating such a fine meal aboard the *Cito*," Frank said.

The shark followed them for much of the day. They actually didn't mind its hanging around; it gave them something different to watch instead of the endless sea. Porpoises played nearby after the shark left, jumping high over the smooth water and landing with a splash. They swam close to the *Fox* and gazed up at the men with eyes that looked almost human. The sea life around them made the men feel less isolated.

They called to the porpoises and laughed at their antics. When they, too, left, George and Frank were disappointed at the loss of their diverting games.

Early Friday morning, while George was on watch repeating the ritual of the kettle, a noise in the water nearby and the sound of something landing in the boat startled him. He stopped rowing and listened. He heard some kind of fish thrashing in the bottom of the boat. He reached down to grab it, but it slithered under the water tanks. Frank slept soundly a few feet away. Not wanting to awaken his friend, he let the fish stay where it was. During the rest of his watch he wondered what type of fish had come to visit them. In the tropics, flying fish leap skyward from the sea to escape the jaws of the dorado, big, square-headed fish with sharp teeth designed expressly for the fleet little flying fish. Unless it was quite lost, this little fellow could not be a flier, he thought.

When the sun came up, the men captured their dead visitor. It was not like any fish they had seen in all their years at sea. It was round, like an eel, about eighteen inches in length. It was ugly, but they both missed their frying pan very much at the sight of it.

"We'd have had us a fried fish for breakfast if it wasn't for the storm," Frank said, smacking his lips.

"We could spare kerosene for him, that's certain. But how can we cook him without a pot or pan?"

Not caring to eat the visitor raw, they consigned him to the deep. He floated away astern of the *Fox* as they rowed on into fog so thick it hid the surface of the sea beyond the blades of the oars. The monotony of the work, though welcome after the perils of the westerly gales, caused them to slip into their own thoughts. Afloat in the gray mist there wasn't much to keep them locked into the present. The sameness of it invited musings on the past and future, leaving the hours of the day behind in the little wake of the boat.

George's mind kept summoning images of Anine, Andrew, Annie Louisa, and Fritz. Dearest Fritz, now nine months old, would be getting bigger. What was his family doing in Brevik at this moment? Were they all well? How was Anine getting on with her parents and other relatives? Had the ships he and Frank met reported them to the newspapers so that Anine would know they were alive? The questions nagged at him. No answers. No way to know except to get across the Atlantic as quickly as possible. He felt sure they would make it now. He knew it with more certainty than anything else.

He pictured their faces, could hear their voices and laughter, and longed to hold his family close to him again. At times, he thought about Agnes Grace, his little baby that God saw fit to take away. Her spirit was somewhere in heaven, but a bit of it necessarily lingered close to the sea, where she had died five years ago. He pushed aside the pain of these memories to make room for others more cheerful. He remembered the early days in New York, moments such as the one at the harborside, Anine with Andrew cradled in her arms as the city celebrated the unveiling of the Statue of Liberty; that first spring at Nauvoo; back further to his days in Brevik, when he met Anine, fell in love with her, and promised to bring her to America; where anything could happen, where there were no limits to a man's ability save his own short-comings. Moments like that burned into his mind.

Memories haunted Frank as well. He wondered about his father, Emanuel, and how he was managing with their little dairy farm in Elunde. Was his mother, Elizabeth, in good health? Had his brother and Caroline in the United States received news of him? In Norway his sister Severine, two years younger than he, and his sister Jenny, only nine years old, and little Kristine. His brothers there, too. He missed them all. Though he had not been around much, having left home at age seventeen, he was still close to his siblings. Caroline, especially, so filled with ideas and hope. So ready to be an American girl, there in Brooklyn, the big city at her feet.

He thought back to his early childhood, back to the days when he was only three or four and Severine had just been born. The family lived in a tiny house deep in a fjord that cut into the coast near Farsund. There was no town in Sellegrod, the locale where Emanuel had built their home and started his family. To get to Farsund for supplies, he took a small rowboat down the fjord to the busy port. Frank loved to ride in the bow of the boat, watching his father at the oars. He often went to the boathouse and played at rowing the family's boat while it was tied up. Frank pictured himself rowing and found himself smiling. Rowing had come early to him indeed, and it seemed to have served him well. His brawn had contributed greatly to the progress of the *Fox*. He gave George all the credit for such matters as navigation and for his tenacity and determination at the oars. But in neither man's mind was there any question as to which of them was the strongest.

After a long stint deep in reverie, the thoughts tire out. They become thinner, like wisps of fog under the heat of a rising sun, until the mind blanks. At such moments the men felt the pain in their hands, which had become increasingly sore. Pain in their buttocks. Just about every inch of their bodies hurt in a dull, aching way. To get their minds focused elsewhere, the men sang songs. They tried anything to ease the passage of time, which, as the day progressed and merged into the next and the next, became an enemy as much as it was a friend.

The fog lifted just enough for them to see two ships on Saturday afternoon. One headed northwest bound for Canada or the United States; the other, southward toward the Azores. The men watched the vessels as pleased as if they had met an old companion. They each hoped the fog would stay away, for they felt certain they would see ships every day if it did. The sightings reinforced their connection to humanity, made them feel less alone and that the voyage was soon to end.

On Sunday, the sea provided another diversion. About sundown, they spotted an object floating on the surface. They rowed over to investigate and found it was a cask covered in barnacles. Curious about what it contained, Frank worked his knife into the top. It was filled with kerosene. But there was no way to get it out of the cask into their container. For some moments the situation annoyed them. They could practically taste a hot cup of coffee.

"We'll soon see a ship, and maybe the captain will give us some kerosene for the stove," George said.

"I hate to leave it," Frank said. "There must be a way to get some of that oil."

But there wasn't, and they had to leave it to the sea. The weather favored them with a warm, clear night. The stars shone above them in a carpet of sparkles. A shooting star, almost bright enough to reflect off the ocean below, would flash across the sky and vanish in the celestial sea. Well fed, well rested, and ever closer to Europe, the men were in very good spirits. They each wondered if the sea would turn on them again. It seemed to have let up on its goal of wearing them down, though, so they let themselves hope for the best and without the reservations they had had before. It is dangerous to trust the sea, but it is difficult to resist the temptation when it caresses you.

The sea reminded them of its power the next day, Monday, July 20. The wind blew strongly from the north, and soon the waves built high. But it was noth-

ing to worry about, just a half gale of around thirty
knots, with slightly higher gusts. The wind shifted
back to the west and hurried them on their way.
Since they met the *Cito*, George guessed, the *Fox* had
traveled another 270 miles, leaving roughly 700 miles
before they closed with the English Channel.

22

Ever since men have fashioned vessels out of reeds, the tanned hides of animals, and finally wood, iron, and steel, the sea has contained its share of mysteries. It is so vast, so deep, that a man floating on its surface feels as if he is suspended on his back at the rim of the atmosphere, looking into the black depths of space. He hovers, caught at an interfacing of a natural boundary. There is little else on earth that can stir the imagination with such vigor than to linger on the watery hinterland and let the mind wander. In a small boat, the sense that there is much unknown about the sea becomes magnified; on a large ship, the workings of mankind's machinery interferes with the impulse to wonder just what lies below far beneath the waves.

After proceeding along for an uneventful two days at the heels of a little westerly blow, the *Fox* came upon a patch of calm that seemed at once unnatural. Seldom does the sea rest, its surface undisturbed by even a whisper of wind or the long swells from storms raging hundreds of miles away. But in the early evening of Thursday, July 23, the ocean stretched out on all sides in an unbroken sheet. It shimmered in the fading light, with patches of indigo splashed with orange and white, reflected from the sinking sun.

As George rowed, he admired the splendid calm. He glanced off to the right of the boat and saw a most remarkable apparition abreast of them about two hundred feet away. He blinked his eyes and stopped rowing.

"Look, Frank," he whispered. "Do you see that?"

Frank stopped rowing as well and scanned the water. There a creature could be seen at the surface, its head black and shaggy, its snout like that of a Newfoundland hound. It appeared to lie in peaceful repose, enjoying the calm, rather balmy evening, just as the men were. They quietly backed the oars to bring the boat in close to get a better look at it. The blades scarcely rippled the water. The *Fox* slid silently toward the creature.

When they were about fifty feet away, it seemed to examine them and slowly sank into the deep without leaving a trace on the water. Not a ripple or ring marked its position. The men rowed to where they thought it had been and leaned over the railing, but they saw only the impenetrable blackness of the ocean. They didn't say anything for a long moment. The silence hung heavy. Each could hear his heart beat in his inner ear, the breaths escape from his lungs.

"What do you suppose that was?" Frank said at last. Although he spoke in barely a whisper, his voice sounded loud.

"It couldn't have been a seal. We're still at least five hundred miles from shore, and we're way out of the track of icebergs, where a seal might have been stranded."

"Let's wait to see if it surfaces again."

The *Fox* floated as still as if she were back in the shed at William Seaman's boatworks, snug in a cradle. The men couldn't help but feel a creepy sensation on their skins and up their spines. Though they did not believe in sea serpents, giant squid, or mermaids, they knew that men through the ages had discovered all manner of fish and mammals living in the oceans. No seal could live long so far out to sea. No whale or porpoise looked like what they had seen. The sight of whatever it was mystified them and filled them with a deep-seated feeling of wonder.

The sun dropped below the horizon. The world around them turned to deep blue and black. They lit the lamp for the compass, comforted by its yellow glow. The men rowed away into the night, leaving behind the mystery of what they had seen, knowing they would never forget it. Nobody would believe their story. Too fantastic, they would be told. Impossible. Such things don't exist. It is easy for landsmen to laugh, far too easy. They have never experienced the power of an ocean gale or the glory of a sunset at sea. At times, as the sun vanishes below the horizon, it does so in a brilliant flash of green, like an enormous bulb of a cosmic camera taking the image of the last seconds of day. The eerie green of Saint Elmo's fire as it crawls up the masts and spars and washes down the decks, even the most basic and simple flash of phosphorescence, are mysteries to the landsman and would frighten him if he ever saw the phenomena with his own eyes. No mariner would deny that the men had seen something strange, and many would wonder what exactly it was.

A fitful west northwesterly wind came up during the night. But the sea remained calm. Friday, July 24, brought a morning of relative peace. The wind, it seemed, had abandoned them. But since they did not need it, its absence didn't bother the men in the least. They rowed on through the early hours of the day, and in late morning the sail of a ship appeared over the horizon, just off to their left. Their long days at sea with so little contact with people had bred in them a very sociable streak. They craved the sound of voices, the connection to others. They also wanted to procure some kerosene, if any could be had.

They made up their minds to row up to the ship, which proved an easy task. Its sails hung limp on the yardarms. On this day at least, the *Fox* had the advantage over the sailing vessel, a bark, larger than the *Cito*, bound for England with a load of lumber from the forests of Canada. Like the *Cito*, the ship hailed from Norway. It was the *Eugen* out of Christiania, the capital of the country. The captain, Axel Bache, was about thirty-five years old and wore a full black beard. He peered over the bulwarks at the two men and listened as they told him their story. Like all the other sailors George and Frank had met, the captain and crew expressed great surprise that such a small boat could go so far with oars only. He invited them aboard and fed them a large meal. He also provided them with some extra stores and, most important to the men, a few gallons of kerosene for their temperamental stove.

George and Frank stowed the gifts from Captain Bache and invited him to examine the *Fox* and make a notation in the log. He climbed down the side of the ship and stepped gingerly into the boat. The added weight made her sink low. She rocked from side to side as he poked here and there. Convinced the men were telling the truth about having no mast or sail, he confirmed his findings in their log.

This is to certify that we met the rowboat Fox, of New York, on this day and examined her and found nothing that she could be propelled with except the oars.

July 24, 1896.

Axel Bache,
Master of the Eugen, of Christiania

Captain Bache began to look a little green. He steadied himself and said, "I don't believe I could stay an hour in this boat before I would get seasick."

"It's a calm day! You should have been with us during some of the storms we met, then you'd really know if you'd get seasick or not," George said, laughing.

"She's a quick boat," Frank said, smiling.

"Well, it's a little too much for me," Captain Bache said, and quickly climbed back aboard the *Eugen*. He seemed very happy to stand again on a stable deck that did not move at the slightest shift of weight.

"Thank you for the kerosene and the provisions," they shouted. "We'll now be able to enjoy a bit of coffee and warm food."

"We'll report you to the London papers when we reach Swansea."

The *Fox* left the *Eugen* in her wake. The sailor becalmed is never an experience one would wish on another. Wind breathes life into a sailing vessel and, under a press of canvas, drives it forward and the waves are felt less. Without the wind, the sails hang lifeless against spars and rigging as the ship rolls in the swell. But the men welcomed the calm, knowing it would not last for long and that the *Eugen* would soon have the wind she needed. That was the way of things at sea.

For the next six days the *Fox* traveled at a good clip, averaging well over fifty miles per day. The weather remained fair for the North Atlantic, meaning that no gales assaulted them. Spots of clear weather intermixed with squalls and rain showers. Occasionally the seas showed their malice, tumbling down in boiling white froth. The sea itself changed color, looked more green than black now. Even the waves appeared different, not as long now. They were steeper and more dangerous near the coast, particularly when driven before a high wind against an opposing tide. The men suffered from cold during the predawn hours on most days. The clamminess of the air chilled them; the rain soaked their clothes.

The signs of life nearer to shore increased. They sighted sunfish. Huge, over ten feet long, and flounder-like, the fish rested languidly on the surface of the swells, taking in whatever warmth the weak beams of the sun had to offer. The common seagull, known throughout much of the world for its strident cries and insatiable appetite, became more numerous, as did species of seabirds that only fly a few hundred miles offshore. Ships also increased in number. Like their winged counterparts, both served as harbingers of land. The spirits of the men soared. According to George's figures and based on several sun sights taken during this time, they were right on course for the Scilly Islands, where they intended to stop and report their successful crossing.

Nearly two months at sea in a boat no larger than an inshore fishing skiff seemed incredible even to them. That and the fact that they had nearly made it across the fierce Atlantic, and at such a quick rate of speed, flooded them with pride. By now barnacles had begun to grow on the boat's bottom. They had to adjust her trim by shifting the water more evenly in the fore and aft tanks, even filling one of them with seawater to add extra weight. The *Fox* had left heavily laden, but she rode high and light now, and that could create problems if a gale arose. She would skitter across the waves, difficult or impossible to control, especially without a sea anchor. The men wisely took every precaution lest their joy dare the sea to rob them of a victory so close at hand. They still had many miles to row before the Scilly Islands loomed up out of the English fog and still more to row across the English Channel to Le Havre.

On Friday, July 31, the men sighted a weather-beaten, three-masted schooner near enough to justify a course change to intercept it. As they got closer to the ship, they tried to read its name, painted in large letters on the stern. The language was unfamiliar to them.

"It looks like Japanese," George said. "I can't make out what kind of letters these are."

"Give it up. We'll be alongside any minute and we'll soon see what nationality the ship is."

Eight bearded men lined the rail, looking at them without the surprise George and Frank had noted upon meeting vessels much farther out to sea. Small boats routinely fished off the English coast. The *Fox* now had assumed an air of the usual. She might have been just another of the local fishing fleet.

"What is your longitude?" George shouted.

In broken English, a large man whom they identified as the captain asked, "Longitude? You are fishermen, no?"

"Not fishermen," George said. He tried to explain who they were and where they had come from but to no avail. The captain didn't understand.

"What is our position?" George asked again, a little frustrated that the man didn't seem to comprehend the meaning of the word longitude. At last he understood and went below. The crew of the *Fox* attempted to speak with the crew of the *Jacob*, which hailed from a port deep inside Czar Nicholas's Russia. Although they had not much success in their efforts, they understood that the schooner had come from Mexico and was bound for Falmouth in Cornwall to receive orders on where to pick up the next cargo. The captain returned to the afterdeck and confirmed their position, roughly thirty-five miles east of Bishop Rock, which marks the southern reefs along the Scilly Islands and the outer approaches to Bristol Channel leading up the western shore of Cornwall and the English Channel to the east of Land's End.

"If the weather holds, we'll have our feet on dry land tomorrow!" George said.

"Then let's row, George. We're closing a dangerous coast. It would do well to make landfall in daylight," Frank said.

Throughout the rest of the day the men enjoyed the warm, sunny weather. They watched ships steam past at regular intervals, more often than at any time since they set off from New York City fifty-five days ago. Around sundown a thick haze reduced visibility to several miles around sundown. Toward midnight, they started looking for the loom of Bishop Rock Light, its revolving white beam visible on a clear night for up to twenty-four miles out to sea. Craning their necks over their shoulders, they peered ahead of the *Fox* every few minutes. No light appeared long after they should have seen it.

23

Too excited, and anxious to reach land, the men set no watches through the night and early morning of Saturday, August 1. George's shoulders and arms moved in tandem with Frank's strokes on the oars. Every now and then Frank corrected for deviations in the compass course, trying to keep as due east as possible, which George had said would put them south of Bishop Rock Light but still within range of sighting it. When they were sure of their position relative to the light, they would work their way up the east side of the Scillies, where there were fewer shoals to concern them.

George had been accurate in his navigation for three thousand miles of the crossing, and Frank trusted beyond a doubt that he knew what he was doing. Nevertheless, the misgivings common among mariners when they close a coast for the first time after months at sea still found a home in his thoughts. A coast brings with it swift tides, reefs, and shipping which pose a danger of collision. Although Frank had never been to the Scilly Islands, their reputation was well known among all mariners who plied the sea long distances in sailing ships.

In proportion to their size, no other island group on earth boasted more shipwrecks per square mile. The bones of hundreds of stricken ships dotted the rough granite bottom of the sea around the Scillies, a scant twenty-five miles west of Land's End. In certain places among the 140 islets and rocks crammed into an area of just six square miles, layers of wrecks stacked one on top of the other beyond the sheer cliffs, pocked with sea caves. During winter gales, a ship caught west of the Scillies either ended up on the rocks there or suffered the same fate farther north, on the western reaches of the Cornwall coast, embayed with a lethal west wind to drive the vessel to ruin. Ships bound for Falmouth, Plymouth, Southampton, and other ports along the English side of the channel separating the island from mainland Europe had to skirt the Scillies as well. Only a fool would navigate them lightly.

The position the Russian captain furnished the day before could have been erroneous. If the *Fox* did not keep on a course to set them south of Bishop Rock, the men could find themselves among the reefs on the west edge of the Scillies. To end the voyage with the boat broken on the sharp outcrops, the last fingers of Cornwall protruding to seaward, was simply unthinkable. The near loss of their charts during the storm added to their anxiety. Before the journey they had sewn a canvas tube to hold the charts and painted it. When the paint hardened, it formed a waterproof seal, much the same way decks were constructed with a layer of canvas on top which was then painted. Yet the seawater easily found its way in while the tube was completely submerged during the capsize, rendering the charts almost illegible.

The men rowed on through a light fog. As the first hints of gray to the east formed on the horizon, the flash of a lighthouse punched through the mist just off the left side of the bow, exactly where George said it would be. They rested on their oars for a moment and gazed at the light, checking the pattern of its flashes to be certain it was the one they had been looking for all night. Neither of them took for granted that it was Bishop Rock. Tides run fast in the waters around England and France. The currents, churning unseen except in the notorious tidal races found in these parts, accounted for many of the wrecks that littered the reefs; the set of a rapid current can make even holding a steady compass course lead to disaster.

"We've made it, Frank. We've made it right on course with a whole ocean behind us!" Although George was not an inordinately proud or arrogant man, he felt justified in rejoicing at his accomplishment. To navigate a rowboat across three thousand miles of open sea, compensating for the push and pull of the Gulf Stream, the influence of wind and wave, the mistakes that are all part of dead reckoning and shooting the sun, was something his teachers at the navigation school he had attended in Brevik and his fellow pilots in New York harbor would have commended. He laughed out loud and smiled at Frank in the dim light.

"You hit the nail on the head," Frank said. "And people said it couldn't be done!"

They rowed slowly and steadily without unduly exerting themselves. The long days at sea had sapped most of their energy, leaving them exhausted but in good spirits at the prospect of an imminent landfall. The skin on the backs of their hands, rubbed raw from the chafe of the oilskins, pained them greatly. They desired relief and rest for their bodies and minds.

The hundred-foot tower of Bishop Rock became visible as the sun came up and thinned the fog. It stood as a lonely sentinel out in the midst of a sea of rocks. Six years earlier, it had been rebuilt after serving for thirty years without fail. Even during a wicked spring storm in April 1874, when waves rose high enough to reflect the beams of the light back into the faces of the two frightened lighthouse keepers on station at the time, the light stood strong against the elements. Seeing its comforting flashes on this calm morning, the men were filled with gratitude that the sea had let them pass. It had tested them, but ultimately it had been a friend.

The black craggy cliffs of the Scillies emerged from the lingering wisps of fog about two hours later. The rumble of the groundswell breaking on the reefs reached them. The white streaks of broken waves contrasted against the grayish hue of the weak sun pushing through the layer of mist that hung close to the surface of the water. Thousands of seabirds surrounded the *Fox*, both in flight and in repose atop the swells. Gannets, razorbills, gulls, terns, and shearwaters winged over head. The birds covered the water ahead of the *Fox* and seemed disinclined to get out of the way. The men took care not to hit any with the oars as they rowed along the edge of the reefs.

They were struck by the warmth of these islands after spending so long a time in the cold, wet embrace of the North Atlantic. Situated in a weak arm of the warm North Atlantic Current and blessed with the balmy prevailing winds blowing from the south and southwest during the summer months, the Scillies enjoyed average temperatures in the low sixty degree range, mild enough to allow subtropical plants to grow. The Scillians grew flowers and vegetables for sale in London, and since they were available much earlier than any produce from farms on the mainland, some of the islanders earned a modest profit from their labors. The main industry of the Scillies, however, was fishing, and one of the local fleet drew into view as the *Fox* got close to the shore.

As the charts the men had were practically useless, they rowed over to the boat to ask the three men in it some questions, not the least of which was if these islands were equipped with a telegraph station. Since 1866, when the Great Eastern completed laying the first truly functional transatlantic telegraph cable across the North Atlantic, the Old and the New Worlds had been linked with a means of instant communication. Some more poetic journalists at the time termed it "a thread of thought" linking the continents. More than one dozen cables had been laid subsequent to this incredible feat of engineering, which entailed laying cable from Valentia, Ireland, to Heart's Content, Newfoundland. The proliferation of the telegraph had reached deep into the American countryside and spawned the advent of wire services, such as the United Press. It did not seem unreasonable to George or Frank to expect to find a communications center on these remote, windswept islands.

"Good morning," George and Frank said to the men.

They returned the salutation.

"Is there a signal station on these islands?" George asked.

The men nodded, and one of them pointed north toward St. Mary's, the largest of the Scillies and not very large at that. They gave George and Frank directions around the reefs. "Look for the light at Peninnis Head; you'll see it plain. There's a striped buoy off the entrance to Hugh Town's harbor. Make your turn in from there. . . . Are you men shipwrecked? Is that what you're doing out here, then?"

By this time George and Frank were used to repeating their story. They had gotten it down to the very epitome of brevity. Later, when they exhibited the *Fox*, they would add a little more drama to their tale. The fishermen looked more closely at the Fox and its crew.

"We heard about you fellows in the papers last week. It's a wonderful thing you have done. Your boat—she's a trim little craft, I'd say. A real beauty."

Captain Bache had been true to his word, then, the men thought. He had reported them as soon as he had reached Swansea. They looked at the *Fox* with discerning eyes. In truth, the fishermen were right. She did look very good despite the long passage. Better than the men who had rowed her, in fact, their skin burned almost black, their oilskins worn and tattered. Much of her paint was still in good shape. Only the barnacles along the waterline revealed that she had been in the water for a long time. Inside, the gear was stowed in good order; shipshape and in Bristol fashion.

"What are you men fishing for?" Frank asked.

An elderly man, obviously the father of the younger men, spoke in a kindly way, with a thick Cornish accent quite distinct from that of a Londoner or Scot. He said he came from his little house in Penzance, on the mainland of Cornwall, to the Isles of Scilly to fish for lobster during the summer months. "We ship 'em out of here from St. Mary's on a steamer which calls regular. We got a little hut to live in. We do the best we can with what we have," he said.

"Well, we should get on our way," George said. "Thank you for the directions."

A short time later, George and Frank spotted another boat working close along the shores of the islands, which, while rugged and remote, held an austere beauty not unlike that of some locations in Norway. They decided it was high time to show the ship's colors. Up went the pole with its wet American flag. The light breeze caused the material to flutter and dry as the men rowed toward the boat they had seen. Strangely, the two men in the boat appeared frightened at the sight of the flag. They rowed away from the *Fox* as fast as they could.

"We'll show them who's fastest in a rowboat, eh, George?" Frank said. He put his muscle into it, and his friend followed suit. The *Fox* flew across the water toward the other rowboat, gaining on it with every pull of the oars. The men in the other boat stopped rowing and waited, convinced that these two strangers could outrow them even on their best day.

"Are we on the right course for St. Mary's?" George asked.

The man nodded, then asked, "You strangers here?" Thinking there might be some money to be made, he offered to pilot them into the harbor "real cheap." The Scilly Islands, and for that matter the people along the Cornish coast, lived very difficult lives. Much of the wealth of England never trickled down to its southernmost reaches. In days gone by, the peasants worked in the tin and copper mines for little pay, and many still did. Their poverty induced them in certain cases to take to wrecking, to luring ships onto the rocks with false beacons, adding to the peril of ships caught off the shores during a bad storm. The man hoped to cash in on the ignorance of these two disheveled-looking seamen, but George and Frank had other ideas.

"No, we're in no need of a pilot. The day is calm, and if we do run aground, we'll have no trouble getting our little vessel off again," George said.

"Well, since there will be no job for me and my boy, I'll tell you how to go." He warned the men about a nasty rock directly ahead and confirmed the directions they had received from the lobstermen. "But for only three shillings I'll guide you right into the harbor," he said in a last attempt to receive some pay for his trouble.

After declining his offer again, George and Frank cheerfully thanked him and were on their way. Soon the *Fox* rounded a small headland, and the men could see Hugh Town spread out before them. The wreck of a steamer, crushed and broken, with its masts poking up out of the smooth water, lay at the feet of a fortresslike building constructed on high land above the harbor. It was Star Castle, built in 1593. The men could see a man on the ramparts looking down at them as they passed and rowed through the fleet of small fishing boats anchored off a large stone pier where ships loaded and offloaded their cargos.

"It seems seeing the Stars and Stripes flying from a rowboat has caught people's attention," George said dryly. "Look at the crowd gathering there on the pier."

Frank looked over his shoulder and back at his friend. He smiled. "We'll have a warm welcome to England."

Once alongside the pier, the men secured the *Fox* to ring bolts built into the stone. Stairs had been cut into the stone to allow crews of small boats to climb up and down as the tide ebbed and flooded. At low tide, a square-rigged vessel drawing twenty feet would be left on the bottom, with much of her copper sheathing below the waterline bare to the sun. The small fishing boats closest to shore would rest on the mud and float free as the tide rose and fell every six hours.

The crowd of people peered over the edge of the quay at George and Frank and shouted down to them.

"What is the meaning of your American flag? Where do you hail from?"

"We are the rowboat *Fox* en route from New York to Havre!" George yelled, his voice exuberant, as though he were making a formal announcement, and indeed he was. "We've come here for a few provisions and to let the world know we are alive and well and have accomplished the extraordinary task of crossing the Atlantic Ocean in a rowboat!"

The crowd cheered. The men let the sound of the shouts and clapping sweep over them, soaking up every word of praise. This was the first of many such experiences, and they were filled with hope for the future. The crowd milled around on the wharf above the *Fox*, buzzing with excitement. In St. Mary's the pace of life was slow, and any type of happening out of the ordinary was bound to attract a good deal of attention. Anxious to get ashore at last, George climbed the steps leading to the pier. His knees felt weak, and a dizzy spell hit him. Mortified, he felt himself about to fall overboard in front of all the people—the great seaman takes a splash! He caught hold of the handrail at the last moment and hauled himself to his feet, swaying to and fro as sailors do when setting foot on land after a long voyage. It took all his strength to keep from falling down.

Frank joined him on the pier, and the two of them shook hands all around. Some wealthy gentlemen approached them, and after another warm round of congratulations, they asked what might be done to help the *Fox*'s crew. They took George and Frank to see John Banfield, the U.S. consul agent stationed on the Scilly Islands, a very accommodating man with the greatest respect for their accomplishment. He changed some of the money George had brought with him to English pounds and agreed to come down to the boat to examine it.

"Won't you join me for tea at my home?" he asked. "I would like to hear about your adventure in more detail."

George and Frank looked at the fellow, all dressed in fine clothes, his skin as clean as if he had just bathed, not a hair out of place. Then they looked at each other, decked out in grimy oilskins and pants and seaboots. The clothing they wore underneath was all they had with them, nor did they have any shoes. "No, we couldn't possibly come to your home as we are now," George said. "We wouldn't think it right."

"Oh, nonsense. It would be my pleasure to serve you a good meal after you've bought your groceries."

Not wishing to insult the official, they accepted. As they walked down the street, swaying like drunks because of their unsteady legs, the people of Hugh Town stopped and stared. Back at the boat, they loaded their fresh provisions and rested, at least as much as possible in view of the steady stream of Scillians who stopped by to chat and look at the boat. Banfield wrote his certification in their log.

Scilly, 1st August, 1896

I certify that at 11:00 a.m. the boat "Fox" of New York arrived at this port having onboard George Harbo and Frank Samuelsen, who stated that they had rowed said boat from New York, and on examination I have every reason to correct this report.

John Banfield, U.S. Consul Agent

Banfield, his wife, and daughter treated the men to a pleasant tea. It was an honor for both men to sit in the parlor of an American consul, and the hour or so passed quickly. They gave Banfield brief notes to telegraph to their families to let them know they were safely across the Atlantic. After the commotion of the day, fatigue settled over them, and they walked back to the *Fox*, where photographers waited to take pictures of them and the boat for the London papers. Soon the news of their arrival would be telegraphed to the major papers in western Europe and across time zones back to the United States.

While the men slept at anchor out in the harbor ready to depart the next day on the rest of their voyage, the reporters for newspapers in New York and New Jersey typed their stories. Most of the accounts were not voluminous, but many did appear on the front pages. Harold, George's brother, in Jersey City, saw the dispatch in the *Newark News*. The headline read simple, plain, and to the point—"Rowed Across The Ocean"—with a subhead tailored for the New Jersey readers: "Harbo and Samuelsen, the adventurous Jerseyans, have about successfully completed their hazardous voyage."

Caroline, Frank's sister, and the relatives she was staying with read of it in the *Nordisk Tildende*, a large-circulation paper serving the enclave of Norwegians living in Brooklyn and the surrounding area. The families of both men in Norway read of their safe passage early the following week.

By August 2, a stack of the daily papers in New York sat on the desk in Richard Kyle Fox's commodious offices in Franklin Square. He picked up the Sunday *New York Times*, that ever-so-staid paper. It was the antithesis of the *Police Gazette* if anything was. Nestled in among the front-page headlines about corruption in Tammany Hall, steamships damaged on their passage across the Atlantic, and London's quivering about the status of the Russian czar, was a story about his two intrepid Norwegians.

Have Rowed Across The Ocean

Harbo and Samuelsen Reach the Scilly Islands Worn Out.

He had to laugh at that. Worn out. So typical a statement of the obvious. Would the men be anything but a bit tired after rowing for three thousand miles? He read on.

London—Aug. 1—A dispatch from the signal station on the Scilly Islands states that the rowboat *Fox.* . . .

Ah, he thought, the *Fox!* How it must have rankled the editors to print the name of the man they all thought beneath them, not worthy of the respect paid to a copy boy. He continued reading.

> The rowboat *Fox* passed there at 11:00 o'clock this morning after a passage of fifty-five days from New York. The two occupants of the boat were well but somewhat exhausted from the effects of their long row. The masters of the Norwegian barks Cito and Eugen, both of whom spoke the *Fox* at sea, examined the boat when they spoke her and gave certificates that oars were the only propelling power used. . . .They are the first men to cross the Atlantic in a rowboat.

Fox scanned the rest of the story but found no mention of the promised *Police Gazette* medals or any direct reference to his support and encouragement of the adventure. But then, he really hadn't expected that from the *New York Times*. The *New York Herald*, maybe, but not the *Times*. As he went through the rest of the story, he smiled the thin smile of a man who has won on a tricky roll of the dice.

> Battery boatmen were greatly surprised yesterday when they learned that the rowers had reached the other side. They had all given best wishes to the adventurers, but predicted to a man that their destination was Davy Jones's locker.

24

Late Sunday afternoon, August 2, the *Fox* got under way with a fair tide behind her to help boost her progress out of the harbor and down the English Channel. The men had waited for the favorable tide, which turned at around six o'clock, and took advantage of the quiet aboard the boat to rest. Ashore, a crowd cheered as Frank hauled in the anchor. Both men unshipped the oars and set out toward Wolf Rock Light.

Le Havre lay about 250 miles to the east. George decided against a direct, nonstop passage through the often rough waters just north of the Channel Islands and Cherbourg, France. The tidal range of forty feet in the vicinity of the islands creates fearsome tidal races, most notably the Alderney Race, between Alderney and the Normandy peninsula. On an incoming tide the current there runs nearly ten knots, a phenomenal speed which turns the ocean into a seething cauldron of standing, breaking waves. With a strong easterly or northeasterly wind the conditions would be far more dangerous for the *Fox* than a gale in the open sea.

Instead, he thought it best to hug the English coast as much as possible and cross the channel from Start Point, a headland that would give them at least a little help in that it somewhat narrowed the crossing between England and France. The coastal course also gave them the option of putting into a harbor at night to rest if the weather turned foul. Frank agreed with the strategy. Neither had any stomach left for battling the sea or an ill-tempered English Channel. They rowed on through the night, sighting Wolf Rock Light at around midnight and passing it at daybreak. This, too, was a lonely, rugged light built on rocks and ledges, with no land in sight.

In good health throughout the entire crossing, both men now felt sick. The tremors and chill of fever caused them to break out into cold sweats. They each suffered the effects of bad colds and not only found their symptoms an additional hardship but also quite a surprise. Their contact with their fellow man had been welcome, needed. It hadn't occurred to them that their disease-free environment had spared them from the common maladies of life ashore. They tried to ignore the symptoms and kept to the oars in spite of their desire to sleep.

The morning of Monday, August 3, ushered in a strong northeast wind. With all of the English Channel to cross, soon the waves began to build, but not in the same way as they did far from land. The waves came very close together and were steep. The lines of them marching across the channel resembled the serrated teeth of a wood saw. Cold spray flew over the bow, drenching Frank and blowing back at George. They rowed hard toward Lizard Point, a land-mass that juts out from the coast to create a prominent headland. With wind and waves against them, the progress had been slow, and when they got out from under the protection of the land, the seas and wind strengthened. They were close enough inshore to see the waves send sheets of spray into the air around Lizard Point. The tidal stream flowing past the headland churned the water into confused, dangerous breakers.

"I'm tired of these waves," George yelled to Frank over his shoulder. "What do you say we put in for the night. There are plenty of harbors close by."

Frank needed no convincing. They made for a little fishing port at Coverack Cove and entered the harbor just before dark. Tied up to a rickety old pier, with plenty of line fore and aft of the boat to allow for the rise and fall of the tide, the men breathed easier and rested. News of the *Fox*'s arrival spread quickly through the village, and soon a crowd gathered around the boat. The villagers peppered the men with questions, which, though they were dog-tired and still feeling ill, they answered freely and with as much good cheer as possible. A young girl brought them apples and a large chunk of fruitcake. Her kindness touched them, and they thanked her and her family for the gift. Before turning in for the night, they had eaten most of the cake.

The following day, the wind still blew from the northeast as the *Fox* set off at around six o'clock in the morning, again with a favorable tide. The people of England were kind, but the coast, it seemed, was decidedly inhospitable. The men considered themselves lucky, however. If they had still been out to sea when the winds shifted to their present direction, the *Fox* would have been blown back for many miles in the wrong direction. Without a sea anchor, every hour would have marked a terrible loss of energy and effort, and their spirits certainly would have suffered from it. As it was, the weather induced them to lay up instead of bashing against the elements. George and Frank hugged the shoreline, and toward noontime they nosed under the protective lee of Gull Rock and dropped anchor. They enjoyed a leisurely dinner of fresh food purchased at Hugh Town, including the last of the fruitcake for dessert.

The wind blew even stronger in the afternoon, right in the direction they wanted to row. The sea once again seemed intent on driving their bodies and minds to the limit. However, there was land with many harbors nearby. The prospect of putting into one at the end of the day for another good meal and a full night's rest comforted them as they slogged onward, wet, tired, and miserably sick. They had been granted safe passage across a mighty ocean, and for all intents and purposes their voyage was finished. Neither of them desired further testing. They simply wanted to end the journey and get on with their lives, hopefully reaping some reward for being the first to cross the sea in a rowboat. Toward evening, they rowed into the fishing port of Goran Haven. With the *Fox* safely tied up to a dock, they prowled around the waterfront for a little while before getting another night of undisturbed rest.

The wind shifted more to the east during the night and still did not let up on Wednesday, August 5. Nevertheless, the men pushed on, and to their immense relief the wind slowly diminished during the afternoon and shifted to the south. Confused seas resulted, making the *Fox* pitch and roll frightfully. They passed the forlorn-looking Eddystone Light, whipped with driving spray from breakers on the shoals to the south of the bustling port of Plymouth. The setting sun caught the tiny droplets of spray in an orange light that bathed the structure in showers of diamonds; a long, dark shadow extended eastward where the light blocked the sun as it sank quickly down beyond Land's End. On three separate occasions the storms of the North Atlantic destroyed this light, killing its keepers, and its attendant history added to the scene that at once inspired majesty and awe.

The night passed in familiar hardship. The wind switched back to its northerly quarter and commenced to blow at nearly thirty knots. The long hours they had spent weeks on end out in the North Atlantic had been nothing compared to these. The closer they came to the completion of the voyage, the slower time seemed to pass. It is well known among sailors that time is merely a relative term; it either dashes past like a well-bred horse or plods along like a stubborn mule, intent on moving at a crawl. The cold and wet leeched their strength. The good meals and rest could make up only just so much for the toil they endured. They desperately needed time to recoup their energy.

Foot by foot they rowed the *Fox* toward Start Point. The headland loomed ahead in the early-morning gray and came abreast of them at around eight o'clock. Both men yearned for some fresh bread, fruit, and other foods they did not have with them. Not far away was the port of Salcombe. Its close proximity and the comforts it offered proved far too much of a temptation for George and Frank to resist. They laid a course into the harbor.

Again, a crowd gathered on the quay shortly after they arrived. The warm welcome and the appreciation among the people for what George and Frank had accomplished lessened the physical pain, allowing them to feel that the ordeal had indeed been worth the undertaking. The newspapermen in the town interviewed them and sent reports of their progress back to London, where it was telegraphed to those publications that had been following the story. The news that the men were at last on the final leg of the voyage to Le Havre set the waterfront in that port alight with excitement.

After buying the provisions they wanted, George

and Frank reluctantly put back out into the English Channel for the last long row in open water. They had roughly 160 miles to go before reaching Le Havre. It could take at least three days, possibly more if the north winds continued to blow—one reason they had put into Salcombe. If they were to spend another three days at the oars, at least they could ensure that they had enough good food to eat.

About four miles off Start Point, a small steamer hove into view, the *Bamburgh*, out of Newcastle. It laid a course directly for them and slowed to a stop upwind of the boat, creating a lee and some smoother water with its hull. George and Frank stood ready to row the *Fox* out of danger in the event the steamer drifted down on them; out of the wind, the *Fox*'s drift slowed significantly. However, the ship's movement through the water was quite slow—her master knew what he was about. George had lain under the lee of many a ship in a small boat while serving as a pilot in New York, and he recognized the seamanship behind how the captain had positioned his vessel.

"Have you any fresh fish aboard?" the captain called down to them, thinking they were fishermen.

"No, we don't," George said. "We've come from New York and are bound for Le Havre."

"New York?" After a moment, he said, "Well, I guess you haven't any fish, then. We're bound for Rouen. We'll pass right by Le Havre on our way up the Seine. If you want a tow in, we'll take you."

Without much thought to the matter, the men agreed that a tow sounded like a fine idea. They called back to the captain, "Thank you very much. That would be good."

One of the crew threw a long, thick line over the side. The men rowed the *Fox* over to it, picked it up, and Frank made it fast to the bow. When the captain was certain his little charge was securely linked up with his ship, he ordered the engines to slow ahead and gradually increased his speed to full. Far astern, out of the wash of the propellers, the *Fox* sped through the waves, sending buckets of spray over the foredeck into the boat. The long line acted much like a lever. The boat tracked first to the left, then to the right, and each time a wave hit her just at the proper angle, she tried to dip her rails under.

"Hold on, George, we're in for a rough ride to Le Havre!" Frank yelled, the wind whipping his words aft to George. He looked over at his friend and found him smiling, absolutely beaming. He was wedged in low to add stability to the boat, his hands on the rails, the wind tousling his straggly red hair.

"Happy to be free of the oars at last!" George said. "At this rate we'll be in France tomorrow morning."

The steamer plunged through the water at a little over ten knots. Towing a small boat at such speeds was not safe. The captain looked back periodically to see that the men were coping well. He had a schedule to meet and couldn't proceed any slower. Besides, he thought, the boat looked as if it was handling the waves just fine. Those were tough men aboard. As the hours passed and the boat still did not capsize, he satisfied himself that all would be well when night came and he couldn't see the little craft any longer.

The night was as wet as any George and Frank endured except during the worst blows. Sleep was impossible. The boat required constant bailing. But they didn't mind much, not now that the end was counted in hours instead of days, weeks, and months. As the sun came up, the men got their first view of France. The land emerged from the Baie de Seine ahead and on both sides of the boat, and before long it became more distinct in character, quite unlike the rocky Scillies. These lands appeared inviting, almost gentle.

The *Bamburgh* passed the lights marking the Banc de Seine, where the water starts to grow shallow as a result of the aeons of silt carried down the meandering river out into the estuary to its mouth. It flowed nearly five hundred miles though northern France from its source at Mont Tasselot in Burgundy, through Champagne, down to Normandy and the sea, carrying with it the waters needed to quench the thirsts of millions along its shores and to transport goods aboard small steamers and barges above Rouen to Paris. The port of Le Havre lay just three miles ahead, south of Cap de la Heve. The men felt the *Fox* slow. The line went slack.

"We'll be off now," the captain cried from the stern. "Good luck with the rest of your adventure!"

George and Frank waved. "Thank you for the tow . . . Thank you!"

The *Bamburgh* retrieved its towline. Whitewater churned under the transom as she gathered way. The men watched her slide eastward toward the mouth of the Seine. They unshipped their oars for the row into Le Havre. About a mile off the harbor entrance, George proudly put up the American flag, and as they continued to row, it lifted to the gentle west wind that had come in during the night to replace its cold, harsh counterpart from the north.

25

Le petit bateau! Le petit bateau! Shouts and cheers from the crowd gathered at the large pier in front of the American consulate rang out over the smooth water of Le Havre. Neither George nor Frank spoke French, but they understood the words "little boat" well enough as they rowed toward the throng among the schooners and barges and steamers moored in the harbor. The sheer size of the crowd overwhelmed them; a wall of bodies blackened the top edge of the wharf from which stone buildings rose to form a backdrop. This was no little village but a thriving port filled with people, all of whom seemed to be present on the pier, waving and jumping and pushing to catch a glimpse of the two men and their *petit bateau*.

The scene struck them as surreal. They had longed for this moment ever since the idea for the voyage took root that hazy day on Sandy Hook Bay, and yet its full impact did not make itself felt in the way they had imagined it would. Tired, wet, and hungry, the men were joyous at the end of their trip and somehow depressed at the same time. The achievement of any goal after great travail does not necessarily bring forth feelings of ecstasy. Rather, it is often a sense of relief and wonder that settle over one's mood at such moments.

George and Frank tied the *Fox* fast to the quay and stepped unsteadily into the mass of people, barely able to stand. The crowd pushed in close, clapped them on the back, and shook their hands. They spoke in quick, unintelligible bursts of words, gesturing with their hands. They seemed more excited at the arrival of these two weather-beaten seamen than the two men themselves. George and Frank stood there, stunned at the reception and deeply moved by the warm smiles of the people. They tried to move through the crowd, but to no avail. A sea of humanity, growing larger and more boisterous with each moment, pressed in on them. After their time on the open ocean, the situation induced a desperate need for space, to think and breathe, to take in the moment in peace.

"You are very great men," a man who had managed to shove his way not too gently through the crowd said. "You want to go to the consulate, no?"

"Yes, we would like that, sir," George said.

The man shouted in French to the people nearest them to make way. With some additional shoving, the three men forced their way through the crowd to the American consulate, a short distance from the water's edge. Inside, the staff ringed them and offered their congratulations as well. C. W. Chancellor, the American consul responsible for administering the business of the United States in the harbor of Le Havre, shook their hands enthusiastically.

"I have heard all about you gentlemen," he said. "Your country is proud of you."

He handed George a letter. Before leaving New York City, George had sent a registered letter to himself care of the American consulate in Le Havre. In

it was a small sum of money, which he rightly thought
would come in handy.

"Thank you very much. This will be much needed,
I think," George said.

He put the letter unopened into the pocket of his
oilskins. He looked around at the fine appointments
of the room, the decorative wood and stonework, the
carpets. There they stood in dirty, worn oilskins, the
clothing beneath them rank with the odor of sweat
and salt and worn to tatters, their feet encased in
damp seaboots. The backs of their hands revealed
raw deep-red flesh. Their faces were burned black
and covered with weeks of stubble, their hair long and
matted. What a sorry sight we are, George thought as
one of Chancellor's clerks photographed them. The
flash of the camera momentarily blinded him, and
in that instant the impact of the moment hit him.
The men standing around them and every detail of
the room burned itself into his brain, and he knew
he would never forget, not ever, what it was like to
be welcomed to France in this way.

"There are a bunch of reporters here to see you two
fellows," one of the consulate staff said. He grinned.
"You're the talk of the town, it seems."

"Talk of the nation, more like," another man said.

"You go tell the press your incredible story," Chancellor said. "I'll see to getting you a cab so you can
find lodgings."

The newspapermen pressed close, asking what
seemed like a thousand questions so quickly that
George and Frank could barely understand.

"Why did you row across the ocean?" was among
the first queries.

George could have tried to sound noble, to inflate
the reasons to the point of incredulity. But he didn't.
He simply stated that they had wanted to prove that
it was indeed possible to row across the North Atlantic,
that he and his friend wanted to set the record straight

for those who thought it impossible. He also said he hoped to lecture and exhibit the boat.

"You believe the attraction will bring lines to the theaters?" a reporter asked.

"We think so. It will be something for people to see us and our little boat. Perhaps then they will believe nothing is impossible," George said.

"The boatmen at the Battery in New York City told us not to try our hand at this," Frank said in an unusual departure from his tendency to remain silent and in the background. "They said we'd end up in Davy Jones's locker. Our families tried to talk us out of the journey, too. Even when things got pretty bad out there, we felt we'd make it. We had to believe we would; otherwise, we would have died out there."

Satisfied for the moment, the reporters hurried off to file their stories. By nightfall the telegraphs in major newspaper offices on both sides of the Atlantic hummed with the story. Two Americans had rowed across the ocean and made their final landfall in France at 9:45, Friday, August 7, in the port of Le Havre after sixty-two days at sea. A new world record had been set and another "impossible" feat dispensed with.

The contribution to humanity of such feats was itself intangible, though the undertaking was in fact quite easily grasped. Did these two Americans compare to Charles Bonin, a Frenchman who just the previous year had crossed Tibet and Mongolia, opening up new vistas on the makeup of the world and its peoples? Did they compare to Englishman William Conway, who was the first to climb 23,000-foot peaks deep in the Himalayas in 1892, or to Hans Meyer of Germany, who scaled Kilimanjaro in 1889? And what of Fridtjof Nansen? He had set out to explore the North Pole in 1893 and presumably was still at sea.

Did these contemporary adventurers really give something to the world with their stunts and their often bombastic attitudes about their blessed ability to achieve what mere mortals could not?

The questions were sound, for no one really can understand what lies at the roots of a great achievement, not unless one has set out to undertake a personal journey and failed. It did not require individuals to scale great peaks, traverse barren, strange lands, or navigate the seas or snowcaps to catch a glimpse of why achievements such as George and Frank's held merit and not a little magic. It is the simple effort, the trying, even the failing, and the trying once again that often gives dull reality a modicum of meaning. It is the hope that though life may appear senseless, goodness may be impossible to grab for more than an instant, that the trying and dreaming and, sometimes, the succeeding lead us all to a better place.

The news reports rang out cheers for George and Frank. They held forth the notion that the impossible was breached once again by the tenacity of the human spirit. They sang the praises of the men's strength and courage and called them conquerors of the sea. Both of them knew all too well that the truth was different. They had conquered nothing but themselves, their own weaknesses. The sea was no more vanquished than the sun, the moon, or the stars. It had let them pass, but by no means was it tamed.

They climbed into a private cab and asked the driver to take them directly to the nearest public bathhouse. The hot water streamed over them, washing away the touch of the sea. The water soothed their split and chapped skin and the pain that shot through them whenever they walked or moved their arms too quickly. After cleaning up, they bought some clothes. The smell of the fresh garments pleased them. They began to feel more themselves, with a renewed connection to civilization. A good meal with some French wine reinforced their cheer.

Later in the afternoon, they sent telegrams to their families advising them that the voyage had come to a successful end and of their plans to exhibit the boat in Paris, London, Antwerp, Hamburg, Berlin, Stockholm, Copenhagen, and finally Christiania. They also telegraphed Richard Kyle Fox. He had hinted that he might lend a financial hand if they made it across and required his assistance. While the men were highly confident that the exhibitions would make them rich, they had very little money at the moment. If Fox would help them, so much the better. C. W. Chancellor made the final entry in their log.

United States Consulate, Havre, August 7, 1896

The rowboat *Fox*, George G. Harbo and Frank G. Samuelsen, arrived here at 9:45 a.m. today from New York, 62 days out.

C. W. Chancellor, consul

Chancellor also scrawled a detailed report of the voyage in his typically illegible, tight handwriting and filed it with his official documents. He described the men as exhausted but in good shape for all they had been through, though he remarked that their hands were in horrifying condition. When he had grasped their hands in congratulation, the skin felt like hardened leather.

George and Frank deposited their oilskins and old clothes in the *Fox* and placed the logbook back inside the aft watertight compartment. The crowd had thinned out considerably. However, many people still paused at the wharf and excitedly pointed at the boat.

They moved the *Fox* to a schooner moored in the harbor, where it would be away from any souls intent on procuring a souvenir. The captain and crew agreed to watch over her while the men slept ashore in soft featherbeds. For this day at least they lived in the lap of luxury.

26

The port of Le Havre had come far since its early days as a rugged little fishing village four centuries in the past. Its humble beginnings as one of the most important harbors in France began in 1517 when Francis I ordered a harbor of refuge built there to shelter the shipping that called at the mouth of the Seine with the staples needed upriver in Paris. The large ships, too deep and cumbersome to navigate the sweeping meanders of the river through the rich, verdant flatlands and low hills to Rouen, offloaded cargos for transport aboard smaller craft. Rouen's position seventy-five miles from the mouth of the Seine, at the eastern edge of the estuary, placed it above Le Havre both in geographic terms and in its importance to the great city, about 150 miles farther inland.

Still, later kings fortified the harbor and dredged its approaches to facilitate the comings and goings of cargo vessels through the Banc de Seine. It saw public-works projects to improve its maritime appeal through the reign of Napoleon III, when its stature and importance finally surpassed that of Rouen. Le Havre had become an outport of distant Paris, a key facility second only in importance to Marseilles, the jewel on the balmy Mediterranean Sea. The harbor's prosperity spawned a thriving town with splendid buildings, such as the Church of Notre Dame, built in the seventeenth century. A beautiful city, it impressed George and Frank as they walked the streets, taking in the bustle. The new mingled with the old everywhere they looked. It was very unlike New York, where the old buildings were torn down to make way for the skyscrapers, where the present gobbled up the past at a breakneck pace, displacing all that stood in its way.

On the docks, immigrants lined up to buy tickets for the trip across the Atlantic in one of the ships of the Compagnie Générale Transatlantique. The sight was familiar to both men. It reminded them of how far they had come since they had left their homes in Norway so long ago. They had great hopes for the future now. Even with only a few francs in their pockets, the same enthusiasm that seized them in their youth bubbled up in their souls—the world seemed to lie at their feet, was theirs for the taking. To Paris they would go. To Paris!

They arranged to exhibit the boat for just four days in Le Havre, thinking the financial rewards would be far greater in Paris. The crowds came to see the *Fox* and to hear their tale, and they made a sum of money that inspired further hopes for what lay ahead of them on their tour through Europe's shining cities. Anxious to be on their way, they stored some fresh provisions in the *Fox*, paid the port captain the taxes due, and headed upriver from Le Havre, leaving the English Channel astern in the boat's tiny wake. They could have paid for road transport; it would not have been difficult to secure. But they were practical down to their bones and chose to row instead of incurring unnecessary expenses.

The seamen round the wharves of Le Havre raised their eyebrows upon hearing that the men had decided to row all the way to Paris. Hadn't these men had enough time and toil at the oars? But they understood the self-reliance that the sea breeds and proffered advice the men dearly needed. La Seine, they said, was home to the formidable mascaret, a tidal bore similar to that found on the Severn River in England and the Petitcodiac River in Canada's Bay of Fundy.

Like these other rivers, the Seine empties into the sea where the tidal range is measured in yards, not simply feet. The fresh water flows down the narrow channels into a wider gulf, and it is here that the tide displays a strange kind of behavior. As it reaches the constriction of the land, it rolls itself up into a wave and surges upriver. Its power reverses the natural flow of fresh water and pushes it in front of the wave as it moves upstream. In the spring, when the moon tides are at their highest, the mascaret had been known to kill the unwary caught out on the dry flats at one moment and the next inundated under the cold weight of the flood. The men could expect to feel its power all the way to Rouen.

They listened carefully to the men of the Seine and timed their trip upriver to ensure that they did not get caught in front of the bore. When it passed, they set out, riding the current round bend after bend in the river. Coming in all at once as it does, the tide did not exactly cohere to its usual six-hour cycle, rising and falling at equal intervals. This meant the tide ran against them more than it favored them, a hardship they overcame by keeping as close to shore as possible, in the shallows where the current ran with less vigor. In fact, the Seine, they found, did not run swiftly at all, except at times of the mascaret. It proved quite an easy river to navigate, one filled with natural beauty and the intriguing culture of rural France.

Beyond Rouen, the Seine narrowed. It continued to twist and turn through the countryside for a time, then ran straight for some miles and commenced its twisting again. Tiny towns dotted the shore. Land birds filled the sky. After so long seeing nothing save the grim, cold colors of the sea all around them the greenery of their surroundings captivated them. The air hung heavy with the smells of farms, of life itself that had thrived in the rich alluvial soil left from the earlier days of the Seine, long before Paris took root on a tiny island tucked in a bend of the river.

The waterfront gradually began to show signs of the city beyond. Towns came closer together until they covered the shore. Behind them low hills created a picturesque view as the river valley spread out on either side of the boat. They passed the Oise, a major tributary below Paris. Barge traffic swarmed up and down the channel on either side of them, and boatmen shouted greetings. The *Fox* passed from the country into the heart of Paris. Stone quays and bulkheads fronted either shore as she glided under the arched bridges linking the sprawling districts on each side of the Ile de la Cité. Parisians out for the day rowed tiny boats on the river, sunned themselves along its banks, and lingered on the bridges to gaze at the shimmering reflections of the city's buildings in the deep black water. Pockets of squalor intermingled with the wealth, but that was the way of things in any big town, and it didn't surprise the men. They hardly noticed it as they took in all that their eyes beheld. Ashore, they walked the crowded streets, alive with horse-drawn cabs, omnibuses, open carriages, bicycles, and trams. Cafes, theaters, stores replete with all imaginable goods, palaces, businesses, and factories, all spoke of vitality, a modern center of one of the great countries of western Europe.

Above the city skyline loomed the Tour Eiffel, the tallest building in the world. Its wrought-iron skeleton narrowed into a single spire twice as high as the Great Pyramid of Giza. The Parisians had come to take the tower for granted since its construction in 1889 for the Centennial Exposition, a time of great celebration in memory of the changes that occurred as a result of the French Revolution a century earlier. But for any newcomer to the city, it was a marvel, and George and Frank admired its beauty.

The *Fox* went on display in a richly appointed room of an exhibition hall. The papers wrote of the event. George and Frank plastered fliers in the public parks, cafe windows, virtually anywhere they could. They had expected large crowds. These never materialized. Some visitors appeared disappointed.

"Is this all? It is only a little rowboat. This is nothing."

Others, most particularly the boatmen of the city, appreciated the *Fox* and the courage it took for George and Frank to put to sea in her. But the public's response failed to give rise to any bountiful rewards the men had envisioned prior to setting out from the Battery. They stayed for three weeks, trying to fan interest in their boat and their story. Finally, they gave up and left Paris by rail for the coast. They crossed the English Channel aboard a steamer and arrived in London still hopeful that the people of England, who had been so kind, would find the *Fox* sufficiently interesting to pay to see her.

Sensing that they required a little more drama in their act, George and Frank hatched a plan they hoped would work to their advantage. They billed themselves as Sons of the Sea. An actor, whom they hired despite the added expense, played the part of their father. He read and sang a monologue of the voyage while the men pretended to row the boat through calms and storms. At the height of the gale of July 10, the flash powder used in cameras puffed and blazed behind them to simulate a smoky lightning. Cymbals crashed to create a metallic thunder. The audience cheered and clapped. It seemed the idea had worked. The Sons of the Sea were a success at last.

However, the shillings charged for admission did not pile up in any significant way over the two months they spent in London exhibiting the *Fox* at the Royal Aquarium. The expenses involved in renting places to exhibit the *Fox*, the fee for the fliers, the pay for the actor, as well as travel and lodging costs, added up as they moved from London to Portsmouth, and other cities on the coast. A traveling show proved more expensive than either had considered. It was a deep disappointment to them both.

One night after counting up their lackluster take for the evening's show, they swallowed the bitter pill of their disappointment and canceled their plans to tour the other big cities originally on their schedule. No Antwerp, Hamburg, Stockholm, or Copenhagen. Their fame had burned brightly for mere seconds; their great voyage, so long and painful, had failed to live up to its imagined potential. The stress and crushing weight of it ate away at the men. George took up smoking. Frank grew more quiet than usual. At the exhibitions, with both of them dressed in their tattered oilskins and rain hats, he got a far-off look in his eyes, as if he were seeing a distant world unrelated to anything there in the thick of the audience, anxious for a thrill.

They could not fail, they simply couldn't, not after all they had been through to get to this point. It hadn't seemed possible at sea that the voyage would end in disaster no matter how terrible some of those long days and nights got. Now, though, once ashore in the cold reality of the city, it seemed that the physical undertaking of the crossing had been easier than the profiting by it. It had enriched the newspaper publishers, like Richard Kyle Fox and his promised *Police Gazette* medals, more than it had them.

The men sorely missed their families and yet had been ready to tour Europe for as long as it paid. Now they simply wanted to go home to Norway. Fridtjof Nansen had arrived in Christiania in September to great acclaim for reaching the highest latitude north yet reached by any expedition. George and Frank had every reason to believe they, too, would receive a warm welcome. They booked passage aboard a steamer bound for Christiania in the late fall with hope flickering back to life in their hearts.

27

The steamer slowly made its way toward the southern edge of Norway, leaving the lighthouse at Lindesnes miles off its port beam as it pressed on through the Skagerrack toward Christiania. The warmth of summer had gone from the coastal region of Sorlandet, one of the richest agricultural areas of the entire country and a favorite vacation retreat for much of the populace. Still, the last vestiges of the North Atlantic Current exerted a moderating influence on the climate compared to that found in Finnmark to the north. Up there above the Arctic Circle a cloak of darkness descended on the land, submerging it in the chill of an everlasting night, not to vanish till the following spring. A cold westerly wind whipped off the North Sea astern of the steamer, as if to hurry it on its way to the capital and the shelter of Oslo Fjord.

George and Frank stood on deck and watched the coastline take shape. Blue mountains rose up behind the flattish lands, punctuated with bays and smaller versions of the fjords farther north on the western shore of the country. These were home waters, where each of the men had grown up to learn the ways of the sea, and they each stared at the waves, lost in memories of the past and hope for the future. The look and feel of the sea and the land beyond helped foster a deep feeling of coming home. Though they had embraced America, their roots still clung to the mostly barren soil of Norway. Many a Norwegian had answered the call within his soul and reunited with their homeland to pursue a simpler, but more rewarding life than was possible to carve out in the whir and whoosh of the United States.

George's son, Fritz, whom he had never seen, would not know any English. His roots would first lie in Norway, where he was born. Did Andrew and Annie Louisa still want to return to America? Did Anine? Did he? George thought of the money earned so far on their exhibitions of the *Fox*. Deep in his heart he longed to open a store in Brooklyn. He had spent his life on the sea, and while he still loved it, he had had enough. If he and Frank could only earn enough money, then he would change his life, his whole way of looking at the world. From ashore, the family could grow and prosper, and he would be there to take part in it. He would have his childhood sweetheart at his side, and together with their children, they would be happy at last.

Frank, too, harbored a desire to leave the sea behind for a life ashore. Like his friend, he still loved it. Who could not? It was, after all, so powerful and fearsome and beautiful all at once. It couldn't help but make a lasting impression, and create a special place inside one's very being impossible to banish. However, he had come to America to start something new and ended up caught in the mire of economic unrest in a country that seemed intent on reinventing itself in periodic spasms. Great changes were taking place there, and he wasn't sure he wanted to be part of them.

The idea of leading a quiet life on his father's farm, maybe owning it one day and raising a family there, had taken hold of him during those long nights at the oars. The solid feel of the earth beneath his feet, the warm hide and pungent smells of the cows and horses in the barn, the clucking of chickens, the squawk of geese, the fragrance of meadow grass carried in the moist spring air. The sight of gray-white woodsmoke rising from the chimney on a cold winter day, so cold his boots squeaked as he walked in the snow. The sun rising over the mountains beyond the fjord, casting the carpet of freshly fallen snow in pale orange, only to turn to a glaring brightness hours later. All of these images had played out in his mind. But without money his dreams would never be realized. He would lead a life caught up with the sea, and that unsettled him for the first time. It was one thing to seek the sea out; another to have it trap you.

The steamer pushed on through the chop and eventually turned for its passage inland up the sixty-mile length of Oslo Fjord, which funnels a cone of blue deep into the fertile lands of Vestfold on the western side, where George's hometown of Sandefjord hugged the sea. To the east, in the county of Ostfold, farms mingled with stands of forest. The ship passed the points of peninsulas, the scrape of bays and scratches of creeks running into the sides of the great fjord, where the Norse had long made their homes, wisely choosing a sheltered location for settlement. At the head of the fjord, the vessel entered the Aker River and Christiania, named after King Christian IV, spread out on either side of the waterway in a pristine expanse of well-kept white clapboard shops and homes with red stone roofs pitched to force snow to drop when it weighed too heavily on the beams. Squat gray buildings poked the skyline upward over the red roofs.

Like so much of southern Norway, industrialization

had started to change far more than the economics of cities and towns. It altered the very look and size of them. Jobs had become plentiful in the more urban locales, and young men and women forsook the country to put down roots in more comfortable and civilized environs. Dense forests had once surrounded the low hills at the fringe of the city, but these were slowly disappearing under the ax of progress. The expansion had come so quickly that the city's districts, even the very streets, took on a haphazard configuration, and so it was without the pens of organized planners that the capital of Norway retained a unique appearance and ambience. It was no Paris or London or New York, all so orderly. It was entirely Norwegian, clean and unpresupposing, with a quiet sense of dignity and pride.

After the men disembarked from the steamer, they set about planning their exultant tour through Norway. They arranged for space to exhibit the *Fox* in Christiania and contacted the newspapers, hoping to attract the crowds which so far had eluded them. The newspapermen of Christiania met the men with less than enthusiastic questions and subsequent articles. Some wrote that the prevailing view of the people held the two men as crazy risk takers not deserving of attention. Others implied disloyalty to Norway because the voyagers had proudly flown the Stars and Stripes instead of the Norwegian flag. Never mind that George was an American citizen and that as master of the tiny vessel he had every right and an obligation to fly the colors of his adopted country. Though Frank was still a Norwegian citizen, he, too, did not see anything wrong with flying the American flag; he had adopted America, too.

There were words of praise among the barbs, and crowds did come to see the men and their "little cup of a boat." Among the visitors was King Oscar II, the monarch of Sweden and Norway. He entered the

exhibition hall with his entourage and caused quite
a commotion. It was not often that this man mingled
with the common folk. Dressed in a military uniform,
complete with a chestful of medals, he strode over
to the two men for a chat. He stroked his long beard
as he listened to their tale, taking their measure.
George and Frank both were impressed by how
friendly he was, how much he appeared to be interested in their accomplishment. King Oscar presented
each of them with a ten-kroner bill, a pittance worth
less than ten American dollars. They accepted the
money with gratitude; it was not the amount so much
as the individual who had offered it that made the
gift special.

Even with the king's tacit endorsement of their
voyage and their performance at the exhibition hall,
the crowds did not pour in. The world had moved
on to focus on other news. The exploits of Fridtjof
Nansen had created a tidal wave of press in September, when the entire country celebrated his arrival
home from the North Pole. The exploration of the
frozen lands to the north aboard the *Fram*, which
Nansen deliberately allowed to freeze into the pack
ice, the epic trek he and F. H. Johansen undertook
with dogsleds and kayaks, and the triumphant return
of the ship and crew eclipsed George and Frank's
efforts. Dejected at the lukewarm reception in Christiania, they exhibited the boat in other cities, hoping
for a better response, but to no avail.

In December, the two men went to Skien, where
Anine had moved from Brevik with the children. The
homecoming cheered George. He held Anine,
Andrew, and Louisa close for the first time since 1891.
Fritz, a beautiful little infant, did not know him, but
that was to be expected. He would know him soon,
when the family returned to America. The long years
of separation appeared over at last. Finally, they would
be together again and move on through the years,

with no more time apart. There was still hope that the exhibitions they planned to hold in America would turn out well. The American public, in spite of the fact that many were in dire financial straits, was endowed with a surplus of upper-class swells who had plenty of cash to spend to see a show. They did it all the time for performances much less entertaining than the tale of the *Fox*.

The Christmas holidays passed all too quickly. The need to leave and continue touring the larger cities of Norway exerted pressure on George, and his friend had not yet been home to Farsund. Frank understandably wanted to get there as soon as he could to spend time with his parents and siblings.

In early January, they set sail for Farsund aboard the *Arendale*. They had let the papers know of their plans in advance and hoped for the best. The ship nosed out of the great fjord into the open waters off the coast of southern Norway and soon reached the bustling port of Farsund. As the steamer slowed and edged into the harbor, members of the Seaman's Union touched off an eleven-gun salute. White smoke belched from the guns as they boomed. A crowd quickly gathered on the stone quays. All of Farsund had turned out to welcome them. The sound of cheering and music from a brass band reached the men across the water. They turned to each other and smiled, grateful beyond words as they faced the people waving at them from the piers.

28

All was a tumult of confusion and unbridled enthusiasm on the docks at Farsund as the *Fox* was brought ashore. A group of brawny seamen hoisted the boat atop their shoulders and carried it through the town, up the hill to the gymnasium, where it would be on display. The band led the way. Norwegian and American flags flew from many of the buildings. The crowd parted to let the small parade pass, waving and cheering the men. This was their moment, and they savored it. At the gym, George gave a little speech about the voyage while Frank stood by, quiet as usual but brimming with happiness at the welcome the people of the town had gone out of their way to provide both him and his friend.

Over the next several days, the boat remained on display. The kroner piled in, though after the initial excitement the crowds diminished. The port was one of the busiest in Norway, and as such it had its share of seamen curious about the boat. They gathered around and expressed their surprise that such a little craft could make it across the North Atlantic. A party was held in George and Frank's honor at the Seamen's Club. More than four hundred people attended, and a crowd gathered outside, unable to get in for lack of room. There were speeches and more speeches. George gave a brief lecture on the voyage and the travails they had suffered. The men were presented with a massive silver platter, a gift from Farsund and her seamen.

Frank spent time with his family at Elunde before he and George departed. He looked at the fields, the few outbuildings, the tidy home Elizabeth kept, and felt a deep sense of longing. It was even more acute than before. But there was no place for him there, not at the moment. The same reasons he had left still remained. The farm produced only just so much, and whatever revenue it generated went to support the family. Land taxes had ballooned out of control. Emanuel had to work extra hard to pay them. He hugged his family good-bye and left with his friend, ultimately hanging his hopes on whatever America had in store for them when they arrived back there with the *Fox*. It was ironic, in a sense, for he left Norway a second time with the same hopes for new opportunities he had back when he was seventeen and shipped out with the merchant marine. Although everything had changed, nothing had.

The remainder of the tours proved as disappointing as most of the others. The men packed up the *Fox* and shipped out on the *Island*, an old iron ship built for the Thingvalla Line in 1882. At sea in her day, she must have seemed the epitome of speed and glory—the three masts with full canvas spread, the yardarms on the foremast rigged with square sails, and black smoke running out the single funnel. Now rust streaked her black hull, and her rigging needed repair. The paint on the superstructure peeled, and bare wood showed through in places. She set sail from Copenhagen on February 15, reached Christiania on the eighteenth, and Christiansand on the nineteenth, where George and Frank boarded her for their trip home to the United States.

Richard Kyle Fox generously paid for their passage, and both of them were grateful to him. They were to exhibit the *Fox* at Huber's Museum in New York and would be paid twenty dollars a day. They would have their gold medals from the *Police Gazette*. Maybe in New York the tide would at last turn in their favor.

Their ship left on February 19 and almost immediately encountered a gale. The vessel drove its bows deep, sending green water across the deck. The passengers huddled seasick and scared belowdecks as the storm raged. A succession of gales, all from the west, screamed for days, then weeks. Massive seas raked the steamer, smashing three of its lifeboats. Waves carried away parts of its bridge, injuring three of the deck watch. The steam engines consumed coal at an alarming rate.

As George and Frank stood inside the luxurious saloon and watched the waves sweep the decks, they understood how lucky they had been. The gales that the *Island* was encountering were far more severe than even the worst one on July 10. The ocean had granted them the greatest gift of all, life. It wasn't something either of them took for granted, and seeing the full fury of the ocean last for a seeming eternity drove the concept home. Passengers knocked on the door of their stateroom during the dark hours of the predawn, haggard and trembling with fear.

"Will we survive the storm?" they asked. "Are we about to sink?"

The men comforted the people. "We have a firm keel below and solid decks above. This is a large ship, not a rowboat. If a rowboat can make it, so we shall, too."

The passengers went away with a little less fear.

The westerlies roared on, bad even for late winter.

Terrific waves washed over the ship, pushing her far over on her sides. Captain Thompson could do nothing but keep the ship's head to the wind with enough speed to maintain steerage way. Day after day the coal stocks in the bunkers diminished even as the succession of storms increased in intensity. If the ship ran out of coal to fire the engines, she would lie helplessly in the trough. Most likely she would capsize in that position, sending 144 passengers and the crew to their deaths. Even if it were possible to launch the remaining lifeboats, with three of them smashed . . . Thompson tried not to think about such a calamity.

When it became clear that he would not make it to New York with the present supply of coal, he altered course for St. John's, Newfoundland. He refilled the coal bunkers and set off again, crossing the Grand Banks through fog and strong west winds, skirting Georges Bank off Cape Cod, and steaming down the southern shore of Long Island to New York harbor. The ship arrived off Sandy Hook at two in the morning, the weather calm and foggy. Captain Thompson hove to and waited for a pilot from the new steam-powered pilot boat, the *New York*, which was on station.

In the gray predawn light, a crew of burly oarsmen rowed a yawl out to the vessel. The pilot charged with taking the *Island* in looked at the battered ship and shook his head. This had been a winter hard on the transatlantic steamers, with some of the worst weather on record. This one obviously had seen some terrible storms. He climbed up the ladder slung down the rust-streaked hull of the ship and met Captain Thompson on the bridge, noting the repairs made to the structure.

"It was a bad voyage, I see," he said as he ordered the ship to proceed slowly and lined her up with the buoys marking Gedney Channel beyond the Sandy Hook Lightship.

Captain Thompson nodded, his face creased with wrinkles, his eyes hollow and dark. "This is the last voyage for the ship, you know. She's to be decommissioned. The sea gave her a good thrashing as a send-off."

Twenty-seven days out of Norway, an incredibly long passage for a steamer, the *Island* limped into New York harbor and came to rest at the fog-shrouded piers in Hoboken, New Jersey. Tiny droplets of water covered everything. The passengers began to disembark. Many swore never to take a steamer across the ocean again. Longshoremen boarded the ship and set about unloading the holds of luggage and cargo. Atop the roof of the vessel's aft cabin the *Fox* remained strapped down next to one of the lifeboats. The wind had blown the canvas covering off, revealing the rusted and blackened kettle, the matted old oilskins and hats, the worn-out oars, splintered and cracked. The keel of the little boat had split somehow. Her paint had faded, and in places bare, weathered wood showed in uneven splotches.

Learning that George and Frank were aboard, reporters gathered to interview them. They asked the now familiar questions, Why did you do it? What was it like?

"Do you want to try it again?" asked a reporter from the *New York Herald*.

George looked at him as if he were crazy, then said with feeling, "Not much. I've had enough."

The following day, reports on the *Island*'s arrival and the repatriation of the two rowers appeared in some of the city's newspapers. They were short stories, though, buried on the back pages. Many papers didn't report their arrival at all. New York did not sit up and take notice of the men. It was a replay of Paris, London, and Christiania. The men were determined to play the venture out to the last, but they fully realized that it had failed from a financial standpoint.

They took the defeat in their typically stoic manner and even in private didn't speak of it much to each other.

The *Fox* went on display at Huber's Museum in late March and early April. On a Wednesday evening, just prior to a lecture on transatlantic navigation held at the museum, George and Frank received their *Police Gazette* medals from Sam Austin, the sports editor of the paper. Forged from solid gold, the medals reproduced the hull of the rowboat. Suspended from gold chains attached to the keel below the bow and stern was a pendant topped with an eagle and the words "Police Gazette Trophy" engraved across a top banner. Set in the center of the pendant was a portrait of the two men standing side by side.

George and Frank faced the crowd and thanked Richard Fox for his generosity. The publisher had helped them with their passage home and in getting the boat expeditiously released from customs in Hoboken upon their return. They then climbed into the boat and gave an exhibition row, pulling the oars in thin air, much to the delight of the crowd. The act too closely resembled the antics of clowns under a big top. It belied the true value of the achievement, which went far beyond the ring of cash registers, but the men did it, anyway. It was just part of the show.

29

The spring of 1897 brought with it its usual fresh northwesterly winds and clear blue skies interspersed with days of gray cold rain. The fishing fleets off Nauvoo and Galilee put out to sea in their little skiffs. The conical icehouses on the beach were crammed full with blocks cut from the frozen rivers and creeks during the winter. The clammers and oystermen dotted the calm waters of Sandy Hook Bay, tending their beds of shellfish with unerring proficiency. Demand for the catches at the Fulton Fish Market fueled an economic boon for the boatmen. The lists of suicides, so lengthy on the pages of newspapers during the early 1890s, grew shorter; the lot of the common man appeared less gloomy, though the chasm between rich and poor still existed and probably always would. The military slaved feverishly on the gun batteries at Fort Hancock and at other harbors along the coast, readying the nation for a conflict with Spain.

George and Frank worked the clam beds together, as they always had. Frank dug deep with the tongs and hoisted great clusters of gray shells, lodged in the ooze, to the surface of the sea and deposited the contents onto the culling board, where George bent to his work. The men repeated the process as smoothly as if they had never stopped. Time had moved forward. The country had elected a new president, William McKinley, and a renewed sense of hope took root for what lay ahead in the new century. Yet for these two men time had stood still, despite their intense effort to push through and effect a significant change. It was as if they had walked in the blazing light of a desert, found an oasis where the greenery of life gathered around a pool of crystal-clear water, and had somehow seen it vanish into a mirage as they stooped at the sandy banks to drink. The work on the clam beds was all they knew how to do, was all that society offered in return for dollars to sustain them.

George received word from Anine shortly after he and Frank arrived in Hoboken that she was pregnant. The child must have been conceived in late January, when he had come to say good-bye before setting off on the *Island* a couple of weeks later. The baby was due in October, and Anine did not want to leave Skien. The separation would continue, and it pained George. He wanted his family near him, to hold his wife close to him at night, to share his disappointments and hopes with her. He wanted to take Andrew sailing, and Fritz, too, when he grew big enough. He longed to see Annie Louisa mature into a young lady. He wished he could be there to see his new baby born; he had missed so much, so much.

The separation he put to good use, however. He did not give up trying. He felt he had no choice. He worked hard with Frank harvesting their crops of hard gray shells. He signed on with the Sandy Hook Pilots Association, now a formal organization rather than the ragtag band of private companies that had presided over the pilotage of shipping prior to 1895. He served aboard the pilot boat when he was called and earned good commissions for his work. The age of the great liners had arrived, and with the channels to the harbor so shallow, only twenty-four feet deep at low water, it required skill to bring the ships safely in and out of their berths in the upper harbor.

One of the only benefits he received from the voyage aboard the *Fox* was the deep respect for his navigational abilities among the seamen of the port of New York. This stood him in good favor. Many of the pilots could buy beautiful homes on Staten Island and in New York City with their earnings. He lived simply and saved as much money as he could in order to set up a comfortable household for Anine and the children. In late October he received word from Anine that she had given birth to a baby girl on the twenty-fifth, whom they had agreed to name Grace Almira. Their baby girl could not replace Agnes Grace, who had died at sea, but she would bear her middle name.

Frank set aside his dreams of farming, but he did not forget them. On April, 28, 1898, just three days after Congress declared war on Spain, Frank was awarded U.S. citizenship at the district court in Brooklyn. It was a day of great joy that was celebrated with his two brothers, Jake and Jakob, his sister Caroline, and his close friend George.

The long separation between George and Anine ended on August 1, 1898. He met them at the docks in New York harbor, overjoyed at the fact that he at last had his family with him. They settled in Brooklyn, where Anine felt comfortable among the many other Scandinavians living there. So many had come that the enclave was often called "Little Norway."

As time progressed and the new century arrived with great fanfare on New Year's Eve, the two men fell into the routine of life most everyone holds dear. No lasting fame or fortune had come to them as a result of their voyage. It did not chart a path to a better future, as they had hoped. But with the hard work and persistence needed to carve out a comfortable existence in America, each had cultivated the required values and ethics to succeed. In this way, the voyage contributed to their lives in an intangible, but far from worthless manner. It formed their characters and shaped their view of the world in that it allowed them to see how fickle it can be, how much chance plays a role in the outcome of virtually every effort a man undertakes.

Frank met and married a beautiful Norwegian girl named Anna Lovisa Isackson. He had continued fishing off the Atlantic Highlands, and he and his new bride lived there in simple comfort. He missed his friend George, but he got up to Brooklyn to see him as often as possible. George now had quite a big family. Anine had given birth to a daughter in 1899 and a son in 1901. Frank and his wife wanted children as well, and on October 2, 1902, Anna gave birth to a baby boy, whom they named Sigurd Emanuel. He grew up with the sea in his blood, accompanying his father on outings aboard his boat at an early age.

The years passed. George and Anine bought a nice home in Brooklyn, which they needed to house their growing family. Anine gave birth to three more daughters between 1903 and 1906, bringing the total number of the brood to nine, excluding Agnes Grace. Andrew was a young man of twenty, and Annie Louisa was a beautiful young lady of eighteen in 1906. But Anine still had her hands full with the other children. Fritz was only eleven, Grace Almira was nine, Beatrice was seven, Harold was five, Ethel was three, Hendrikke was one, and Vivian was an infant. With his earnings as a pilot, George could afford to buy Anine a baby grand piano, and he hired a maid to help his wife keep house, which she greatly appreciated.

Two years later, in 1908, Anine gave birth to

another daughter, Georganna. Their home was filled with the laughter of children, the playfulness of youth. At night, the gentle notes of the piano filled the sitting room. Anine watched over her little ones as she knitted pretty articles of clothing. With the early spring came cold northwesterly winds and rain. Out on the sea, aboard the pilot boat, the men worked in any kind of weather. It was often dangerous. The waves drenched them as they climbed up the sides of the ships, water streaming down on them as it drained through the scuppers.

After guiding a ship safely into port, George came home feeling feverish and weak. Anine put him to bed. The next day, the fever increased. He trembled and soaked the sheets with his sweat. The family doctor, a man by the name of Malone, came to George's bedside.

"He's down with pneumonia, Anine," he said quietly. He did all he could for George, but his condition worsened.

On April 4, 1908, George Harbo died. A shadow passed over the family. The house was silent, the happiness gone. He was a man who had crossed an ocean in a rowboat, had beaten the odds, had dared the sea and came out a winner, only to die at the age of forty-three from the power of an invisible enemy that had taken up residence in his body.

Family and friends gathered for the church service and proceeded to Greenwood Cemetery in Brooklyn. Frank stood at the edge of the grave, his head bowed.

"Good-bye, old friend," he whispered. "Good-bye."

Frank felt as if a link had broken, setting him off in a lonely way into a world filled with life and things to do but somehow empty. He knew this would pass with time, as it always did when the pain of loss grew tamer with age. Yet he could not help but think of his time aboard the *Fox*, the determination of his

friend, the laughter and the misery, and the long
struggle that was now over for George. He looked at
his friend's family. These were fine children, and so
many. Anine cradled little Georganna in her arms, a
distant look in her eyes as she gazed at the open scar
in the earth where her husband would soon lie. It
saddened him to think of them, now very much at
the mercy of a world much crueler than the sea ever
could be.

Approximately one year later, pneumonia took
Georganna, dealing Anine and the children another
loss to reckon with. She was buried with her father
in Greenwood Cemetery.

The long chain of events in Anine's life stretched
out behind her. She could not look back without
seeing the series of hardships. There were happy
times, but there weren't enough of them. How can
there ever be enough happiness? The world had so
little of it that one was always wanting more. She
worked hard to keep the family together, made sure
the clothes were clean, that the children were fed.
But the vitality of her youth had gone long ago, and
the deep love she had felt for George lingered and
caused her heart to slowly break.

Despite the presence of so many young children,
the house appeared empty. It had lost its former
comfort, its feeling of peacefulness. Anine kept the
piano spotlessly clean, dusting its ivory keys, the deep
brown wood, and the trinkets placed on top of it. But
she seldom played it, if ever, after George's death.
To hear its notes could only remind her of the days
gone forever, of George's quick smile, his deep blue
eyes. The way he laughed quickly, always catching the
humor of a joke.

Time crawled on, joyless and apparently without
meaning. Anine lost herself in her family. But the
children noticed a change, particularly Andrew and
Louisa, who were old enough to comprehend the

impact of their father's and sister's deaths on their mother. In April 1911, Anine took ill. The older children and their relatives recognized the symptoms. Pneumonia had not yet finished with the Harbos. Anine sank into the depths of the fever, never to fight her way back to good health. Three days after her forty-sixth birthday, on April 17, she joined her infant daughter and her beloved husband.

The deaths of both parents shattered the Harbo family. The children were separated and went to live with relatives and with Harold, George's brother. Doctor Malone adopted Hendrikke and changed her name to Harriet. She was kept from seeing her brothers and sisters, and told little, if anything, about them or her parents as she grew up in the Malone household. The other children were shuffled from the homes of relatives throughout their childhoods, though they did remain in close contact with one another. In the course of just over three years, all that George had worked for and dreamed of vanished. His obscurity was complete.

30

The year of George's death brought great change in the Samuelsens' household as well. Frank purchased half his father's farm in Elunde, acting on a dream he had nursed since 1896. He booked passage for his wife and son on a steamer bound for Norway and crossed the North Atlantic for the last time. At home after more than twenty years, the hiatus spent at sea and in America, he quickly took to the slow, simple life on the outskirts of Farsund. The cows needed milking; the soil, tilling; and the crops, harvesting. Wood for the stove had to be chopped. The routine he slipped into gave him immense peace. Never again would he put to sea to brave the storms and the bone-chilling cold. He hoped Sigurd would follow a different path as well. The sea was a dangerous lover. It bewitched men and tricked them into lives with little to offer in return for the long hours on deck tending the nets, tonging for clams, or riding the great ships to exotic ports around the world.

The years passed by. World War I came and went. Time for Frank, though, stood still. He enjoyed his

quiet existence, watching his son mature into a man.
Sigurd left for America, lured in part by the boon
times of the Roaring Twenties. There were many
opportunities there which did not exist in Elunde.
The cycle so familiar to Frank repeated itself. He
wished his son luck and bade him good-bye.

In 1927, Frank's mother, Elizabeth, died, leaving
him the entire farm.

Another death marked that year. He lost his wife,
Anna, to a prolonged illness. Frank continued to work
the farm alone. His life may have seemed empty, and
for a time it was. But he had found the one place in
the world, after years of seeing many parts of it, that
gave him peace. His hair began to grow white and
thin, but he still had his health and the strength that
had helped him get the *Fox* safely across the Atlantic.

In 1930, Sigurd married Anna Hansen, whom he
had met at the Atlantic Highlands, where he had
settled down to a life as a fisherman, just like his
father. Late that year, Frank became a grandfather.
Sigurd and Anna had given him a little boy, Spencer.
In 1932 the couple had another boy, whom they
named Norman.

Times in the United States had soured since the
stock market crash in 1929. The Great Depression
changed the fabric of life for nearly every American,
and for Sigurd it was no different. He worked as a
cook aboard a scallop fishing vessel to make ends
meet. It was dangerous work, and it kept him from
being with Anna and his two young sons. In the spring
of 1935 he had managed to line up a job as a lighthouse tender. His last trip was in April, when he
would have a new shot at life ashore, safer, more
comfortable, and for better wages.

The night Sigurd went to sea, a severe spring
nor'easter blew up. It raked the coast with high surf
and damaging winds. Sigurd's boat went down, and
the crew of five died. The bodies of the men washed

ashore or were picked up out of the sea, but the ocean did not return Sigurd. Anna, devastated at the loss, did not even have her husband to bury. The sea had spared the father, but it had taken the son.

Anna had no choice but to bring the two boys back to Norway, where they stayed with her mother. Times were so difficult in America that there was no way she could support the boys herself. She went back to America, found work as a housekeeper, and saved money to bring her sons home. Frank often visited his grandsons. He took them fishing and often gave them a ten-kroner note. The boys loved him and found that his propensity to sit for hours in silence, his quiet but stern manner with them, engendered a deep and abiding respect. They knew about his row across the sea but asked him very few questions. They got the impression that it was a subject their grandfather would rather not discuss.

The Germans invaded and occupied Norway in April 1940. Anna and her new husband tried to get the boys out of the country, but the Germans refused to let them go. Through the war years, Frank lived in a home for old people, though he was not ill. He had lost his second wife and sold his farm. In his seventies, he desired the comforts available to him in Farsund. He saw his grandchildren as often as possible and watched with resigned belligerence as the Germans marched through the streets of his much-loved town. Far away in France, the beautiful port of Le Havre lay in ruins.

Frank lived to see the Germans ejected from his country. He saw the joy among the people as they celebrated the end of the war, and he toasted the victory with his friends. Weak from a series of illnesses that landed him in the hospital, Frank went to sleep on the night of June 6, 1946, and did not live to see the sun rise. He died in peace, as he had lived most of his seventy-six years.

On June 11, Spencer and Norman joined the relatives and friends of Frank Samuelsen in the funeral procession from the church to the adjoining cemetery on a hill in the heart of Farsund. It was a balmy June day, the air fragrant with the scent of the grass and trees. A horse and a closed buggy took the casket to the grave. One member of each family held an arrangement of flowers, and one by one the men and women, selected to dedicate the flowers, stood up and gave a short speech in Frank's honor. More than one hundred people attended the funeral, and they all spoke of Frank's great adventure aboard the *Fox* fifty years earlier.

A reporter for one of the Norwegian newspapers wrote: "The world will not see his like again. Ours is an effete age."

Afterword:
The Contemporary Fox

What happened to the *Fox* remains a mystery. Some say Andrew Harbo kept her and installed an engine, a most reprehensible outcome for such a splendid craft. Others insist she is on display in an obscure museum in Great Britain or that she was destroyed while being exhibited in Coney Island, New York. It is known that the Smithsonian Museum tried to find out what happened to her. Curators wanted to include the boat in the museum's collection. But they were unable to track her down, and it must be said that they didn't try all that hard. George Harbo and Frank Samuelsen had made history, but their story was not equal to others in the eyes of some.

Quite possibly the boat was left out in the weather in Brooklyn or in the Atlantic Highlands and slowly the elements ate away her cedar planks and oak frame. It would not take long for the *Fox* to have looked like any other forgotten rowboat, and it does seem sadly fitting that she would simply fade away into obscurity in the same way her crew had. Out in the back of boatyards, behind storage sheds, one can find many skeletons of the past, the ribs weathered white and adorned with the greenery of tall, hardy grass growing up around a once-sturdy keel. She blended in with her less traveled peers and probably ended up in the belly of a stove as fuel on a cold winter's day.

The story would certainly have ended on this disappointing note were it not for William Seaman's son, Harold. Harold was thirteen years old when he helped his father build the *Fox* in 1896. He stayed in New Jersey and continued working with boats, carrying on the Seaman tradition of building skiffs for the fishermen and recreational craft for those who wanted and could afford them. In 1901 he became a charter member of the Long Branch Ice Boat and Yacht Club, which sprang up on the Shrewsbury River, in the environs of Sandy Hook. Harold Seaman was like many other characters one can find along the waterfront of any coast, a bit salty and weather-beaten, and filled with yarns to pass the time in the coffee shop or on the pier.

The legend of the *Fox*—and as the twentieth century progressed, the story did truly take on elements of the fabulous—remained a mainstay of the stories told in the area where the two men had fished and where the boat had been built. It was the stuff that turned the heads of local yachtsmen. Harold, nicknamed "Pappy," found a river of interest in his part of the tale, and he told the story often.

In the late autumn of 1974, members of the yacht club decided to build an exact replica of the *Fox*. Why is unclear. Members say it was just something they wanted to do, a fun kind of project to celebrate two local fishermen who had set a world record and were almost forgotten to the world. It was also a wonderful project for Pappy. At the age of ninety-one, Pappy once again found himself at work on the rowboat *Fox* through the winter and into the early spring of 1975. Too old to actively build the boat, he still participated in its design, working out the details that went into the vessel from memory and with the help of blueprints dug out from the records. About twenty volunteers from the club worked on the boat weekday evenings and on weekends.

The replica was built to the exact specifications used to construct the original, and no modern materials went into her except an occasional dab of epoxy. Copper rivets held her cedar planks in place. Every detail, from the watertight compartments to the handrails mounted on the bottom of the hull, was faithfully reproduced, right down to the forty-six-star flag the men carried across the Atlantic with them and proudly displayed along with the boat.

Word reached the relatives of George Harbo and Frank Samuelsen regarding the yacht club's intention to launch the "new" *Fox* late in the spring of 1975. For the first time in nearly seventy years, members of the two families came together to celebrate the voyage and remember the men who had made it. Frank Samuelsen's four great-granddaughters gathered at the bow of the boat and broke a bottle of champagne to the cheers of onlookers and the clicking cameras of the local press.

In July, a nine-man crew rowed the *Fox* in shifts the 130 miles from Sandy Hook up Long Island Sound to Mystic, Connecticut, taking approximately five days to cover the distance. Two larger boats escorted the *Fox* and saw her safely into Mystic, where she was put on display at the Seaport Museum. It remained at Mystic Seaport, with a brief stint at a boat show the following year, until it was loaned to the Twin Lights Historic Site in the Highlands of New Jersey in 1979.

The *Fox* remained at the Twin Lights Museum until 1996. Members of the yacht club repainted her and set out on a row to New York harbor as a way to celebrate the centennial of the voyage. Again the grandchildren of Harbo and Samuelsen attended.

The Harbo family donated the records of the voyage to the museum, including a detailed account of the journey dictated by George before he died. The yacht club still has the replica, and it is something of a local attraction. There is talk that it will end up at another museum, one slated to open in an old lifesaving station set on the beach. But that's another story which has still not found a resolution. What remains clear, however, is that at least along the north shore of New Jersey the legend of the *Fox* will never die, and that is a good thing.

APPENDIX A
Small Craft Daredevils

The epic voyage of the *Fox* earned George Harbo and Frank Samuelsen a place in the *Guinness Book of World Records*, and a place in history, though their accomplishment has remained far more obscure than that of some of the men and women who grace the same pages under the category of marine achievements. They are recorded there as the first men to successfully cross the North Atlantic in a rowboat, completing the transatlantic journey in a record fifty-five days, from the Battery in lower Manhattan to the Isles of Scilly in England, a distance of approximately 3,000 miles. No team has beaten their speed across. Several have tried, and several have died in the attempt. The last leg of the voyage to Le Havre was not considered part of the crossing because their landfall in France was not their first and possibly because they received a tow for more than half the distance across the English Channel.

One year before George and Frank left New York, a crusty old New Englander, heralded as the father of small-boat voyaging, departed from Boston aboard a thirty-seven-foot sloop called the *Spray*. His name was Joshua Slocum. Three years later, he returned to New England, having set a world record as the first man to circumnavigate the globe alone, traveling under sail a distance of approximately 46,000 miles. He is listed in the *Guinness Book of World Records*.

Slocum was a born showman and a talented writer. His book *Sailing Alone Around the World* was a big hit and is still a classic among all true stories of the sea. He exhibited the boat throughout the world during his voyage to earn money. Once he killed an enormous shark and exhibited that, too. He did not earn a chestful of gold, but he did do a lot better than George and Frank. It is thought he committed suicide at the end of his life. Discontent with his lot ashore and out of place in the new century, he sailed off in a gale toward Nantucket Shoals, one of the worst places to be in a storm. He was never heard from again. Some might hotly debate whether he died on those shoals. Slocum has taken on a quasi-Elvis status, reportedly showing up in exotic ports well into the twentieth century.

In the twentieth century there have been spates of small-boat crossings at various times and in a wide variety of craft, some of them quite ludicrous if one considers the dangers of the sea. The 2,700-mile rowboat race in October 1997, from the Canary Islands to the West Indies, was the most recent but by no means the only one of note over the last one hundred years.

In 1928 a German named Franz Romer earned himself immortality in the pages of the *Guinness Book of World Records* when he crossed the Atlantic from Lisbon, Portugal, to San Juan, Puerto Rico, in a nineteen-and-a-half-foot foldboat, a rubber canoe or kayaklike vessel equipped with sails. He had to sit or lie down for the entire fifty-eight days it took him to make the crossing; he could not stand up.

Boils covered his skin, which was almost always wet. His legs cramped and lost strength. At the end of the voyage, he had to be pulled from his boat because he could barely move. The same year he set his fantastic record, he had the misfortune to tangle with a hurricane in the Caribbean. Neither Romer nor his foldboat was ever seen again.

In 1952 a French physician, Alain Bombard, set off from the Canary Islands bound for Barbados in a rubber raft equipped with sails. He took no supplies to speak of, subsisting on fish, the occasional seabird that got too close to the raft, plankton to ward off scurvy, and rainwater. Why cross in a rubber raft with no provisions? The good doctor was intent on studying the effects of exposure and a lack of food and water on castaways, so he decided to put himself in a situation in which all he had to sustain him was whatever the sea provided. According to his research, as many as 90 percent of the poor souls cast adrift in provisionless lifeboats die within three days despite the fact that it takes far longer than that to die of hunger and thirst. Bombard wanted to prove that it was possible to live off the sea, that shipwrecked sailors need not die in such large numbers.

Sixty-five days after his departure, Bombard arrived in Barbados. A rash covered every inch of his skin, which was shrunken around his bones; he had lost fifty-five pounds. His toenails fell off, his vision went bad, and he suffered a severe case of anemia. Yet he made the 2,700-mile journey across alone and with nothing save the scanty fruits of the sea. People thought him crazy, and the scientific community discounted his theories.

True, he must have been somewhat daft to attempt such a voyage. However, he proved that a human being can exist in impossible conditions, that sheer will and resourcefulness can overcome seemingly insurmountable odds. Even if his theories were met with derision, Bombard reinforced the notion that to live is to push onward to the edge, look down, and see what might be learned to forward the path for us all.

Hannes Lindemann, a German physician, earned himself the distinction of being the first man to sail a dugout canoe alone across the Atlantic in 1956. He left from Las Palmas in the Canary Islands and arrived in St. Croix sixty-five days later, a distance of just under 3,000 miles when all the zigs and zags of his course were added up. Lindemann also lived off the sea, but he did take supplies. He crossed again in 1957, this time in a foldboat.

It is important to note here that the racing teams last October, Romer, Bombard, Lindemann, and countless other mariners in small craft chose what sailors call a "downhill" route to cross the Atlantic. Their course from east to west took them happily through the northeast trade wind belt which blows during summer from below latitude thirty degrees north, right in the neighborhood of the Canary Islands. These winds pushed the sailing craft across the sea, with lots of help from the waves rolling westward. There is also a favorable current.

In 1970, John Fairfax, a British adventurer, found his way into the pages of the *Guinness Book of World Records* when he completed the first solo rowboat crossing of the Atlantic from east to west. He, too, took the "downhill" route. However, it took him 180 days to row 4,500 miles, from the Canary Islands to Miami, Florida. The actual mileage between the Canary Islands and Miami is roughly 3,600. But Fairfax found it rather difficult to keep a good course by himself, which frustrated him no end. Every time he tried to sleep or prepare a meal, the wind blew him to and fro, and on several occasions he rowed in circles for days. His main inspiration to undertake the voyage stemmed from his reading accounts of the

Fox's perilous trip. The daring of the two men, their many adventures, and their final triumph filled his heart, and he cast away everything to make his own attempt at a "first" passage.

To understand the stupendous nature of George and Frank's time across, it is important to realize that their route took them west to east through some of the roughest waters of the Atlantic. No balmy trade winds or azure seas. No puffy white clouds and flying fish for breakfast. They battled for every mile under conditions many of the others taking the more southerly route from east to west never encountered.

George and Frank chose to ride the westerly belt of winds ranging from the fortieth parallel to north latitudes well into the fifties, and in 1896 and 1897 these winds blew with a fury even in the summer months. The series of gales they encountered were highly unusual in terms of frequency and strength, more like weather systems expected in the late fall or early spring. The exceptional weather almost killed them, but that, combined with their discipline and brawn, accounts for their incredible speed. Small sailing vessels have taken longer to cross. One could argue that they, too, had taken a "downhill" route, though it surely was more akin to stepping over the edge of a cliff than coasting down a slope.

Prior to John Fairfax's voyage, four men set out to make the crossing under oars alone in 1966. It was the first time since George and Frank's odyssey that anyone had attempted to row across the Atlantic from west to east without sails. All hailing from Great Britain, two-man teams set out in a sort of race to see who could cross the fastest. Aboard the rowboat *Puffin* were David Johnstone and John Hoare. Aboard the *English Rose III* were John Ridgway and Chay Blyth. Both boats were self-bailing and had all the other benefits of modern technology. Puffin had a small cabin; the twenty-two-foot *English Rose III* had only a canvas cover, a contemporary version of that used aboard the *Fox*.

The crew of the *Puffin* left Norfolk, Virginia, on May 21, 1966. Leaving from Virginia would put the boat much closer to the Gulf Stream, which the crew could ride northeastward up the coast and out into the Atlantic Ocean. With its strong force behind them on the coastwise leg of the voyage, they expected to pick up at least one knot per hour, quite a boost for a rowboat. The Gulf Stream would add about twenty-five miles over the ground per day. It seemed a good plan, one that would show the other team of Britishers just who was the best. From the start the *Puffin* had a bad go of it. The winds were from the east, and despite their efforts, the boat was still just offshore in the turbulent, shallow water after a week of hard work.

Up in Cape Cod, the crew of *English Rose III* readied their little craft for the race. They departed on June 4 and suffered the same ill fate of their competitors to the south. The wind practically blew them back to the sandy cape, but they pushed on, even skirting the edge of a hurricane. The voyage dragged on far longer than either man aboard the *English Rose III* had anticipated, lasting a total of ninety-two days to cross under 3,000 miles to Inishmore, Ireland. Both men were starved and exhausted, and like George and Frank, neither particularly fancied another go at it to see if a better time could be achieved.

The other team never reached land. Their boat was discovered capsized and adrift in the Atlantic. The sea had taken one crew while sparing the other.

In 1969, when Fairfax began his row across the Atlantic from east to west, taking that "downhill" route so popular among cruising yachts bound from Europe to the Caribbean, another man set out to row the ocean solo from west to east. His name was Tom McClean, a robust and greatly knowledgeable Irish-

han. He took a northern route through the dense
og and iceberg zone from St. John's, Newfoundland,
o Black Sod Bay, Ireland. In these high latitudes
ales are more frequent, it is freezing even in the
ummertime, and the likelihood of rescue is remote
n the event of a mishap. On the upside, the distance
etween Newfoundland and Ireland is under 2,000
niles, as opposed to rowing the 3,000 miles from New
York to the Isles of Scilly, as George and Frank did.
McClean took seventy days to get across in his twenty-
oot boat. Again, he had all the conveniences of modern technology to aid him.

As long as there are human beings on the face of
he earth, there will be adventurers. They are few
among us. It is hard to break the chains of conven-
tional life to pursue the unknown, to risk life itself
to find a sense of peace and harmony with the natural
world. It is best left to those few, for death is an all
too real possibility when man pits himself against the
forces of nature. Yet we all owe a deep debt to the
brave-hearted men and women who undertake the
seemingly impossible, whether it is here on our brilliant blue planet or in the dark reaches of outer space.
These are the truest of us, the ones unafraid to cast
off the mundane and safe for the thrill of pushing
the limits of human endurance, emotion, and powers
of intellect. They are the heroes we all can admire,
for they do it not for money or fame as much as for
the noble quest that we all share and aspire to in our
attempts to lead lives that bring out the best qualities
of humanity while leaving the detritus behind in our
wake.

APPENDIX B
On Sea Serpents, Mermaids, and UFOs

The sea has long held a high degree of mystery. In the days before Christopher Columbus sailed in 1492 on his voyage of discovery, the prevailing wisdom among the uninformed maintained that the world was flat and that ships sailing too close to the edge would plummet into the darkness of the unknown. Charts drawn in those early days of sail clearly show areas where sea serpents were likely to rise up from the depths to devour the crews of hapless vessels. Not every mariner agreed with these supposed wisdoms, including Columbus. Pytheas, the first Greek to discover Iceland in 325 B.C., was a keen mathematician who is thought to have known that the earth was round. The most common belief, however, lay in the myths put forth, and fear ran rampant among those who shipped out on anything but a coastwise journey.

Today science tells us that no strange monsters lurk beneath the ocean's surface. Creatures yet undiscovered are thought to live deep down on the abyssal plain and in the volcanic undersea mountains along the mid-Atlantic Ridge. But they are more docile in nature, though no less fantastic when deep-sea explorations manage to discover them. Giant squid are known to exist as well. They are quite rare and very shy. No one has ever seen one alive, only dead, washed ashore or floating in the sea.

But monsters? No, science says they don't exist.

What strikes the observant student of small-boat voyages is the repeated reports among the travelers of seeing very odd denizens of the vast wasteland of the open sea. No report indicates the sighting of a monster, but many tell of sighting creatures, often quite large, with which mankind remains completely unfamiliar. The report George Harbo and Frank Samuelsen gave about the sea serpent is not unusual when considered in the context of dozens of voyages in which such sightings have occurred. The *New York Herald* reported that a ship sighted a similar-looking creature roughly in the same area of ocean as the *Fox*. To his credit, the journalist drew no conclusions as to the validity of both reports.

John Ridgway, on his row with Chay Blyth across the Atlantic from west to east in 1966, reported seeing a "sea serpent" one dark night. Ridgway was a captain in a British paratrooper regiment and not a man to dream up such a fantasy. He wrote of sighting the sea serpent in the book *A Fighting Chance*, written together with Blyth: "Through the ages mariners have returned with tales of such creatures, only to be told that what they had seen was the product of an overwrought imagination. I can only tell what I saw with my own eyes, and I am no longer a disbeliever."

Howard Blackburn also wrote about sighting a sea serpent. It was reportedly a baby. He saw it eating a very large fish. Hannes Lindemann, the first to sail the Atlantic in a dugout canoe, reported sighting a creature he thought was a giant squid. A physician and an avid oceanographer, Lindemann would know an enormous squid if he met one.

Strange sightings occur in the skies as well. John Fairfax, the first to row the Atlantic solo from east to west, recorded sighting two UFOs in his book *Britannia: Rowing Alone Across the Atlantic.* He described the objects as two bright blue spheres—brighter than any star—that shifted their course through the night sky in an erratic way no satellite could attain. He had the sensation they were above him, that his body was "floating in a void . . . struggling against a terrific, mental, esoteric force" that was willing him to abandon himself.

Fairfax's account also tells of strange dreams, and he admits he did hallucinate once when he was very ill. However, he swears he saw the UFOs in a perfectly conscious moment. His adventure required no sprucing up with reports of strange unidentified flying objects. He was matter-of-fact about them and wrote the sighting off as just another mystery of the sea.

Joshua Slocum wrote of a strange man at the helm of the *Spray,* whom he identified as one of the sailors aboard the *Pinta.* Ann Davison, the first woman to sail across the Atlantic solo in 1952, wrote of feeling the presence of another person aboard her twenty-three-foot sloop. She even heard voices. Other sailors have reported auditory hallucinations, such as telephones ringing, bells, whistles, and car horns. Reports of sailing upward toward the sky and down into great holes, islands that weren't there, icebergs inverted above the horizon, and countless other tricks of the mind litter the true stories of the sea.

Did George Harbo and Frank Samuelsen see a sea serpent? Hannes Lindemann a squid? Did Ridgway see his oceangoing monster, and did Fairfax really have a close encounter with UFOs? Of them all, it seems Lindemann's sighting was probably the most believable, since science tells us the giant squid does live. But the other tales should not be discounted entirely, either. The sea can play tricks on the mind, but it can also reveal its secrets to the lone mariner close to its embrace. It is so vast a place, its depths still virtually unexplored, that only the most devout landsman could fail to appreciate the magic of the possibilities it may hold.

Bibliography

Anuta, Michael J. *Ships of Our Ancestors*. Baltimore, Maryland: Genealogical Publishing Co., 1996.

Bergmann, Leola. *Americans From Norway*. Philadelphia: Lippincott, 1950.

Blanchet, Christian. *The Statue of Liberty: The First One Hundred Years*. New York: American Heritage, 1995.

Bookbinder, Bernie, Robert Snyder, and Harvey Weber. *City of the World: New York and Its People*. New York: Abrams, 1989.

Brendon, Piers. *The Life and Death of the Press Barons*. New York: Atheneum, 1983.

Coe, Lewis. *The Telegraph: A History of Morse's Invention and Its Predecessors in the United States*. Jefferson, North Carolina: MacFarland, 1993.

Coles, K. Adlard. *Heavy Weather Sailing*. New York: John de Graff, 1989.

Davison, Ann, David Lewis, and Hannes Lindemann. *Great Voyages in Small Boats: Solo Transatlantic*. New York: John de Graff, 1982.

Derry, T. K. *A History of Scandinavia: Norway, Sweden,*

Denmark, Finland, and Iceland. Minneapolis: University of Minnesota Press, 1979.

du Maurier, Daphne. Vanishing Cornwall. New York: Doubleday, 1981.

Dunne, Thomas. Ellis Island. New York: Norton, 1971.

Elsy, Mary. Brittany and Normandy. New York: Hastings House, 1974.

Fairfax, John. Britannia: Rowing Alone Across the Atlantic; the Record of an Adventure. New York: Simon & Schuster, 1971.

Fowles, John. Shipwreck. Boston: Little, Brown, 1975.

Guthorn, Peter. The Sea Bright Skiff and Other Shore Boats. Exton, Pennsylvania: Schiffer, 1982.

Hammick, Anne. The Atlantic Crossing Guide. Camden, Maine: International Marine, 1992.

Moscow, Henry. The Street Book: An Encyclopedia of Manhattan's Street Names and Their Origins. New York: Hagstrom, 1978.

Ridgway, John, and Chay Blyth. A Fighting Chance. Philadelphia: Lippincott, 1967.

Roberts, Russell, and Rich Youmans. Down the Jersey Shore. New Brunswick, NJ: Rutgers University Press, 1993.

Rudjord, Kåre. Atlanterhaus Roerne. Farsund, Norway: Forlaget Lister, 1988. (Special thanks to Spencer Samuelsen for reading me the text, most of which is in Norwegian. Among other items, this slender book contains newspaper interviews with Norwegian reporters while George Harbo and Frank Samuelsen were in Norway. These interviews were quite helpful.)

Slocum, Joshua. Sailing Alone Around the World. New York: Sheridan House, 1954.

Smith, Gene, and Jayne Barry Smith, eds. Police Gazette. New York: Simon & Schuster, 1972.

Stigen, Terje, and Bert Boger. Norway. New York: Viking, 1961.

Tute, Warren. *Atlantic Conquest: The Men and Ships of the Glorious Age of Steam.* Boston: Little, Brown, 1962.

Vecoli, Rudolph J. *The People of New Jersey.* Princeton, New Jersey: Van Nostrand, 1965.

Villiers, Alan. *Men, Ships, and the Sea.* Washington, D.C.: National Geographic Society, 1973.